D0060057

DEMYSTIFYING SHARIAH

DEMYSTIFYING
SHARIAH

WHAT IT IS, HOW IT WORKS, AND WHY IT'S NOT TAKING OVER OUR COUNTRY

Sumbul Ali-Karamali

BEACON PRESS ■ BOSTON

BEACON PRESS
Boston, Massachusetts
www.beacon.org

Beacon Press books
are published under the auspices of
the Unitarian Universalist Association of Congregations.

23 22 21 20   8 7 6 5 4 3 2 1

This book is printed on acid-free paper that meets the uncoated paper
ANSI/NISO specifications for permanence as revised in 1992.

Text design and composition by Kim Arney

Library of Congress Cataloging-in-Publication Data

Names: Ali-Karamali, Sumbul, author.
Title: Demystifying Shariah : what it is, how it works, and why it's not
taking over our country / Sumbul Ali-Karamali.
Description: Boston : Beacon Press, 2020. | Includes bibliographical
references and index.
Identifiers: LCCN 2019037396 (print) | LCCN 2019037397 (ebook) |
ISBN 9780807038000 (hardcover) | ISBN 9780807038017 (ebook)
Subjects: LCSH: Islamic law.
Classification: LCC KBP144 .A4424 2020 (print) |
LCC KBP144 (ebook) |
DDC 340.5/9—dc23
LC record available at https://lccn.loc.gov/2019037396
LC ebook record available at https://lccn.loc.gov/2019037397

For my husband

CONTENTS

INTRODUCTION

Upon completing the first draft of this book, which I had provisionally entitled *Shariah in America*, I realized that almost none of it had to do with shariah in America. That's because there isn't any. Not taking over our country, anyway. I laughed, envisioning a book called *Shariah in America* filled with blank pages.

Islam is difficult to write about in my country—that's the United States—because we are none of us here, not even Muslim Americans, completely unconditioned by the negative stereotypes so normalized in our culture, educational system, news media, and entertainment industry. Any positive discussion of Islam is dismissed as propaganda. I often ruminate on how Muslims are perceived to be aliens from *Star Trek*'s evil parallel universe, the "mirror" universe, where mass murder, despotism, and conquest are the norm—as opposed to the "real" (non-Muslim) universe, which we rosily view as valuing peace and cooperation. Although it's not true that Muslims come from the mirror universe (in case you were wondering), so many loathsome misconceptions adhere to us that I cannot adequately explain shariah without also unwinding stereotypes, eliminating presumptions, and providing historical background for current events.

Human psychology periodically obstructs these explanations, because we all prefer comfortable information that bathes us in approbation and absolves us of transgression. I would love to believe that when my husband and I argue, it is always 100 percent *his fault*. No one likes acknowledging responsibility, but a discussion of Islam in the world today is not possible without explaining the colonialist role of European and American powers in Islamic history.

In defending Islam against stereotypes and countering negativity with positive examples, *never* do I intend to give the erroneous impression that I'm declaring my religion to be better than another. *Never* is proselytizing my purpose. If spiritual and moral perfection—God, if you wish—resides at the top of a mountain, then I believe many paths lead there, meandering variously up the sides. As the Qur'an says, "To me my religion, to you yours!"

Of course, I'm writing as a Muslim American and not, say, a Muslim Indonesian or Jordanian. As such, I'm as much a cultural product of my environment as anyone. A Christian Ugandan might practice a markedly different interpretation of Christianity than a Christian American. My culture and my diverse, wonderfully multicultural, American environment, in which I am fed and clothed and housed, influences the interpretations of Islam I choose. But I am no less authentically Muslim for being American.

This book is not a compendium of all the rules of shariah on all subjects and in all countries but an introduction to the principles, goals, and general development of shariah—as well as the relevance of these topics today. I include the examples of shariah in quotidian life, such as the Islamic view of same-sex relationships and what Muslims eat, to give you a sense of how Muslims engage with their religio-legal tradition; but these examples are illustrative rather than comprehensive.

Understanding Islamophobia is also crucial to any discussion of shariah, because it birthed the shariah panic. But Islamophobia is complex, and this book allows for only the merest summary. Because it affects us all, though, I urge you to read one of the excellent sources named in the suggested reading list on my website.

One of my father's closest friends was Jewish. He read my first book on Islam, *The Muslim Next Door: The Qur'an, the Media, and that Veil Thing*, with tremendous interest, delighting particularly in the stories of my father as a new immigrant. When I despairingly felt as though I were chipping away with a teaspoon at a great granite wall of misconceptions about Islam and Muslims, he told me, "When I was a kid, they said that Jews drank the blood of Christian babies. You just have to keep fighting! Keep fighting those stereotypes!"

This book is a defense against the stereotypes and, I hope, a relatable discussion of shariah. The information herein isn't my personal opinion; it's academically reliable, based on established scholarship and facts. And defending against stereotypes doesn't mean I'm arguing that Muslims are perfect—we're just not the ogres of the modern world.

It's always been easy to buy into vilification of minority groups. On the starship *Enterprise*, after a Starfleet admiral persecutes an innocent person solely because he is fractionally Romulan, Captain Picard converses with his chastened security officer, who has finally realized that his wholehearted embrace of the admiral's tactics, shown to be bigotry and McCarthyism, was misplaced.

"At least it's over," says Worf, shamefaced.

"She or someone like her will always be with us," responds the captain grimly, "waiting for the right climate in which to flourish, spreading fear in the name of righteousness. Vigilance, Mr. Worf! That is the price we have to continually pay."

Let us be vigilant! Learning about Islam as *Muslims* understand it—not as the anti-Muslim propagandists deform and twist it—will deflate the sails of those spreading fear and open new avenues for intercultural and interreligious understanding. That's what Captain Picard was fighting for—the evaluation of everyone for their integrity, not their religion or ethnicity or cultural background. Thank you for being on board.

PART I

THE BASICS AND FOUNDATIONS OF SHARIAH

CHAPTER ONE

SHARIAH IN A NUTSHELL

NEARLY A DECADE AGO, attending my Stanford reunion, I stood self-consciously but optimistically in the campus bookstore beside a table piled high with copies of my book, alongside other alumni authors, when a white-haired, blue-eyed couple sporting badges labeled "50th Reunion" approached me to say politely, "You look like someone we could talk to. We're very much afraid that shariah law is taking over the United States."

Momentarily speechless, I struggled to address a statement that was problematic on multiple levels. Why assume that most Muslims were *not* people they could talk to? Was it such a surprise to see a professionally dressed Muslim woman with a nice haircut? And *where* did they see "shariah law" taking over the United States? Could they see it? Define it?

Ruthlessly suppressing these questions, I settled for assuring them that the First Amendment of the Constitution prevented *any* religious law from taking over our country. Not to mention, I added brightly, the Supreme Court and Congress!

I smiled engagingly. Their brows remained furrowed, their eyes troubled.

"But Rush Limbaugh said it could," they said simply.

They left without buying a book.

Shariah hysteria has only worsened in the intervening years. Prior to the publication of my first book, the term *shariah* (or the simplified "sharia") was known in some circles but absent from the American layperson's vocabulary. In the intervening ten years, though, the terms "shariah" and—the Western construct—"shariah law" have acquired monstrous meanings in the West, virally infecting media and internet.

You might reasonably assume that the reason for the fear comes from groups like the Taliban and ISIS, who claim to apply shariah. It's certainly easy to point to these criminals when making the argument that shariah is fearsome. But vilification of shariah began long before the birth of these groups—hundreds of years ago and even earlier, depending on how you look at it—and besides, using religion to justify violence is not unique to Islam. Groups around the world commit crimes and justify them with religion; this is nothing new. The current American-European defamation of shariah is the result of another factor: a thriving, intentional disinformation campaign (discussed later in this book), which, in the last decade, has sought to spread fear of shariah as a predatory, backward, Draconian legal system that Muslims strive to impose on Muslims and hapless non-Muslims alike.

This is ironic, because, as Harvard law professor Noah Feldman writes, "For most of its history, Islamic law [shariah] offered the most liberal and humane legal principles available anywhere in the world."[1]

I know that may be difficult to believe for anyone following the American public discourse. But it's true.

The Islamic legal system based on shariah was a remarkable achievement. Otherwise, it couldn't have succeeded as spectacularly as it did for over a thousand years. It counts as one of the world's three major legal systems—defined as widely influential legal systems that grew past their original birthplaces—alongside Roman law and English common law.

When I think of shariah, I don't think of something cruel and vicious. I think of justice, feminism, defense of the weak and defenseless, and a commitment to the rule of law. I'm well aware that these words might be taken by too many to be some sort of joke. But that's because few non-Muslims possess even the most rudimentary understanding of shariah.

What *is* shariah, then? Defining it is difficult, because "shariah" is not limited to a single fixed meaning. "Sky" has a fixed meaning. "Desk" has a fixed meaning. But "shariah" has several possible meanings.

Since 2010, when the word "shariah" was, as I'll discuss later, intentionally catapulted into the Western public discourse, average Muslims have struggled to define and defend its complexities. It's like expecting all Christians to explain canon law. I advise my acquaintances to stash a three-second explanation in their back pockets: "Shariah just means Islam." Because, generally speaking, it does.

In literal terms, the Arabic word *shariah* means "the path to the water-ing place." If you find yourself in the desert, the birthplace of Islam, you will most certainly desire to be on the path to the watering place!

In religious terms, shariah is the path you take to quench your *spir-itual* thirst. It's the "right path" or "the path God wants us to follow." Shariah is God's "eternal and immutable law—the way of truth, virtue, and justice."[2] It's the path you follow to be a good and righteous person. In a nutshell: shariah is the way of God.

And that's why shariah is, loosely, Islam. Because, to Muslims, Islam is the way of God.

Okay, but (you may be thinking), what *is* the way of God? What does that mean? How do you know what it is and how do you follow it?

While the Prophet Muhammad lived, the early Muslims simply asked him to explicate the way of God. He was the Prophet. That was his role. It was easy.

After Muhammad's death, in 632 CE, Muslims set about discover-ing the way of God on their own. They began to formulate educated guesses about how it was defined and how they should behave in order to follow it. They based these postulations on the two clues available to them: the Qur'an, which is, for Muslims, the literal word of God; and the *Sunna*, the words and deeds of the Prophet Muhammad—his prophetic example.

The Qur'an and the Sunna, divine as Muslims considered them, did not necessarily address every detailed question that arose in life. The Qur'an decreed that Muslims should fast, but it didn't specify all the details around fasting. The Prophet's life had contained only finite ex-amples; he couldn't address an infinite number of religious questions ex-tending into the infinite future.

Therefore, to discover further religious answers to life's questions, early Muslims began interpreting and analyzing the Qur'an and the Sunna. Throughout the centuries, they filled countless books with these interpretations of their religious texts. This entire body of interpretive literature is called *fiqh*, or "understanding."

Fiqh is not a rigid set of rules or laws. It's not a code. It's a massive col-lection of opinions, debates, arguments, interpretations, and case studies. It is the collective human interpretation of the divine texts. Fiqh is the result of Islamic scholars over fourteen centuries trying to answer the question "What is the way of God?" or, put another way, "What is wrong and what is right in the eyes of God?"[3]

Shariah and fiqh are not the same, and it's crucial to understand this: shariah does not change, being the way of God, but fiqh changes and develops with time. In fact, fiqh is *meant* to change. Fiqh contains internal methodologies allowing it to change and develop. Shariah is immutable; fiqh is mutable.

That's clear enough, right? But consider this complication: in addition to meaning "the way of God," shariah can also mean the Qur'an and the Sunna together, because these are the divine sources that contain the way of God. So far, that's consistent, because the Qur'an and the Sunna are immutable.

Yet another definition of shariah, however, is actually the most commonly used one: shariah can also mean the Qur'an plus the Sunna plus fiqh. The sum of these equals the entire system of Islamic jurisprudence, the system of engaging with and interpreting the religious texts (the Qur'an and the Sunna) in order to determine religious rules and practices. Shariah in this way is defined as the entire Islamic legal tradition.

Note, however, that the sum of the Qur'an plus the Sunna plus fiqh equals not only shariah but the greater part of Islam. That's why, generally speaking, shariah means Islam. (Substitution property, for those who remember high school mathematics.)

This works even in practical terms. You can usually substitute "Islam" whenever you hear the word "shariah," and it usually makes sense.

"Islamic law" is generally defined this way, as well, to mean the legal aspect of Islam. Sometimes, Islamic law means only fiqh, but sometimes Islamic law also refers to the entire Islamic legal tradition. I myself have a graduate degree in Islamic law, but—

"'Islamic law' is a misnomer," said my Islamic law professor on the first day of class, "because Islamic law is not law in the way we think of law, as rigid and statutory and enforceable."

Neither statutory nor enforceable, neither rigid nor inflexible, shariah often does not even incur earthly penalties. It's not a code of law. You cannot peruse a book of shariah, though you can peruse one of the many thousands of books of fiqh. Shariah defined as the entire Islamic legal tradition is the flexible engagement with religious texts, which results in religious rules and guidelines, designed to guide Muslims along the way of God.

However the term "shariah" is used, it's absolutely essential to understand the following: (1) shariah, defined as "the way of God," is divine, (2) the Qur'an and the Sunna are divine, though the written record of the Sunna (the *hadith*) is not divine, and (3) fiqh is not divine but human-made.

Those scholars qualified to analyze and develop fiqh are called the *fuqaha*, which may be translated as "religious scholars" or "legal scholars" or "religio-legal scholars." Or "jurists." Another word for them is *ulama*. I'm mostly going to call them "the scholars."

I hope it's obvious now that calls for Muslims to "give up shariah" are nonsensical. It's like telling Muslims to give up Islam. It's like telling Christians they have to renounce Jesus Christ and his teachings.

Islam, like all religions, has developed and changed throughout history and according to culture. No religion can survive for 1,400 years, as Islam has, without being flexible and adaptable. Islam has been both, as the profuse variety of global Islamic practices and interpretations attests.

A few years ago, listening to radio news while dressing in the morning, I heard an American reporter relating his travels to Syria. He had interviewed Syrians "on the street" and asked them if they were in favor of shariah.

"Of course," they answered, sounding puzzled. (They were Muslim. It's like asking Christians if they are in favor of Jesus.)

"But what about stoning and cutting off hands?" he retorted.

The Syrian interviewees responded with confusion—yes, they favored shariah, but they didn't know what the reporter was talking about, as no one was being stoned or amputated. The reporter concluded his piece on the radio by saying incredulously, "They're Muslim and they don't even know what shariah is!"

My mind boggled. Just think: an American reporter travels to a Muslim-majority country to interview Muslims and assumes that he knows more about their religion than they do. Clearly, the Syrians thought of shariah as the religion they practiced; the reporter thought of shariah as stoning and amputation, which is the Western stereotype. (I'll explain stoning, amputation, and other punishments later, so stay tuned.)

Although "shariah" loosely means Islam, this is an imprecise, blurry definition. Islam is a bigger category. You might see "shariah" and "Islam" in the same sentence, contrapuntal and contradistinct, such as "According to shariah, and indeed Islam itself . . ." Obviously, in this phrase, "shariah" does not mean Islam as a whole but rather a subset of Islam, usually the subset of Islam concerned with rules, jurisprudence, and the legal order of society.

"Shariah" in common usage doesn't usually refer to the more abstract aspects of Islam, such as theology or mysticism. Or the oneness of God (*tawhid*). Or doing what is beautiful and finding the beauty of God (*ihsan*). Or having faith in God (*iman*). Or, most importantly, submission to God and God's scriptures, prophets, and angels (*islam*).

Sometimes, shariah is used interchangeably with "fiqh," but this is a *terrible* usage. It causes confusion between what is divine (God's law) and what is not divine (human-made religious interpretations). And *that* causes confusion between what cannot be changed (God's law) and what can be changed (human-made religious interpretation). This confusion has resulted in many Muslims and non-Muslims erroneously believing that fiqh is shariah and therefore can never be changed.

In this book, I do use "shariah" to refer to the entire Islamic legal tradition (or "Islamic law"), as well as to the way of God. Because that's the common usage. Just be aware that fiqh is mutable.

Most of shariah concerns rules for individual Muslims to follow in their personal lives, such as rules on prayer. A smaller part of shariah is composed of laws that judges implement in courts to adjudicate crimes like murder. And a third part of shariah is a discretionary set of laws that a ruler can choose whether to implement, depending on the public interest.[4]

Does Islam contain outdated statements of centuries ago? Yes, of course it does; what ancient religion doesn't? What aged text—even our Constitution—doesn't? But all religions, including Islam, evolve.

Fiqh has continued to develop over the centuries. But explaining the development of fiqh and shariah is not possible without first understanding a bit about Islam. Therefore, the next few chapters set a foundation by describing Muhammad and the birth of Islam, the two primary sources of shariah—the Qur'an and the Sunna—and a few of the different groups within Islam, such as Sunni, Shi'a, and the Nation of Islam.

CHAPTER TWO

MUHAMMAD AND THE BIRTH OF ISLAM

WITHOUT AT LEAST a rudimentary understanding of Islam, understanding shariah is impossible—as is evaluating the validity and truth of *any* discourse on Muslims. How can myths like "Muslims are out to convert everyone they encounter" and "Islam is spread by the sword" and "Muslims have always been backward" be intelligently evaluated without an understanding of basic Islamic theology and history?

The media's barrage of reports on extremist Muslims leads many people to naturally but mistakenly assume that they are informed about Islam. Suppose you lived in a country where you never learned the tenets of Christianity, knew no Christians, and had never seen a church—but where *every day* in the public discourse (news media, podcasts, talk shows) you heard about the Ku Klux Klan, abortion-clinic attackers, the Hutaree Christian Militia, the Christian Identity Movement, the Phineas Priesthood,[1] and the Lord's Resistance Army in Africa. Such a situation might well lead you to believe that you were informed about Christianity. But in actuality, your knowledge would be limited to these particular groups.

In the United States and Europe, we hear about bad Muslim behavior every day but know little about Islam or most Muslims. Even Western *Muslims* have been conditioned to understand their own religion as inferior. So please, for a moment, leave behind what you've learned, pretend you've never heard of Islam and Muslims, and let's start again.

BASIC BUT NECESSARY INFORMATION

Human beings allocate various names to God, depending upon the language and the tradition. The French word for God is *Dieu*. The Spanish word for God is *Dios*. The Persian word for God is *Khuda*. And, of course, the Arabic word for God is *Allah*.

Allah simply means "God" or "the God." Allah does not mean "Exclusively Islamic God" or "The Only Valid God in the World." In fact, Arabic-speaking Jews and Christians have historically called their God "Allah," too, because "Allah" just means "God" in Arabic. Some Malaysian Christians, as well, have begun using "Allah" to refer to God. Frequently, I hear the phrase "Muslims worship Allah," but that's like saying, "Mexican Catholics worship Dios."

Islam haters do insist that the Muslim God is different from the Christian God. You might equally say the God of the Old Testament is different from the God of the New Testament, but still we refer to the "Judeo-Christian" tradition. Muslims themselves believe that their God is the God of Christians and Jews.

I'm often asked about the difference between "Muslim" and "Islam." Islam is the name of the religion, and a Muslim is someone who believes in Islam. More specifically, "Islam" means "submission to God," and "Muslim" means "someone who submits to God." Both of these words originate from the same Arabic root, which means "to be in peace." Therefore, "Islam" means "submitting to God's peace" or "the peace that comes from submission to God" or "entering into God's peace." It *never, ever* means submitting or surrendering to another person or another deity.

To be Muslim, one need only believe in one God and in Muhammad as the Prophet of God. Muslims summarize these beliefs in a single sentence: "There is no god but God, and Muhammad is the Messenger of God." Another translation: "There is only one God, and Muhammad is the Messenger of God." This "Declaration of Faith" is one of the Five Pillars of Islam, the main tenets upon which all Muslims agree, the other four being prayer, fasting, donation to charity, and pilgrimage to Mecca.

In the Declaration of Faith, the upper-case "God" refers to a single, supreme being—*the* God. The lower-case "god" refers to a god that might be one of a pantheon of gods. The Qur'an rejects a multiplicity of deities. In other words, "there is no god but God" means "nothing is worthy of worship except God."

Sometimes, I see this phrase translated as "There is no god but Allah," which always makes me grind my teeth, because it wrongly implies that Muslims think Allah is different from God and that Allah is the only valid deity, in contrast with everyone else's deity. Muslims intend to say: "Nothing is worthy of worship except God, and Muhammad is the Messenger of God."

The second part of the Declaration of Faith, "Muhammad is the Messenger of God," means that Muhammad was chosen by God to deliver God's message to the human beings around him but was never elevated to anything beyond human status. Translations that read "Muhammad is His Messenger" are incorrect, because Muslims believe that God is neither a "he" nor a "she" but a different entity entirely.

Muhammad preached many messages, but his main message was belief in one God. Thousands of years before Muhammad, a man named Abraham had also preached belief in one God. Muhammad saw himself as continuing the religion of the Prophet Abraham. Muslims believe that they are descendants of Abraham's son, Ismail, and that Jews and Christians are descendants of Abraham's other son, Isaac.

Muslims always follow Muhammad's spoken or written name with the words, "may peace be upon him." Muslims also utter "may peace be upon him" after the names of Jesus and Moses, whom Muslims revere as prophets. In this text, I have omitted this phrase for simplicity's sake; if you are Muslim, please just say the words to yourself, as I do.

Muhammad's followers now number about 1.7 billion adherents worldwide (though estimates vary), nearly a quarter of the world's population, making Islam the second-largest religion in the world, after Christianity. Approximately 18 percent of Muslims in the world are Arab. The Saudis constitute about 2 percent of the worldwide Muslim population. Over half the Muslims in the world live in Asia. The country with the largest Muslim population is Indonesia, followed by Pakistan and India. Muslims constitute about 5 percent of Europe's population and perhaps 1 percent of the population in the United States.[2]

MUHAMMAD AND THE BIRTH OF ISLAM

Muhammad was undoubtedly a real historical figure. Muslim as well as non-Muslim contemporary sources prove this, and such sources generally, in their broad outlines depicting Islam, differ little from each other.[3] What follows is the barest sketch of Muhammad's life and background.

Muhammad was born around the year 570 CE[4] in what is now Mecca, in Saudi Arabia. He was orphaned at the age of six, at which point his paternal grandfather became his guardian, succeeded by his paternal uncle. Muhammad is said to have been "unlettered," as were many people in the sixth century.

The Hijaz, where Mecca was located, was in those days a tribal society. No central government operated there in the seventh century. Power resided in the tribes, which increased their wealth by raiding other tribes— an acceptable form of income as long as no one was killed. In the case of a killing, blood feuds ensued, sometimes lasting generations. Warfare was the default state.

Most Arabs at that time in the Hijaz practiced a pagan, polytheistic religion, but some practiced Judaism, Christianity, or other forms of monotheism.

Nowhere in the world was the sixth century a hospitable environment for women's rights. In Arabia, a woman could not divorce her husband. A man could marry as many wives as he wished—all that tribal raiding must have produced a surfeit of widows—and this polygyny was practiced by both pagan Arabs and Jewish Arabs, though not by Christian Arabs. When he tired of one of his wives, a man could simply send her away, keeping their children. A woman could be sold into marriage by her male relatives. She had no inheritance rights. She could not testify in court. These norms were not unique to Arabia; some or all were common in many parts of the world, not only in the sixth century but for many centuries afterward.

When Muhammad was twenty-five, he married a widow named Khadija. By all accounts, they had a happy marriage, which lasted for nearly twenty-five years, until her death. Contrary to his polygynous culture, he never took another wife during his marriage to her. After her death, he did marry other women, mostly divorcées or widows—often the most vulnerable women in society—and primarily to form political alliances.

One day, when Muhammad was forty years old, Muslims believe, he retreated to a cave where he habitually meditated, often upon the injustices of society. He had always been concerned with social justice, unsurprisingly, given his orphaned status. On this particular day, as he meditated in the darkness, he suddenly felt grabbed and tightly squeezed, though he saw no one. Just as frightening, he heard, over the haze of his discomfort, a voice commanding him to "Read!" (or "Recite!").

Muhammad responded that he didn't know how to read. Again, he was clutched and squeezed and commanded to read. Again, he pleaded ignorance. After the third time, Muhammad desperately asked the voice what exactly he was meant to read/recite. From the expectant darkness came this answer, which was to become the first revelation of the Qur'an:

> *Read! In the name of your Lord who created,*
> *Created man from a clot of blood!*
> *Read! Your Lord is the Most Generous,*
> *Who taught by the Pen*
> *Taught man what he knew not. (96:1–5)*

Understandably terrified, Muhammad hastened home to his wife, who consoled him, believed him, and conducted him to her Christian cousin, Waraqa. Learned in the scriptures, Waraqa convinced Muhammad that he had heard the voice of the angel Gabriel, the same angel who had appeared to Moses. Waraqa assured Muhammad that he was a prophet, one whose coming had been foretold.

(A Catholic friend of mine, upon learning this, kept asking, "The *same* angel Gabriel? The very *same one*?" "Yes!" I replied.)

Over the next twenty-three years, Muslims believe, the angel Gabriel would bring to Muhammad the words of God. Muhammad would recite the words aloud and his followers would transcribe them onto whatever materials were available. Within twenty years of Muhammad's death, in 632 CE, Muslims would gather together these bits of writing and compile them into a single book called the *Qur'an*, or "Recitation."

Because Muhammad accepted the Judeo-Christian tradition as part of his religion, Muslims believe generally in the Judeo-Christian worldview: heaven, hell, angels, the devil, and the Judeo-Christian prophets—Jesus, Moses, Noah, Adam, Solomon, David, and many more. Muslims also believe in the virgin birth of Jesus, and the Qur'an devotes more space to Mary than the Bible does. Muslims do not believe Jesus was the son of God, but Muslims revere Jesus, one of our five most important prophets. We would never, for example, lampoon him in vicious cartoons.

Muslims do believe in the creation story, including Adam and Eve, but not in original sin. In the Islamic version of the creation story, Satan tempts Adam (not Eve) into eating the apple, though in the end they both eat it. This version of the story represents a significant, deliberate rejection of all the previous ancient views—spanning multiple cultures, religions, and centuries—of Woman as responsible for all the chaos and evil in the world (remember Pandora?).[5]

If you don't wish to view Muhammad as a prophet, you can think of him as a social reformer. He preached that society should take care of the disadvantaged. Because people converted to Islam as individuals and not as clans, he challenged the clan-based hierarchical structure of Mecca and obliterated class distinctions. He bought and freed slaves. He forbade usury, commonly used to enslave the poor.

None of this particularly appealed to the rich and powerful.

Muhammad disregarded racial distinctions too. He freed an Ethiopian slave and appointed him as the first *muezzin* of Islam, the one who calls people to prayer. In his last sermon, Muhammad famously proclaimed:

All mankind is from Adam and Eve. An Arab has no superiority over a non-Arab, nor does a non-Arab have any superiority over an Arab. Also, a white man has no superiority over a black man, nor does a black man have any superiority over a white man, except by piety and good actions.[6]

As if that statement weren't stunning enough for a tribal, clan-based, sexist (as they all were) seventh-century culture, he also said, in the same sermon, "It is true that you have certain rights in regard to your women, but they also have rights over you."

This presented, of course, another problem for the Meccans: Muhammad gave altogether too many rights to women. He and the Qur'an granted women unheard-of rights, recognizing women as *legal beings*—that is, no longer a man's property but *legal entities* who could enter into their own contracts (marriage or otherwise), divorce their husbands, retain their property upon marriage, mandatorily inherit from their relatives (even to the exclusion of male relatives), own money they earned even during the marriage, testify in court, and retain custody of their young children. If these rights were often not absolute or gender-neutral, they were far greater than women's rights before Muhammad and far greater than those elsewhere in the world for centuries to come.

The common derogatory view of "oppressed Muslim women" amazes me in its tenacity, given that Muhammad and the Qur'an gave women more rights in seventh-century Arabia than Englishwomen would have for another *thousand* years. As British historian Norman Daniel notes:

> Before the passage of the Married Women's Property Act of the 1860s it was justly said that in England women had fewer rights than the Qur'an allowed them.[7]

Because Muhammad thus uprooted societal norms in addition to preaching a new religion, the Meccans persecuted Muhammad and his followers, often severely, for twelve years. The nascent Muslims didn't fight back. They exercised nonviolent resistance by refusing to renounce their religion, freeing slaves, turning the other cheek (to borrow the famous phrase), and emigrating.

To escape persecution, some of Muhammad's followers migrated to Ethiopia. Muhammad stayed in Mecca, but when a plot to assassinate him was uncovered, he and his followers fled to Medina. This nearby city had been experiencing political tensions among its communities of Jews, Christians, pagans, and Sabians (another religious group of the time, mentioned in the Qur'an).

These political and religious tensions should be perceived against the backdrop of the brutal war that the two nearby empires, the Roman Byzantine (Christian) Empire and the Persian Sassanian (Zoroastrian) Empire, had been fighting for decades. Some factions in Medina had "declared for" the Persians, some for Rome.[8] Evidence indicates that Muhammad considered himself allied with Rome.[9]

Medinan officials invited Muhammad, as a respected outsider, to help them manage the tensions in the city. Muhammad, his followers, and the various groups in Medina entered into an agreement called "The Constitution of Medina." This document established Muhammad as the political leader and mediator of all Medinans but the religious leader of only the Muslims. Non-Muslims kept their religious practices and customs.

Muhammad could have been an autocratic leader, but he wasn't. In governing Medina, he consulted with all the Muslim and non-Muslim communities.[10] Under the Constitution of Medina, all the groups contracted to function as political allies and defend the city. Muslims consider the Constitution of Medina to be the first charter of religious freedom in the world. Scholars of Islam John Esposito and Natana DeLong-Bas write:

> This model of focusing on the common good while allowing for personal choice provides a flexible framework and broad political overview that can be and has been reinterpreted over time to accommodate changes in societies and cultures.[11]

Even after Muhammad arrived in Medina, the tensions with Mecca continued. Only then, fifteen years into his mission, did Muhammad fight back against the Meccan pagans in three defensive battles. His army consisted of the citizens of Medina, comprising Muslims, Christians, Jews, pagans, and members of other tribes. Certain factions failed to adhere to their agreements: during the third battle, some Medinans broke away from Muhammad to fight with the opposing side. This was treason, according to the Constitution of Medina. (It would be considered treason today.) Late biographers, writing centuries after the events, told tales of Muhammad taking prisoners or putting to death those who had betrayed him, but no evidence of this comes from Muhammad's time, and the Qur'an—which is a contemporaneous primary-source historical document—seems to actually contradict this.[12] Indeed, according to new research, Muhammad was more a man of peace than even his medieval Muslim biographers—who couldn't comprehend a leader reluctant to engage in battles—have characterized him to be.[13]

By the time he died, in 632, Muhammad's followers numbered in the tens of thousands. He was more powerful than the Meccans at that point, but he didn't resort to attacking them. Instead, he treated with them.

When the Meccans surrendered, Muhammad didn't kill or convert them, as his culture and time would have allowed him to do. All he destroyed were the pagan idols in the Ka'aba, an ancient shrine that Muslims believe Abraham built to honor the one God. A fresco depicting Mary and Jesus he specifically protected from harm.[14]

Muhammad never claimed to be capable of performing miracles. I personally doubt that he would have sanctioned the growth of legends around his life. The Qur'an was the only miracle he ever claimed, and that on behalf of God.

CHAPTER THREE

THE QUR'AN

The Primary Source of Shariah

For MUSLIMS, the Qur'an is the literal word of God. It's also the primary source of shariah. And it's a contemporaneous primary-source historical document evidencing Muhammad's life, time, and circumstances.

The Qur'an often bewilders readers, because it's not a narrative document. It doesn't narrate stories. The Qur'an has been described as an "outpouring of divine messages."[1] A. J. Arberry, a British scholar, advised us that—regardless of belief or disbelief in the Qur'anic message—the Qur'an had to be read *as though* it were a single, powerful, divine revelation transcending the pedestrian confines of time and space.[2]

The entire Qur'an is divided into 114 chapters, or *surahs*. Each surah is composed of verses. The surahs are not arranged in chronological order of revelation. Rather, with the exception of the first, they simply progress from longest to shortest.

The Qur'an is also—literally—poetry. It flows in unmetered verse, with its own rhythm. Much of it rhymes. Like all poetry, the Qur'an alludes and implies and refers; it wields metaphor and analogy; rarely does it specifically explain. This makes understanding the Qur'an challenging without background, context, and footnotes.

Even native Arabic speakers cannot easily understand the Qur'an, because word meanings have changed radically in 1,400 years. Shakespeare's plays are only 400 years old, but no one could read them cold, without any familiarity with English history or literature or culture, without footnotes, and yet understand the meaning of every word and phrase—and the Qur'an is many times older than Shakespeare's plays. Not even all Muslims agree on the meaning of every Qur'anic verse. That's one reason it's so ridiculous that non-Muslims commonly cherry-pick Qur'anic verses, with no grounding in Islamic history, language, or culture, and presume to understand what they mean.

Because Muslims believe that the Qur'an embodies the literal word of God, they have expended considerable effort over the centuries to ensure that no corruption enters the Qur'anic text. How logical it would be for someone advocating a particular agenda to simply insert it into the Qur'an! To prevent this, Muslims have always meticulously preserved the exact words of the Qur'anic text. Translations are considered aids to understanding the Qur'an but are not accepted as the real Qur'an, because translation introduces further uncertainty of meaning.

The fact that the Qur'an has been preserved unchanged does not mean that *interpretation* of the Qur'an must remain unchanged. If the Qur'an is eternal, as Muslims believe it is, then it must be relevant to all generations, interpretable in any time and place. Certainly, some literalist or "originalist" Muslims resist reinterpretation, just as some Christians and Jews interpret their texts literally. But literalists and originalists are neither the majority of Muslims nor are they unique to Islam.

I'm often asked why Muslims cannot just rewrite the Qur'an to make it more modern. It's hard to overstate how shocking and offensive this suggestion is to Muslims. First, it implies that the Qur'an is not simply old but backward and anti-modern. Second, Muslims *cannot* rewrite the Qur'an, because we believe it is composed of God's literal words.

Nobody ever suggests completely rewriting the US Constitution, though our debates about it involve some of the same issues that arise regarding the Qur'an. Some Americans believe in more literalist readings of the Constitution, some less. Rather than rewriting the Constitution wholesale, we work with it and reinterpret it.[3] The Fourteenth Amendment's Equal Protection Clause protects women now but didn't when the Founders drafted it. The Founders didn't think discriminating against black people was unconstitutional, but we do think so now. Most judges throughout history have interpreted the Constitution as a document open to reinterpretation; however, a minority of "originalist" judges believe the meaning of the Constitution is permanently fixed by the intent of the Founders, protecting only what it protected at the time of adoption. These are the same kinds of exegetical issues that arise with respect to the Qur'an.

Even though we cannot change the Qur'an, we can reinterpret it in light of our time and place. Islamic scholars have always done this, especially when the Qur'an addresses a particular historical situation that doesn't exist anymore. In fact, the Qur'an *itself* sometimes anticipates a different interpretation for the future; at times, it limits existing seventh-century practices with an eye toward gradually eliminating such practices altogether.

Slavery is an example. The Qur'an accepts slavery as an existing historical condition, as do the Old and New Testaments—some sort of unfree status was prevalent throughout the world until the nineteenth century—but it disapproves of slavery, limits it, and urges Muslims to free their slaves. Muhammad himself freed slaves. In addition, the Qur'an commands Muslims to allow their slaves to purchase their freedom, thus requiring slaves to be *paid* so that they can do so.[4] Slavery was outlawed in Muslim lands in the mid-nineteenth century, before it was outlawed in the US, and virtually all Muslims now view it as a historical relic.

Polygyny is another example of a historical institution that the Qur'an limited and (it can be argued) meant to eventually eliminate. In an era of unlimited polygyny, the Qur'an restricted the number of wives to four ("Only *four*?" you can hear those seventh-century men whining), but only if such wives could be treated with equal fairness. (4:3) But then, in the same surah, the Qur'an states that it's *impossible* to treat multiple wives with equal fairness! (4:129)

Well, that looks like a directive for monogamy to me. Many modern Muslims agree, viewing polygyny as something the Qur'an sought to eventually eliminate.

Nevertheless, traditional fiqh, mostly developed by men, does allow for a maximum of four wives. Still, even traditional fiqh concedes that the Qur'anic verse treats polygyny as the exception rather than the rule, clearly preferring monogamy. For Muslims in the world today, polygyny is uncommon, either prohibited or significantly curtailed in many Muslim-majority countries, and recognized by most Muslims as specific to an ancient time when men were scarce and women needed marriage for economic support.

The Qur'an contains universal statements of fairness and justice, as well as statements responding to particular historical questions or situations. Therefore, when you read the Qur'an, it's crucial to understand the *reason for revelation*, the reason that the Qur'an contains the verse in the first place. Sometimes, the reason has long disappeared, allowing reinterpretation of the verse.

The Qur'an must also be read intratextually. That is, it must be read as a whole, with all its verses relating to each other. This only makes sense. You wouldn't, after all, approach a novel by reading only isolated sentences, here and there; you would read it as a whole, with each part relating to other parts. True, the Qur'an is not a novel, but it speaks to stories, in the form of historical circumstances, in its verses.

That is why cherry-picking verses from the Qur'an is so nonsensical. The only "oppression" I feel as a Muslim woman is the relentless use of Qur'anic verses—particularly those urging Muslims to fight—as whipping posts. Especially since those condemning the fighting verses usually ignore the verses that nearly always immediately follow—that is, those verses that allow fighting only in self-defense—such as: "But do not attack them . . . unless they attack you first" (2:190) and "But do not be the aggressor; God does not like aggressors" (2:190) and "if they desist [fighting], then all hostility shall cease" (2:193) and "Fight during the sacred months *if you are attacked* [emphasis added]" (2:194) and "if you are greeted [with peace], then answer with an even better greeting [of peace]" (4:86) and "if they incline to peace, you must incline to peace." (8:61) Even one of the harshest "fighting" verses in the Qur'an concludes by commanding that if the enemy repents, then let them go their way. (9:5)

Indeed, I am exasperated by the continual mindless reiteration of the Qur'an as a manual for violence. Of the 6,236 verses in the Qur'an, only 47 urge fighting. It seems to me that only a misguided and unsuccessful manual for violence would use less than 1 percent of its verses to urge fighting. Furthermore, most of those 47 are limited by commands indicating that fighting is allowed only in self-defense.

After 9/11, sales of the Qur'an surged. But most purchasers were not buying the Qur'an for its numerous exhortations to peace and forgiveness. They were searching it for verses commanding Muslims to "slay infidels" (though this is a mistranslation, as the Qur'anic word translated as "infidels" does not mean non-Muslims generally but specifically the pagans making war on seventh-century Muslims) or trying to understand the attacks of 9/11 or simply looking for a scapegoat. But, as media and terrorism expert Arun Kundnani remarks dryly, those seeking to understand the events of 9/11 would have done better to read a history of the CIA; it is political history, not religion, that's germane to political conflicts, of which terrorism is an expression.[5]

Finally, all religious texts must be read in their historical context. The Qur'an was speaking to people who understood the world differently, a world where brutal warfare was the norm, where people conquered or were conquered themselves, and where women's rights were not easily conceptualized. So let's please eliminate the double standard here: it's unfair to denounce isolated Qur'anic verses as proof of barbarity and yet completely ignore, dismiss, or excuse the violence in other religious texts. (Even many atheists and agnostics exercise this double standard, because of cultural conditioning.)

What is the Qur'an about, then, if not fighting? The main message of the Qur'an is the exhortation to believe in one God. But it contains other themes, which might be enumerated as follows: human beings as individuals, human beings in society, nature, prophethood and revelation, eschatology (matters of judgment and the afterlife), Satan and evil, and the emergence of the Muslim community.[6] The Qur'an repeatedly stresses God's infinite mercy and forgiveness.

The status of women was also of clear concern to the Qur'an, which unquestionably and quite radically advanced women's rights. The Qur'an never tells women to obey their husbands. The text shows no surprise regarding women leaders and serenely accepts even queens as natural. It places women on an equal spiritual plane as men. And although some Qur'anic verses grant less than equal rights to women and thus seem unfair today, these verses considerably advanced the rights of women for their time.

Over 750 verses of the Qur'an concern nature and the environment— that's over fifteen times the number of fighting verses. The Qur'an deems human beings "vice-regents," or trustees, on Earth; Muslims must channel God's divine mercy into caring for it. The Qur'an identifies water as the origin of life (21:30), a remarkable statement for the seventh century, a thousand years before Darwin. Damaging the environment is prohibited in the Qur'an.[7] Eighty-eight verses specifically place considerable emphasis on the importance of water resource management and water conservation, environmental justice, plant conservation, biodiversity, sustainability, and environmental stewardship.[8]

Muslims believe that the Qur'an is divine. Nonetheless, the Qur'an requires historical, literary, and intertextual context to be understood. In addition, as we'll see in the next chapter, the Qur'an sometimes must be understood through the lens of the Sunna, Muhammad's words and actions.

CHAPTER FOUR

THE SUNNA

The Second Source of Shariah

MUSLIMS CONSIDER THE SUNNA, defined as the words and deeds of the Prophet Muhammad, to be divine—but not because we believe that Muhammad himself was divine. Rather, Muslims believe the Prophet was *divinely guided*. If God sent his words to Muhammad, via the angel Gabriel, and if Muhammad acted and spoke on the basis of those divine words, then his actions and words were divinely guided and therefore of extraordinary importance.

Whereas the Sunna refers to the divinely guided words and deeds of the Prophet in the abstract, the hadith is the written record of the Sunna. "Hadith" can refer either to the entire written record or to individual reports of the Prophet's words and deeds. The Sunna might be divine, but the hadith is not divine, because fallible human beings relied on their fallible memories to recall the words and deeds of the Prophet and endeavor to reproduce them accurately. Islamic scholars strived diligently to sift the accurate from the inaccurate, but they themselves always knew that hadiths couldn't be proved with absolute certainty.

Originally, hadith reports were transmitted orally, from generation to generation, as were other stories and information in Arabia at the time. Muslims didn't start recording hadiths in writing until about a century after the death of the Prophet. Collections of these written hadiths didn't appear until roughly two hundred years after the Prophet.[1] The written documentation was late not because the reports didn't exist until then, or because Muslims thought the Prophet's words not worth the bother of writing down, but because they only learned papermaking—from the

Chinese—in the eighth century. (The Arabs, in turn, introduced it to Europeans in the twelfth century.)[2]

The early Muslims analyzed each hadith report to determine its validity. They knew that human memory was imperfect and that communication lost accuracy in transmission. They understood the difficulty of accurately transmitting a statement the Prophet may have made only once in passing.

Even words as well-heeded as the Prophet's would have been difficult to remember verbatim, passed down over centuries. Most Islamic scholars understood this. Therefore, we can assume that even the most reliable hadith are usually not *verbatim* statements of the Prophet, even when the gist is correct.[3]

If a hadith is not in the Prophet's exact words, then it must have been paraphrased. For me as a twenty-first-century Muslim, here's the issue: did that paraphrasing, however well-intentioned and scrupulous, inadvertently affect the meaning of the hadith? Someone at a particular time, in a particular culture, and with a premodern worldview remembered the Prophet's words according to his or her own understanding of them. Did these factors filter the meaning of the Prophet's words? Create any misunderstanding around them?

In other words, was that hadith report really what the Prophet meant? Even if it were, could we, looking back across fourteen centuries, be missing or misunderstanding the ancient context and cultural understanding of the Prophet's words? Assuming the Prophet did say and mean these words in an ancient context, would he mean them in today's circumstances?

These issues arise even in the case of well-intentioned, scrupulous transmitters. But what if you were unscrupulous and wanted to promote a particular agenda? What better way to amass support than claim that the Prophet had agreed with you?!

The early Islamic scholars understood this. They knew some hadith reports had been fabricated to suit various agendas.[4] They did their best to excavate and eradicate them.

Other fabrications may have resulted from less nefarious motives. Imagine some seventh-century preacher, eager to motivate his listeners to charitable behavior. In the heat of the moment, he prefaces his opinions with the words "I heard the Prophet say . . . !" perhaps never realizing that his words have been forever recorded as hadith.

Despite mistakes and forgeries, however, much of the hadith corpus must indeed be a true reflection of the Prophet's words and deeds. Seventh-century Arabs routinely memorized literature and other information for oral transmission. Pre-Islamic society had already included the concept of a sunna as an exemplary mode of conduct displayed by a distinguished and respected member of society; the sunnas of such members of society, even before Muhammad, would have been followed as a matter of course.[5] It's inconceivable that early Muslims wouldn't have been even more acutely focused on the Sunna of their revered Prophet.

These days, too many people (both Muslim and non-Muslim) wield hadiths like weapons, lifting them from their contexts and brandishing them before unsuspecting people with whom they disagree. But Muhammad did not issue laws in a vacuum. He spent much of his twenty-three years of prophethood defending himself and his followers from persecution, torture, physical attacks, broken treaties, assassination attempts, and armed battles—all against a backdrop of seventh-century politics, a near–world war between two neighboring empires, and the social norms of the time. That was his context; his words cannot be extricated from it without altering the meaning.

I once consulted a supremely learned *shaykh* (another word for an Islamic religious scholar) about left-handedness. Incensed because a Muslim Sunday school teacher had instructed my child's class that left-handed Muslims must teach themselves to be right-handed, I indignantly related this incident to the shaykh. He shook his head, smiling ruefully, and said, "This is based on a report that the Prophet told a man to eat with his right hand and, when the man didn't obey, immediately caused paralysis in his left hand."

The shaykh chuckled, then continued, "This cannot be authentic. Hadith is one part truth, one part mythology, and one part historical attitudes of the time."

The historical attitudes of the time, no matter what the culture or religion, included suspicion regarding left-handed people. Not coincidentally, *sinister* comes from the Latin and old French word for "left." In twentieth-century America and Britain, until the 1960s, psychologists commonly believed that left-handed children should be retrained to be right-handed.[6] Even today, suspicion of left-handedness persists in both Muslim and non-Muslim communities. In 2015 a mother in Oklahoma alleged that her four-year-old's preschool teacher had prohibited him from using his right hand because it was evil to do so.[7] It's still possible to find current Christian websites reiterating that left-handedness is associated with the Devil.[8]

Historically, multiple cultures mandated reserving the right hand for tasks requiring cleanliness and the left hand for dirtier tasks. This helped control disease, especially when water for washing was scarce. In India and many Arab cultures, where people eat with their hands, it's traditional to use only the right hand.

Given this history and social context, a report of a seventh-century Prophet advising someone to use his right hand to eat is unsurprising. If Muhammad did so advise (and this is not certain), Muslims can even then disagree on whether this hadith, originating from a time of superstition and unsanitary considerations, firmly prohibits left-handedness forever or merely recommends right-handedness and whether it was meant only for that particular time and context.

Over the centuries, not even the most devout Islamic scholars assumed that the entire hadith corpus, without exception, was literally and absolutely true. Today, the danger arises when modern Muslims assume that it is. The early scholars understood human error, the human temptation to forge hadith, and the human tendency to create legends around a beloved figure. That is why they rigorously analyzed each hadith report to determine its authenticity.

The scholars subjected hadiths to linguistic analysis. Did the language of the hadith match the language the Prophet would have used? They analyzed the language of the hadith to date it and to search for inconsistencies.[9]

Incidentally, this linguistic analysis of hadith, coupled with the Arabs' advanced knowledge of mathematics and statistics, led to the first invention of cryptanalysis, the science of code breaking. Before the Arabs, no one had ever devised a system to break codes; relatively simple ciphers had remained unbroken for centuries.[10] The first known available treatise on cryptanalysis, *A Manuscript on Deciphering Cryptographic Messages*, was written in the ninth century by the Arab philosopher and scientist al-Kindi; it refers to an earlier, eighth-century, Arab treatise on cryptanalysis, but that manuscript has not been found.[11]

In other words, the early Muslims treated the analysis of hadith as a science. Jonathan Brown, a hadith specialist, describes the following three-tiered system of hadith evaluation, which, he remarks, greatly resembles the system journalists today use (or should use) to evaluate the validity of information.[12]

First, the Islamic scholars asked, "What's the source of this hadith?" Who said it? To answer this question, they examined the "chain of transmission" (*isnad*). The hadith must have been quoted from someone who attested they'd heard it from x who had heard it from y who heard it from z, and so on, down to whomever heard it firsthand from the Prophet.[13]

Second, the scholars evaluated the reliability of everyone who had transmitted the hadith. If the transmitter were a known liar, the hadith would be suspect. The scholars also examined the transmitter's oeuvre: did the transmitter generally transmit sound hadiths or weak ones? And they evaluated the chain of transmission to ensure that it wasn't interrupted.[14]

Third, the scholars searched for corroboration. Had the hadith been transmitted independently via different chains of transmission? The more independent pathways of transmission led to a hadith, the stronger the hadith.[15] A hadith report could not be classified as strong unless multiple reliable people had independently reported it.

The scholars rated the hadith reports along a spectrum from strongest to weakest: "widely and diffusely transmitted," "sound," "weak," and "baseless forgeries."[16] They subjected hadiths about law and theology to a far more rigorous scrutinization process than they subjected hadiths about etiquette, manners, pious preaching, or the meanings of Qur'anic terms.[17] Most people, including most Muslims, don't realize that Islamic scholars employed this two-tiered system! But it's crucial to know: the aforementioned hadith on left-handedness would have undergone much less scrutiny than, for instance, a hadith about inheritance law.

Despite the rigorous scrutiny, authentication wasn't always possible. Sometimes, the hadith compilations included two contradictory hadiths, because it was impossible to determine which was true. The compiler included both, letting the reader decide which was true. Thus, the accuracy of even the strongest hadith was considered only highly probable, rather than 100 percent certain.

The early hadith scholars also distinguished between which words and actions of the Prophet were meant to be followed by everyone and which were not.[18] Sometimes the Prophet was just someone going about his life as best as he could and not necessarily thinking about establishing the rules of a new religion. What would happen if an offhand remark became sanctified as hadith?

I have an example. One hadith reads, "A community that entrusts its affairs to a woman will not flourish."

Ouch.

But let's look at it. First, this is a statement uttered fourteen centuries ago. It's not that different from Saint Paul's advice in 1 Timothy 2:12 of the Bible (New Testament), in which the saint says: "I do not permit a woman to teach or to have authority over a man, she must be silent." Let's face it, antiquity was not rife with women's rights.

Second, this hadith seems to contradict the Qur'anic portrayal of feminine authority and leadership. The Qur'an relates the story of the Queen of Sheba, approves of her power and belief in one God, and never orders her to abdicate, sell her palace, and let someone else lead her people. Indeed, the Qur'an refers to the Queen of Sheba as a female ruler and takes her elevated status in stride, as something to be celebrated.[19]

The hadith also seems to contradict Muhammad's example. His own wives assumed positions of leadership. His first wife was an influential businesswoman, and his widow Aisha commanded an army. Muhammad appointed a woman as *imam** of her household, over other men.

How then could the Prophet have uttered this statement? The answer lies in the context. At the time, the Persian Sassanian Empire was floundering and had gone through eight emperors in four years.[20] When an inexperienced princess ascended to the throne, the Prophet said he didn't think the empire would flourish.[21] His comment was about a specific historical occurrence.

Of course, it's possible that Muhammad never uttered these words in the first place. Not every Islamic scholar believes this hadith to be authentic. This was an isolated hadith, not corroborated by more than one of Muhammad's Companions.[22] And despite this hadith being purportedly narrated during a battle in which a woman was leading an army, none of

---

* *Imam* can mean religious leader or someone who leads the prayer.

the men in the army, upon hearing this hadith, immediately dropped their weapons in protest.[23]

Today, although Muslims do generally consider the hadith corpus to be sacred, they don't always apply it literally to modern life. In fact, most Muslims *must* relegate this particular hadith on women's authority to its historical context, because as of this writing, at least thirteen Muslim women have been presidents or prime ministers in the last four decades alone.

I'm just going to say that again. *Thirteen Muslim women have been presidents or prime ministers.* In the last few decades alone. They have governed over Muslim-majority countries or, in two cases, countries with sizeable Muslim populations. That's a great many Muslim men who have been led by women. Yet, these thirteen women have all been respected according to their office.

I've lost count of the times I've heard—in person, in the media, or from our politicians—offhand remarks about oppressed Muslim women with no rights. No one stops to ask, "Hmm, how could Muslim women become presidents if they have no rights?" Megawati Sukarnoputri, the president of Indonesia, was one of the most powerful women in the world.

That's not even counting the Muslim women queens (like Noor and Rania of Jordan) or the Muslim women rulers of history, such as Razia Sultan of India, Shajar al-Durr of Egypt, Sayyida al-Hurra of Spain (pirate queen as well as ruler), the Arab queens 'Arwa and Asma (who had sermons proclaimed in their names), and the many others who wielded political power in their own right.[24] It's not counting the many Muslim women serving in legislatures or in local governments.

The example of the hadith of women's leadership illustrates the intricacies of hadith interpretation. But it also illustrates that Muslims are not simply the sum of their religious texts. Muslims, like other religionists, engage with their religious texts and are not frozen in the seventh century.

The hadith is the lens through which the Qur'an is understood and interpreted, as well as a source of specific information about the law and theology of Islam. But the hadith is also a connection to Muhammad. Hadith chains of transmission connect present-day Muslims—whether Sunni or Shi'a—with a Prophet who lived fourteen centuries ago.

CHAPTER FIVE

SUNNI, SHI'A, AND OTHERS

MUCH HAS CHANGED in the public discourse since the 2003 US invasion of Iraq. Before that, no one ever asked me about Sunni and Shi'a. These days, I'm frequently asked to explain the difference.

SUNNI AND SHI'A

All Muslims are Sunni, Shi'a, or subsets thereof. No real theological differences separate them; that is, Sunni and Shi'a do not differ in their views of God or the Qur'an or the Prophet. Nor are the two groups markedly different in their practices. That's why I don't believe Sunni and Shi'a should be called "sects" of Islam, though others might.

"Sects" also implies that one group is orthodox and the other has broken off as heterodox. But neither Sunni nor Shi'a are orthodox, as they both developed contemporaneously. Sunnis constitute 85–90 percent of the world Muslim population, the Shi'a, 10–15 percent.

I grew up in Southern California attending a mosque populated by both Sunni and Shi'i Muslims, and my father grew up in India, where both Sunni and Shi'a attended his local mosque. My family is Sunni, but we currently attend a Shi'i Islamic center. Quite a few Muslims identify as neither Sunni nor Shi'a but simply as "Muslim" or even sometimes "Sushi," the latter a term indicating disregard of or impatience with the negligible differences between Sunni and Shi'a. A friend of mine didn't think to ask her father whether she was Sunni or Shi'a until she was in her twenties. "We are *Muslim*," he replied, rolling his eyes.

Before 2003, most non-Muslims I met had never heard the terms "Sunni" and "Shi'a." Yet, today, I routinely encounter the assumption that

Sunni and Shi'a have been at each other's throats for centuries. Why? The reasons are worth unpacking.

First, human beings tend to explain away conflicts they fail to understand or care about—or that concern people foreign to them—with the carelessly simplistic assertion, "Oh, they've been at each other's throats for centuries." I hate this statement. I hear it ubiquitously directed toward situations where Muslims are involved, in the public discourse, news media, television, film, and books.

This one sentence lazily deflects blame onto the victims of misunderstood conflicts and excuses us, as outsiders, from having to cogitate about complicated motivations and circumstances. It excuses inaction—after all, there's nothing one can do with people who have been at each other's throats for centuries. It absolves us of responsibility—after all, *we* had nothing to do with the conflict; they've always been at each other's throats. Finally, it confirms our superiority as people uninvolved in the conflict and confirms their inferiority as people who cannot settle their differences.

It's simply not true that Sunni and Shi'a have been "at each other's throats for centuries." Yes, some tension always crackles between differently identifying groups, between any majority and minority. (Only look at the current tensions between ethnic and religious groups in our own country.) Yes, the minority group always feels the differences more acutely than the majority group. And yes, incidents of oppression between Sunni and Shi'a (mostly by Sunnis persecuting the minority Shi'a) have undoubtedly occurred in 1,400 years of history. But these have been relatively few. Sunni and Shi'a have historically never engaged in campaigns of violence on the scale of, say, the Catholic-Protestant conflicts throughout history. They have never had a program of forced conversion at the level of, say, the Spanish Inquisition.

Sunni and Shi'a have always recognized each other as valid Muslims. It's only rare extremists (a fraction of a fraction of the Muslim world) who do not accept the Shi'a as Muslims.[1] In fact, historically, marriages and interaction between Sunni and Shi'i Muslims have been so common as to be unremarkable. Older Muslim Americans have often expressed bafflement to me about the recent prominence of this so-called Sunni-Shi'a divide.

The Sunni-Shi'a conflict is amplified by journalistic reports on Iraq. It seems that nearly all conflicts in Iraq and other Muslim-majority nations and communities have been reported, in recent decades, as "sectarian conflicts," even when they have little or nothing to do with religion. It's far easier, even for well-meaning journalists, to report conflicts as "sectarian" rather than determine whether they are actually something else—such as fights over resources or infrastructure, political protests spiraling out of control, or general criminal behavior, like theft. After all, human beings fight for all kinds of reasons, and usually not for religious ones.

Our twenty-four-hour news cycle, incessantly reiterating "sectarian violence" in Muslim contexts, brainwashes not only non-Muslims but other Muslims around the world. A Muslim who may never have thought in terms of Sunni-Shi'a differences, but who watches CNN, might become conditioned by the "they've always been at each other's throats" narrative and conclude for perhaps the first time that he *ought* to be at the other's throat. And that is a tragic thing.

These days, as in the past, any "Sunni-Shi'a" conflict has far more to do with political power than religious differences. The US invasion of Iraq in 2003 disrupted the society there: families commonly included both Sunni and Shi'a members, but the war caused a segregation of Iraqi society into Sunni areas and Shi'i areas, generating difficulties for mixed families. The US-backed Shi'i government also began oppressing Sunnis, greatly increasing the fissure between Sunni and Shi'a in Iraq, not to mention giving birth to ISIS. In Syria, the conflict sparked by the 2011 uprising began as a political one, challenging the government of Bashar Al-Assad, but various groups later appropriated the conflict, framing it as religious. Proxy wars instigated by Iran (a Shi'i state) and Saudi Arabia (a Sunni Wahhabi state) have also fueled political conflicts and disguised them as sectarian.

Nevertheless, the only significant difference between Shi'a and Sunni stems from a single question: who holds religious authority?

While the Prophet lived, he held leadership and religious authority. When he died, the question arose: who would lead the nascent Muslim community? One group favored 'Ali, the Prophet's son-in-law, insisting that the new leader remain within the Prophet's family. Another group favored Abu Bakr, the Prophet's best friend, arguing that community consensus should choose the next leader.

The second group prevailed. This group would later become the Sunni. The group that had favored 'Ali would become the Shi'a, short for *Shi'at 'Ali*, or "party of 'Ali."

Thus, Abu Bakr became the first Caliph of Islam. He was not a prophet or king, but the leader of the Muslim community. 'Ali did become Caliph eventually, but not until three other caliphs had served before him. Sunni Muslims consider these first four caliphs to be "the Rightly Guided Caliphs." After 'Ali died, rule in Islamic lands generally became dynastic.

For the Sunni, formal religious authority lies with the religious scholars, those qualified to articulate and interpret the religious law; for the Shi'a, formal religious authority lies with the descendants of the Prophet. The majority of the Shi'a, called the "Twelvers," believe that the twelve male linear descendants of the Prophet Muhammad were divinely guided *Imams*, each Imam designating his successor. The twelfth Imam, it is believed, went into hiding and will return at the end of time.

These divinely guided Shi'i Imams (always uppercase) who are descendants of the Prophet should not be confused with imams of Sunni mosques. Sunni imams are religious leaders of mosques or simply prayer leaders; they may be supremely learned or barely learned. Rare Shi'i religious scholars who have reached the very highest levels of scholarship, called *ayatollahs*, may also be addressed sometimes as "Imam."

Since the occultation of the twelfth Imam, Shi'i religious authority has passed to the Shi'i religious scholars. Thus, practically speaking, Sunni and Shi'a look quite similar now. The difference is that the Shi'i scholars exercise authority on behalf of the absent Imams, whereas the Sunni scholars exercise authority on their own behalf. The Shi'a have separate books of jurisprudence and hadith from the Sunni, but religious interpretation and methodology between the two groups is similar. Traditionally, all Shi'a who have not reached the highest stage of religious education must choose as a guide someone who has reached this stage. Generally, this scholar's opinions are binding for those who follow him, but not for those who do not.[2]

In addition to the majority Twelvers, two other branches of the Shi'a are the *Zaydis* and the *Ismailis*. Zaydis are the most similar to Sunnis and do not believe the Imams are divinely guided. The Ismailis believe the line of descent from 'Ali never expired; since the nineteenth century, in contrast to other Muslim communities, the Ismailis do have an authoritative figure to lead their community—the Aga Khan, believed to be directly descended from 'Ali and Fatima, the Prophet's daughter. The

Aga Khan is the spiritual and cultural head of the Ismaili community and interprets Islamic law in light of modern society.[3]

WAHHABIS

Much of antimodernist ideology in recent Islam has derived from Wahhabi Islam. Contrary to what many assume, Wahhabism—concentrated in Saudi Arabia—is not any kind of "original" or "pure" form of Islam but a relatively recent religious movement. In the eighteenth century, Muhammad bin 'Abd al-Wahhab began to develop an extreme form of Islam that fused the conservative culture of the Arabian Peninsula onto local Islamic practices. He called his result the one true form of Islam.[4]

'Abd al-Wahhab's movement, though identifying as Sunni, differed from the rest of Islam in several particulars. First, none of the other Islamic schools of legal thought (discussed later) had ever proclaimed themselves to be the only true form of Islam. In fact, they had all accepted one another as valid. Yet, the original Wahhabis considered themselves not just a school of legal thought but rather *all of Islam* itself.[5] 'Abd al-Wahhab deemed all non-Muslims, all non-Sunni Muslims, all Shi'a, and all Sufis to be heretics. He also denounced as heretics great Sunni legal figures of Islamic history if he didn't agree with them.[6]

Were it not for two historical factors, Wahhabism would likely have dwindled, as extremist movements usually do. First, the British in the late eighteenth century encouraged the Wahhabis (along with other local ethnic and religious groups) in their campaign to foment rebellion against the Ottoman Empire.[7] Second, the al-Saud family, contending to gain control of the Arabian Peninsula, offered the Wahhabis a partnership: we'll adopt your religion, said the al-Saud, if you fight for us.[8]

The Wahhabis accepted. Thus, when Saudi Arabia was founded, in the early twentieth century, Wahhabism became its official religion. The Saudis also controlled the two holy cities of Islam, Mecca and Medina. Imagine if, in an equivalent scenario, a small extremist Christian sect, such as David Koresh's Branch Davidians, suddenly became the official religion of the United States, flush with money, allied to the world's superpowers, and controlling Christianity's most holy religious sites.

These converging factors rendered Saudi Arabia and Wahhabism disproportionately influential. So did the mid-twentieth-century American decision to bolster the Saudi regime as "the leader of the Muslim world," to further oil interests and fight Communism, which is anti-religion.[9] But Wahhabism is not mainstream Islam.

Wahhabism has become less stringent over the last several decades, though it's still extreme on the spectrum of Islamic beliefs and practices. Since the 1970s, Wahhabis have often called themselves *Salafis*.[10] The Taliban also emerged from the Wahhabi mold, having been commonly educated (if at all) in Wahhabi schools. Though Wahhabism has grown somewhat past its Saudi roots, Wahhabis amount to only a few percent of Muslims worldwide.

SUFIS

The only Muslims who sometimes manage a good-guy image in Western discourse are the Sufis. Yet, Sufi Islam is not a sect or division of Islam; it's a *way*. It's a tendency within Islam, a way to achieve ethical and spiritual perfection. Sufi Islam cannot be precisely defined, but it emphasizes inwardness over outwardness, the spiritual, and the mystical dimension of Islam. The word "Sufi" comes from the Arabic word for "wool," because in early Islam, a group of people began to eschew materialism and wear only rough wool garments, following the example of the Prophet Muhammad.

Here's how you can be a Sufi: imagine a circle with a point in the exact center. That point represents God. The perimeter of the circle represents Islam, or shariah as "the way of God." Infinite radii connect the perimeter of the circle to God the Center. Only once you stand on the perimeter of the circle and accept Islam/shariah can you discover a path (a radius) that leads to God the Center. You can be any kind of Muslim—Sunni or Shi'i, progressive or fundamentalist, liberal or conservative—and be a Sufi.

You do have to be Muslim first, though. Accept shariah, then move along the radius to God.

On more than one occasion, people have told me that they are Sufi but not Muslim. To me, that is cultural misappropriation: taking an Islamic practice and erasing Islam from it. That's equivalent to saying they are Christian but do not believe in Jesus Christ. Adopting Sufi practices is different from claiming to be a Sufi.

The idea that Sufism has little or nothing to do with Islam comes with colonial baggage. Rampant Western misunderstandings about Sufis originated with nineteenth-century Orientalists—those studying "the Orient," often with little or no knowledge of Arabic. They understood neither Islam nor Sufism, but the latter was attractive to them, as they perceived it as a form of "universal spirituality."[11] They concluded—even insisted—that Sufism had nothing to do with Islam (the traditional enemy).[12] Yet, Sufism has been solidly Islamic for over a thousand years and has Islamic beginnings three centuries earlier than that.

The progeny of Orientalist attitudes is the current prevalent belief that Sufis are "the good Muslims," the peaceful ones. Implication: non-Sufis are the bad Muslims. This kind of categorization is silly and insulting. For one thing, Sufis have led military campaigns; for another, most Muslims are peaceful, just like most people of any religious community, whether they are Sufi or not.

THE NATION OF ISLAM

The Nation of Islam originated in the United States in the early twentieth century, independent of mainstream Islam. Indeed, scholars dispute whether the Nation of Islam should be considered part of Islam at all. At its inception, many of its tenets differed from and even violated the basic beliefs of Islam.

The Nation of Islam germinated between 1913 and 1925, a period in which an American man named Timothy Drew changed his name to Noble Drew Ali and founded the Moorish Science Temple. His new religion contained elements of both Islam and Christianity but was separate and distinct from both. Ali wanted to found a religion for black Americans, who were only one or two generations removed from slavery, and distance it from Christianity, the perceived religion of white people.

Ali may also have wanted to reclaim an Islamic heritage. He and his followers adopted Islamic symbols (calling themselves "Moors") and sartorial practices (wearing the fez). In doing so, Ali was reaching back toward a perceived Islamic ancestry. Not so far-fetched, as historians believe that the Qur'anic chanting of Muslim slaves in America, numbering in the tens of thousands, eventually evolved into the shouts and hollers that engendered blues music.[13]

When Noble Drew Ali died, in 1929, his follower Wallace Fard Muhammad left the Moorish Science Temple and established a new group called the Nation of Islam, whose members were often called "Black Muslims." The Nation of Islam had little to do with Islam; certain of its aspects were in fact theologically antithetical to Islam. For example, Wallace Fard Muhammad was deemed God incarnate and his successor, Elijah Muhammad, a prophet.[14]

In 1964, one of the Nation of Islam's ministers, Malcolm X, traveled to Mecca for the pilgrimage, the Hajj. Malcolm X realized, upon pilgrimaging to Mecca, how different "Islam" was from the "Nation of Islam." The variety of different races and nationalities represented at the Hajj stunned him. The Nation of Islam was based on racial differences, but Islam eschewed racial differences. Malcolm's wife, Betty Shabazz, observed that Malcolm went to Mecca as a Black Muslim and came back as a Muslim.[15]

Malcolm X changed his name to El-Hajj Malik El-Shabazz and returned to the Nation of Islam with his newfound enthusiasm for Sunni Islam. Just a year later, Malcolm Shabazz was assassinated, at the age of forty. But his enthusiasm took root, and, in the 1970s, the Nation of Islam changed its name (several times) and transformed, as an entire group, to Sunni Islam.[16]

A small group of Nation of Islam members rejected the wholesale change to Sunni Islam. It broke off from the main group and retained the name and original theology of the Nation of Islam. This group has since been led by Louis Farrakhan.

PART II

THE STORY OF SHARIAH

CHAPTER SIX

WHAT SHARIAH IS
AND HOW IT WORKS

THE FIRST MUSLIMS brought their questions to the Prophet Muhammad. When he died, they took their questions to his contemporaries, called the Companions, those who had known him personally. The first four caliphs were all Companions of the Prophet.

The Companions remembered and transmitted the Prophet's words. They interpreted the Qur'an and answered questions about how it applied to daily life. They issued their learned opinions but also discussed their views, deferred to other learned opinions, and sometimes changed their initial decisions when confronted with additional evidence or other learned viewpoints.

But after the Prophet's contemporaries passed away, who remained to answer religious questions?

The early Muslims looked to the Qur'an and the Sunna to guide them, but these were finite sources. Besides, the Qur'an is not a legal text. Of its 6,236 verses, only about 80 verses deal with law in a strict sense.[1] Relatively few clear and uncontested rules come directly from the Qur'an and the Sunna. Therefore, to find answers to their questions about how to live according to the way of God, the early Muslims began interpreting these religious texts.

The earliest interpreters were private citizens who studied the Qur'an and the Sunna, both in the academic abstract and in response to specific disputes and questions brought to them by Muslims.[2] These early Islamic scholars included women, such as Aisha, the Prophet Muhammad's widow.

Suppose a dispute was not governed by custom or public law or ordinance. Or suppose the disputants wanted an Islamic answer to their dispute. Where could they go for dispute resolution?

They could consult someone with expertise in the law and the Qur'an and the Sunna. They could ask this scholar, this *mufti*, to listen to their grievances and resolve their dispute. The mufti would then consult the religious texts, as well as decisions from other muftis. He would arrive at his own conclusions. The two parties would follow his decision.

The mufti sometimes found and applied pertinent rules that had already been derived or settled by previous scholars. But at other times, no existing rules pertained to the issue at hand. In that case, the mufti exercised *ijtihad*.

Ijtihad was, and still is, independent reasoning applied to the religious texts in order to interpret them. Shariah rules that do not come directly from the Qur'an and the Sunna result from ijtihad, which is not any old independent reasoning but independent reasoning using an agreed-upon methodology of interpretation. More than that, ijtihad must also yield results that align with the goals of shariah.

THE GOALS OF SHARIAH: THE MAQASID

All Islamic scholars recognized that the purpose of shariah was to exclude harm and promote benefit.[3] Therefore, all rules of Islamic law had to further this purpose. Over time, this purpose was articulated as five (or six) categories of goals, called the *Maqasid al-Shariah*. The Maqasid decreed that all human beings had the following rights:

- the protection of life
- the protection of religion (and morality)
- the protection of property (resources and wealth management)
- the protection of family (lineage and progeny)
- the protection of intellect (rationality, knowledge, mind, education)
- the protection of human dignity/reputation[4]

Wording of these shariah goals may vary. Most commonly, they are articulated briefly as the right to life, intellect, religion, property, and family.

If one concept encapsulates the nature of the Islamic legal tradition, it's the Maqasid al-Shariah. If the primary question for Muslims was "What is the way of God?" then the Maqasid al-Shariah is the concise nutshell answer.

All shariah rules, all fiqh, must comply with the Maqasid. Islamic scholars developed laws against slander to further the goal of protecting human dignity and reputation. To further the goal of protecting life, they developed laws regarding food cleanliness and laws against homicide. They developed extensive laws of inheritance to protect lineage and family.

Everyone, the Islamic scholars agreed, was entitled to the fundamental rights articulated in the Maqasid. For me, an American lawyer, these Maqasid principles strongly resemble the principles in our own Constitution, and I'm deeply proud of both. As advanced for its time and remarkable as our Constitution was (and still is), though, the Maqasid al-Shariah was developed a thousand years earlier.

FOLLOWING THE MAQASID: FIQH AND ITS METHODOLOGY

The Islamic scholars developed the rules of fiqh and aligned them with the Maqasid by using multiple "methods" or "tools" of ijtihad (independent reasoning). Scholars agreed on these methods, though they differed in their views of how important each was in relation to the others. They all agreed, though, on the primary importance of *consensus.*

If I were a mufti—and this would be acceptable, as some women were muftis even in early Islam[5]—and I knew that neither the Qur'an nor the Sunna contained a clear answer to my question, then I would examine earlier scholarship to determine whether the past Muslim community had reached a *consensus* on my question. Had the question previously arisen, and had the scholars unanimously agreed on an answer?

I likely wouldn't find consensus on my question. In the totality of the fiqh literature, consensus was reached on less than 1 percent of issues.[6] These issues were regarded as particularly important, since everyone agreed on them; most related to matters of worship, such as the five daily prayers or the prohibition on intoxication.[7] That means, though, that over 99 percent of fiqh was subject to juristic *disagreement*, where scholars reached no consensus and where different scholars reached different conclusions, despite using accepted methodology.

But here's the amazing thing. These differing conclusions were all respected and recognized as possible and correct manifestations of the law. From Muhammad's time onward, Muslims acknowledged that only God knew the right answers and that humans could do only their fallible best to ascertain them. And that's why *all* learned fiqh opinions by recognized scholars, following an acceptable methodology, were acknowledged as valid.

What if I, as a mufti, searched for a consensus on my legal question but found none? I would then progress to the next tool of ijtihad. I would use *analogy* to draw similarities between an established fiqh rule and my own legal issue.

To understand how analogy works, consider this famous example. Prophet Muhammad forbade the trade of ripe dates for the same weight of unripe dates. The reason was that unripe dates would lose weight as they dried, rendering this an unequal trade. The early Muslim jurists extended this ruling by analogy, forbidding the trade of unequal weights or amounts of *any* object.[8]

The permissibility of wine consumption presents another example of analogy. The Qur'an prohibits the consumption of grape wine and forbids people from praying when drunk. Muslim scholars, by analogy, concluded that if grape wine were prohibited because it made people drunk, then date wine (or any wine) should also be prohibited on the same grounds.[9]

In applying analogy, scholars identified *the reason for the rule* (also called *the reason for revelation** if the rule came from a Qur'anic verse) and extended that rule to another set of circumstances. In the case of wine, the reason for the rule was intoxication, not hatred of grapes. Therefore, the scholars forbade any intoxication, from any source.[10]

Isolating and extending the reason for the rule or revelation contributed to the adaptability of Islamic law. If the reason for the rule changed or disappeared, then the law could not necessarily be applied in the same way. Hence the Islamic legal maxim "The law is changed if the reason for the law is changed."[11]

---

* *The reason for revelation* (or the rule) is the "operative cause," called the 'illa in Arabic. For you lawyers, it's the *ratio legis*.

To sum up so far, if I'm a mufti, I know that my decision must comply with the Maqasid (goals) of shariah, and I've taken the first four most important steps in making my decision. I've consulted the Qur'an and the Sunna for clear answers, searched for a previous consensus, and then used analogical reasoning to find my answer. These four steps, incidentally, are considered the proper methodology in the majority Sunni view; in both the Shi'i and minority Sunni views, *reason* (aql) replaces analogical reasoning,[12] though these two are not always completely distinct.

What if I've taken all these steps and exercised rigorous logic throughout—a requirement assumed by the scholars—but I've arrived at an unjust result? Or apprehended a looming unforeseen consequence?

I could use additional tools to help me achieve a more just result. I could apply the principle of *istihsan*, which means "seeking the best."[13] Istihsan would allow me to choose one possible legal solution over another or favor one legal precedent over another on the basis of equity and fairness. I could also apply the principle of *istislah*, which would allow me to take the public good into consideration. In applying these principles, I'd consider factors like *necessity*, *mistake*, and *hardship*.

Necessity would allow for a potential exception to a general legal rule. For example, one general legal rule is that Muslims are forbidden to eat pork. Nevertheless, if a Muslim is starving to death (literally) and can find nothing else to eat, then pork is allowed for that person at that time, in order to further the shariah goal of protecting life.

As a mufti, I could take *needs* into account in making my decision, even if the needs didn't amount to a necessity. Needs might be considerations taken into account to protect society or its citizens. For example, I could choose a legal outcome that gave greater protection to minor children.[14]

I could also create an exception to a general rule by allowing for *mistake*. For example, breaking a Ramadan fast by eating or drinking is not allowed. But, *mistakenly* breaking a fast does not invalidate the fast. (It is surprisingly easy to eat by mistake while fasting! You might automatically pop something into your mouth because you're hungry and tired and not thinking clearly, or you might mistakenly believe the sun has set.)

Considerations of *hardship* would also allow for an exception to the general rule. For example, although all healthy adults must fast during Ramadan, early scholars provided exceptions for those who were traveling, pregnant, menstruating, elderly, ill, or in other conditions in which fasting would constitute a hardship or a health hazard.

Finally, after applying istihsan and istislah principles, I could consider *custom*. Customary practices, though not always formally acknowledged, could significantly affect legal decisions. For example, the Prophet forbade the sale of something that did not exist.[15] Sounds fair, right? But in a manufacturing contract, a person pays another to manufacture something that doesn't exist until it's manufactured. Strictly speaking, manufacturing contracts would be forbidden under the general rule. Nevertheless, Islamic scholars permitted them, recognizing that custom had always allowed them.[16]

Suppose I, as a mufti, had examined all these aforementioned aspects of Islamic law and subsequently arrived at an answer to my legal question. My decision wouldn't necessarily result in delineating one party as absolutely right and the other absolutely wrong. Neither would it likely involve characterizing their actions as illegal or legal. Instead, my solution would fall within a *five-tiered* scale of law.

Islamic scholars categorized human behavior into five areas: required, recommended, neutral, disliked, or prohibited. Fasting during Ramadan is *required* for healthy adult Muslims. But fasting on certain non-Ramadan days might be *recommended*. Committing murder is absolutely *prohibited*. Divorce, though, is permitted but *disliked*.[17] The middle category must certainly be the vastest: the *neutral* category, containing actions on which Islamic law is indifferent, such as wearing pink or watching *Star Trek* or majoring in mathematics.

This five-tiered system made it easier to apply the law to human behavior, which does not always adhere to absolute values of right and wrong. Because cases brought to muftis often involved disputes between community members who would continue living and working together, solutions tended to be practical, allowing the parties to save face and avoid humiliation. Imposing an all-or-nothing solution, like designating one disputant the winner and the other the loser, might have prevented both parties from continuing to live in close proximity.[18]

This goal of preserving relationships, even in conflict, gave rise to the legal maxim "Amicable settlement is the best verdict."[19] To reach an amicable settlement, the mufti could conclude that it would be "more correct" to follow one course of action over another. The Qur'an, with its emphasis on forgiveness, facilitated compliance with this maxim, because forgiveness is always the better course in Islam, even in egregious cases like those involving violence.

The mufti's final decision regarding the dispute, called a *fatwa*, was not "law." The mufti, a private citizen, had no governmental or legal authority. His decision was binding on the parties only because they had *agreed* to be bound by it.

A fatwa, therefore, was a nonbinding, reasoned legal opinion by a recognized, learned Islamic scholar who applied the accepted methodology. It was neither absolute law nor a divine order. It could be disregarded in favor of another fatwa.

This is still the definition of a fatwa. In today's modern world, where law comes from the nation-state, it is less relevant—usually irrelevant—to governance and the state's legal system. It is primarily relevant as a cleric's learned opinion, just as a rabbi's or priest's opinion is relevant to those who seek it. But for most of Islamic history, the fatwa was an element in the governance of society, and it contributed to the development of the law.

Recently, on *The Daily Show*, Aasif Mandvi, describing his acting role in a new comedy series, said breezily, with a sense of great hilarity, "So my character gets a fatwa against him. Oh!" he interrupted himself, turning to the audience, "you know what a fatwa is? It's a death sentence!"

I gasped and cringed like a character in a bad movie when I heard this. A fatwa is not a death sentence! And here was a *Muslim* announcing to millions of viewers on national television that it *was*, hoisting us by our own petards. A fatwa is a nonbinding, reasoned legal opinion by a recognized Islamic scholar! *Not* a death sentence!

Of course, the reason for this misconception is Ayatollah Khomeini's infamous "fatwa" pronouncing a death sentence against Salman Rushdie for the publication of his book *The Satanic Verses*. However, Khomeini's "fatwa," as I'll discuss later, was flawed in essential legal details and criticized by numerous Islamic scholars, in addition to being largely motivated by politics and personal vengeance.

Throughout history, if a mufti issued a fatwa that most other muftis disagreed with, then it remained a minority opinion; or perhaps only an individual opinion; or perhaps an opinion completely forgotten in time. On the other hand, if enough qualified scholars agreed with the fatwa, it might become a strong opinion, or even the majority opinion. It might even, rarely, become a consensus.

From the beginning, Islamic scholars understood that, however carefully they tried to glean the way of God, only God knew the correct answers. That's why they concluded their fatwas with the words "God knows best." With this phrase, they acknowledged, "Here's my opinion. I think it's correct because I've followed established legal methods and because I'm learned in the religious law, but I know it may be wrong because I'm human and therefore fallible. That other scholar with a different opinion might be correct. Only God knows best." Indeed, a legal maxim attributed to Muhammad states, "The disagreements of the scholars are a source of mercy for my nation."[20]

This generally accepted methodology and system of developing the law not only provided transparency but accountability. Strikingly, it also generated legal pluralism and legal flexibility. *Legal pluralism* means that you allow for multiple possible legal outcomes on the same set of facts. *Legal flexibility* means that the law was not rigidly applied, but flexible.

Islamic law was legally pluralistic because a single legal question could have a variety of answers. Different muftis arbitrated the same kinds of conflicts—can I get a divorce? who owns this property?—using the same religious texts and under similar fact patterns. But they arrived at different legal decisions because they differed in how they used the tools of ijtihad.

The law was flexible and adaptable because, as culture, custom, issues of public interest, and other factors changed across time and geography, juristic analysis accommodated those changing factors and thus allowed the law to stay socially responsive.[21] The same facts were evaluated differently in different circumstances, thereby adapting to different societies, customs, and geography, as well as over time.[22] Therefore, this system of developing fiqh had, by its very nature, legal flexibility and adaptability built right into it. There's an Islamic legal maxim for this too: "It may not be denied that laws will change with the change of circumstances."[23]

It's ironic that the Western stereotype of shariah is one of a rigid and backward law, because the reverse is true. The shariah-based legal system flourished successfully and continuously for over a thousand years—longer than most (if not all) legal systems in the history of humanity.[24] Such longevity would have been impossible had the shariah-based legal system's fundamental cornerstones not been legal pluralism and legal flexibility.

Also ironically, not from Muslims did I learn how remarkable an achievement the Islamic legal tradition was but from professors who were not Muslim.

You may be wondering: if there were an array of legal decisions on the same facts, then how did Muslims decide which decision was correct? They didn't. This is how Islamic law differs from the modern law of the nation-state. According to fiqh, *every* decision by a recognized scholar, following the proper methodology, was correct. In fact, a famous legal maxim proclaims, "Every mujtahid is correct,"[25] where a mujtahid is someone who exercises independent reasoning (ijtihad) on the religious texts. As Jonathan Brown remarks, "The statement 'the shariah says . . . ' is thus automatically misleading, as there is almost always more than one answer to any legal question."[26]

If the Islamic legal system were characterized by legal pluralism, then how did those living in Islamic lands know which acts were allowed and not allowed? The big issues of law would have been understood by everyone—general principles against stealing, cheating, usury, adultery, violence, etc., didn't change. It was the smaller issues within the bigger ones that varied. For example, all Islamic scholars agreed that a woman could divorce her husband (this was literally a millennium before a European woman could divorce hers). But scholars differed on what constituted valid grounds for divorce, the procedures of divorce, and the distribution of property upon divorce.

Over time, Muslims began to consolidate opinions to promote predictability in the law. Textbooks of decisions were compiled. Decisions by the more illustrious established jurists carried more weight than opinions of inexperienced scholars. But to this day, there remains wide variation in the religious law.

WOMEN MUFTIS

Women were Islamic scholars, hadith scholars, and muftis from the early seventh century onward. Indeed, one of the most respected of scholars was Aisha, the Prophet's wife.

The authority of women is clearly established by no less than the Qur'an and the Sunna. In Arabic, the masculine form can mean both men and women, just as the English plural "you" can include both men and women. But the Qur'an doesn't simply say "you" when it addresses people; it *explicitly* addresses women so that there's no doubt of their inclusion and—at many times—their equality with men.[27] Here's an example (33:35):

> For all men and women who have surrendered themselves unto God, and all believing men and believing women, and all truly devout men and truly devout women, and all men and women who are true to their word, and all men and women who are patient in adversity, and all men and women who humble themselves [before God], and all men and women who give in charity, and all self-denying men and self-denying women, and all men and women who are mindful of their chastity, and all men and women who remember God unceasingly: for [all of] them has God readied forgiveness of sins and a mighty reward.

In Qur'anic verses like the one above, by explicitly recognizing women at a time when women were rarely recognized, the Qur'an "compels men to recognize [women] as independent moral beings."[28] The above Qur'anic verse clearly equalizes women with men in the moral and religious spheres—a radical and feminist idea for late antiquity.

One of the earliest Islamic scholars was Umm al-Darda, a prominent seventh-century jurist, who sat with men at the mosque and debated religion with them. She famously said, "I have sought worship in everything, but I've never found a better way than sitting with scholars and debating knowledge with them."[29] She stood shoulder to shoulder with men while praying, arrived at the mosque with her hair uncovered, and taught classes in the great mosques of Damascus and Jerusalem to both men and women, including the caliph.[30] As a recognized and respected legal scholar, she issued fatwas, including one that women should pray in the same position as men.[31]

Mohammad Akram Nadwi, a religious scholar researching female Islamic scholars in history, has found records of over eight thousand. Women issued fatwas, taught classes, were cited by the great male jurists of Islam, argued with judges in court, and intervened in court cases.[32] Prominent male jurists sometimes recorded forty or fifty women scholars or jurists with whom they personally studied.[33]

Was Islamic law as much interpreted by women as men, then? Well, no. Male religious scholars still far outnumbered the women. The ancient world everywhere was a patriarchal world, whether or not women scholars were respected.

Moreover, even seventh-century female religious scholars did not necessarily formulate twenty-first-century feminist interpretations of religious law. They would have interpreted the law through the lens of their own patriarchal culture.

Let me give you a modern example. In the 1960s, when my parents first came to California from India, an American (white, agnostic) female friend of theirs, a professor, advised them not to go to a woman doctor because "women doctors were not as good as male doctors."

How could a woman say such a thing about other women? Her opinion was a product of her environment. Even today, as shown by abundant data, women show implicit bias against other women and in favor of men.[34] Seventh-century women would similarly have conceived of their roles in terms of their seventh-century world.

Fatima Mernissi's *The Forgotten Queens of Islam* relates biographies of the Muslim women rulers, regents, and queens of Islamic history that Western scholarship has never known and that Islamic scholarship has, tragically, forgotten. But, thanks to modern scholars like Mernissi and Mohammad Akram Nadwi, their ephemeral forms have acquired some deserved substance.

HOW THE SHARIAH-BASED LEGAL SYSTEM WORKED IN PRACTICE

In the seventh century, communities ruled themselves. Rulers of empires generally couldn't reach remote areas. Police forces hadn't been invented yet. At first, in Islamic lands, people governed themselves in pre-Islamic ways. They used local laws and customs, often grafting Islamic tenets upon them.

The first generations of Islamic scholars also integrated some legal practices of their surrounding cultures, such as those from Persia, Mesopotamia, Egypt and other Roman provinces, Yemen, and Arabia, as well as from Jewish law.[35] Conversely, these early scholars categorically rejected other practices. This makes sense, because although the scholars were starting a new civilizational project, based on the Qur'an and Sunna, their ideas of law and justice would have come from cultures and histories they knew.

The muftis began to develop the law by giving fatwas in response to hypothetical questions or practical disputes. Their fatwas, complete with commentaries, were compiled into treatises. These treatises were used as references in court.[36]

Muftis were also professors. They conducted *halaqas*, or "study circles."[37] Both men and women learned from muftis. When a student had learned enough, the mufti issued the student a certificate. To deepen and broaden his learning, the student would then find another mufti with whom to study and earn another certificate. This process continued until the student became a recognized mufti (or shaykh) himself.[38]

Why did these people study and teach religious law for no remuneration and in addition to their day jobs? It was their passion, and they took to heart the words of the Prophet Muhammad, who famously said, "Pursue knowledge, even if you have to go all the way to China!" (A near-inconceivable distance from Arabia back then.)

In Islam, all learning (*'ilm*) and knowledge is a path to divine knowledge. It was Muslim "society's valorization of learning and the community's recognition of those deemed to possess it"[39] that produced the class of Muslim religious scholars. And since the muftis didn't charge fees, learning was accessible to everyone.

What if you and your neighbor had a conflict resolved by a mufti, but then your neighbor refused to abide by the fatwa? Then you could take him to court.

The *qadi*, a judge usually appointed by the ruler or his officials,[40] would hear your case. The qadi and his court were an established element of Islamic society by the ninth century.[41] He issued enforceable legal decisions, but he was more than a modern judge:

> [The *qadis*] were not only justices of the court, but the guardians and protectors of the disadvantaged, the supervisors of charitable trusts, the tax collectors, the foremen of public works, and the informal mediators in social and family quarrels. They resolved disputes, both in the court and outside it, and established themselves as the intercessors between the populace and the rulers.[42]

The qadi was generally chosen from the scholar class, though he wasn't always a mufti. He enforced agreements, resolved disputes, and adjudicated crimes. To adjudicate his cases, the qadi consulted treatises of muftis' fatwas on similar issues in similar fact patterns. He conferred with the muftis and decided which fatwas were most relevant to his case.

Even early Islamic law allowed a woman to be a qadi, with some limits.[43] Some scholars even asserted a woman's *unlimited* right to be a qadi.[44] The great majority of qadis were men, but a few examples of female qadis have survived the erosion of history. Umm Muqtadir Billah, who maneuvered to get her thirteen-year-old son recognized as caliph and ruled in his stead, appointed a woman as a qadi in the early 900s.[45] Less than a century after that, Malikah Arwa' bint Ahmad governed the province of Yemen under three different caliphs and was appointed to *hujjah*, which was the highest religious office under the Fatimid caliphs of Egypt.[46]

The qadi lived in the societies where he held court, so he was connected to the people and liaised between them and the ruler. Like the mufti, he avoided zero-sum results that granted the winner everything and humiliated the loser. Sometimes this required compromises between the parties. When compromise wasn't possible, such as when a crime was committed, the system allowed for the convicted loser of the dispute to at least explain his motivations or circumstances and bring witnesses, friends, and neighbors to testify to his character. This allowed him to save face[47] and preserved community relations.

For those versed in the English and American common-law systems, the Islamic system might seem familiar. Judging cases by consulting legal decisions in similar cases? Isn't that like our case-law system?

Yes, it is! The shariah-based legal system, with its inception in the seventh century, and the English common-law system, with its inception in the twelfth century, have much in common. They are both *case-law systems*, in which muftis or judges examined individual cases and the legal questions they posed. The Islamic legal system and the English common-law system both differ from the *civil-law system*, which is based on statutes rather than cases and is in effect throughout most of Europe.

In both the Islamic legal system and the common-law system, judges developed the law by interpretation rather than by following a code of laws. However, whereas English common-law judges looked to previous court cases as authoritative precedents to follow, qadis were not bound by previous court cases. Instead, qadis gathered the law from the muftis: from their fatwas, from consultations with them, and from legal treatises—the books of fiqh.[48]

In addition to issuing decisions based on fiqh, the qadis also enforced *siyasa* laws. These were administrative laws that the ruler enacted for the efficient running of society, such as tax laws and traffic laws.[49] Siyasa laws could not contravene shariah; indeed, they were a facet of the shariah-based legal system, as laws promoting the public good.

The difference between siyasa and fiqh is like the difference between the laws Congress passes and the laws our courts develop by deciding cases. Congress identifies a matter of public interest and passes a law about it; this is like a siyasa law established by a Muslim ruler to further the public good. In contrast, our judiciary today—at least in the US and England—develops the law by interpreting cases, similar to how qadis enforced the law gleaned from the muftis, who developed fiqh by evaluating cases, applying and interpreting religious law, and issuing fatwas. Both kinds of law—congressional law and case law—are enforced by our courts, just as both siyasa and fiqh were enforced by qadi courts.

This model of the shariah-based legal system varied over the centuries and across geographical areas, with shifting power and political currents. Bureaucracy played a later role. But the basics of how it worked remained the same.

Some scholars have suggested that the English common-law system originated from the Islamic shariah-based legal system. This would explain certain mysteries. Why, for instance, despite Roman rule in England, did England develop a common-law system when the rest of Europe developed legal systems based on the Roman civil-law system?

First, some context. The English common-law system germinated in the twelfth century. By this time, the Islamic shariah-based legal system was five hundred years old—mature, developed, and extending over thousands of miles and far beyond its birthplace.

Second, England had connections to the Islamic legal system through its king. The Normans who invaded England also invaded Sicily, which had been ruled by Muslims for two hundred years. When Roger II took over Sicily, he retained and integrated Muslim culture and infrastructure there, including governmental structure, finance, and judicial institutions. He retained judges for Christian matters alongside the existing qadis for the Muslims.[50] As legal scholar John Makdisi writes, "The influence of Islam on Roger II was significant in all aspects of his reign."[51]

In the twelfth century, then, England and Sicily were the only two states that both had Norman kings.[52] They talked! Frequently, officials made both England and Sicily their homes.[53] Both kingdoms exchanged court personnel, as well.

When, in the twelfth century, King Henry II overhauled the legal system in England and planted the seeds of the English common-law system, it only makes sense that these exchanges with the sister kingdom of Sicily (which still retained much of the Islamic legal system) would have influenced him. This theory makes especial sense when you consider the structural similarities between Islamic law and common law—and how both differ structurally from Roman civil law.[54]

If we do *not* take Islamic law into account, the sudden birth of the English common-law system is a mystery, as Makdisi writes:

> Until now, historical research has focused almost exclusively on Roman, Germanic, Anglo-Saxon, and other European legal systems as potential origins for the revolutionary changes introduced by King Henry II to English law in the twelfth century. Yet, despite hashing and rehashing the modes by which transplants could have taken place between these legal systems and English law, historians have had to admit that the fit is just not there.[55]

But the fit *is* there, according to some scholars, when it comes to Islam and English common law. Some of the principles hypothesized to have come into English law from Islamic law include the following: the assumption that everyone is innocent until proven guilty; the right not to incriminate oneself; the inadmissibility of hearsay; and the right to a fair trial.[56]

Civilizations are influenced by other civilizations all the time—there is no shame in this!—and less advanced societies naturally learn from more advanced ones. In Islam's first centuries, the Arab Muslims learned papermaking from the Chinese and studied the philosophy of the Greeks to develop their own philosophy. By the twelfth century, Muslim civilization was advanced, with a centuries-old, sophisticated legal system; in Europe, though, justice was commonly served by employing "trials by ordeal," such as trial by water (innocent if you sank, guilty if you floated) or trial by fire (innocent if you could walk barefoot onto flames or red-hot metal without injury). Europeans learned from Muslims in other areas, as is well documented, so why wouldn't they have learned about law, as well? Why wouldn't the English, searching for a new legal system to implement, have been influenced by and even adopted a version of the five-centuries-old, well-established case-law system they'd heard about from their fellow Norman king in Sicily?

It was, as journalist of legal history Manlio Lima remarks, "a considerable improvement over trial by ordeal."[57]

DEVELOPMENT OF THE SCHOOLS OF LEGAL THOUGHT

To sum up, in the first century or two of Islam, muftis issued fatwas and taught students in their study circles. Thus, fiqh developed and the community of scholars grew. Qadis, situated between the ruler and the muftis, developed the shariah-based legal system in practice.

In the mid-eighth century, some study circles grew into larger centers of learning. These were clustered in particular geographical areas and organized around famed scholars.

By the mid-ninth century, scholars began coalescing around legal doctrines of analyzing and developing fiqh, rather than around individual scholars. These "interpretive communities"[58] following particular legal doctrines were called *madhabs*, or "schools of legal thought."

All the schools based their development of religious law on the Qur'an and the Sunna. They all used the legal sources and legal methods of independent reasoning (ijtihad) discussed above. But they differed in the importance they gave certain legal methods over others. Some schools used analogical reasoning extensively, whereas others preferred to rely more heavily on hadith. Some schools were more skeptical of using hadith. Some especially valued close linguistic readings of the Qur'an. But they were all accepted as valid interpretations of shariah.

The Shi'i schools developed, as well, though for the first few centuries, Muhammad's male descendants, the Shi'i Imams, issued the Shi'i religious rules. After the line of Imams expired, religious authority devolved to the religious scholars, essentially the same as in Sunni Islam, with the exception of the Ismailis. The Shi'a have their own books of hadith and fiqh, but the differences between Sunni jurisprudence and Shi'i jurisprudence are not generally significant. The Shi'i hadith collections include sayings of the Imams as well as of the Prophet Muhammad.

To reiterate the important point, though: all schools of Islamic legal thought recognized each other as valid. As a Muslim, I can choose to follow any of the schools. Historically, Muslims tended to associate themselves with one particular school, and rulers often adopted adherence to one school over another. Nevertheless, strict adherence to one school was not always the case; this position makes sense to me personally, because if all the schools recognized each other as valid, I believe I should be able to follow any of them on various issues.

At one time, many hundreds of schools of legal thought thrived. Most have since disappeared or merged with other schools. Today, four main Sunni schools (Hanafi, Shafi'i, Hanbali, and Maliki) and one main Shi'i school (Jafari) survive. A few smaller schools remain, as well, such as the (Sunni) Ibadi and Zahiri schools and the (Shi'i) Ismaili and Zaydi schools.

The Zahiri school is actually extinct but still considered influential.[59] That's not a bad epitaph!

THE MADRASA AND WAQF

Aside from the schools, two institutions influenced the development of fiqh: the *madrasa*, which I'm often asked about, and the *waqf*, which nobody asks me about.

When, as a student, I first learned about waqf, the Islamic institution of charitable endowments, I confess to thinking, "Who cares?" If you're feeling the same way, I empathize. Bear with me, though, because waqf is key to understanding both the strength and the demise of the shariah-based legal system.

Recall that, especially in the first centuries of Islam, most of the learning occurred in the study circles, or halaqas, held in private homes or in mosques. Fiqh education continued this way until the nineteenth and even, in some places, the twentieth century. But, starting in the tenth century, a madrasa system started growing alongside the halaqa system.

The madrasa was a law college where students studied fiqh. Madrasas could accommodate more students than traditional halaqas. Mosques began to be enlarged to accommodate classrooms, libraries, dormitories for the students, and food.[60] The money for all this came from a charitable endowment, called a waqf.

The Islamic institution of waqf was established to facilitate charitable giving. Giving away property "for the sake of God" was one of the most pious actions a Muslim could undertake. Property donated to advance education or build a hospital or establish a homeless shelter all counted as property given away for the sake of God. Waqfs could not be set up to benefit the wealthy—only the needy.[61]

Because education was commonly considered an obligation to God, donating property for educational purposes qualified as donating it for the sake of God. Therefore, madrasas were commonly supported by waqfs.

Suppose I lived in Islamic lands sometime between, say, the eleventh and nineteenth centuries. I could donate my property, as a waqf, for religious education—that is, for a madrasa. But then I would lose all ownership of it. I could appoint myself or my family as the trustee to manage it, but I still wouldn't be able to control the madrasa's budget or operations or otherwise act as the owner of the property. My madrasa (as waqf property) could not be sold or transferred or divided; it would therefore last for generations, even centuries, supported by my waqf endowment.[62]

In 859 CE, a Muslim woman named Fatima Al-Fihri founded the oldest university in the world still operating today, the University of al-Qarawiyyin, with a waqf charitable endowment. The second-oldest university in the world, Al-Azhar, was founded in 975 CE and has benefited throughout its history from waqf endowments.

Many waqf donors were not wealthy, but the wealthy could inevitably afford larger donations. Rulers also established waqf madrasas, appointing themselves as trustees because they wanted to woo and influence religious scholars. This eroded the boundaries between the judiciary and the ruler somewhat, and every so often the ruler could find religious scholars willing to rubber-stamp their actions. But even so, developing fiqh remained exclusively the purview of the scholars.[63] After all, though the ruler could appoint and dismiss scholars in his madrasa, he could replace them only with other scholars from the same (stubborn) scholarly class.

Understanding waqf is essential for three broad reasons. First, by the time of colonialism, waqf properties amounted to an enormous segment of society—between 40 and 60 percent of all real property![64] Second, waqf endowments ensured the continuation of Islamic legal education and provided a structure for it. Third, between 30 and 50 percent of waqf founders were women, and even more waqf beneficiaries were women.[65]

That's why, when colonialism destroyed the waqf system, half the economy of Muslim lands disintegrated, Islamic legal education and development was arrested, and women were dispossessed of property and income. In other words, understanding waqf charitable endowments is crucial to understanding not only how Islamic society worked but—as we'll see—how it was shattered.

POWER STRUGGLES AND THE RULE OF LAW

In Sunni Islam, then, and eventually in Shi'i Islam (after the line of divinely guided Imams expired), the answer to the question of who would make the religious law after the Prophet turned out to be this: the scholars. But whyever would a ruler concede lawmaking power to a group other than himself?

Not all the early rulers did concede. About a hundred years after Muhammad, Caliph al-Ma'mun attempted to garner religious authority for himself. He endeavored to impose his own religious views on the population, persecuting, jailing, and even executing religious scholars who disagreed with him.

But the scholars, heroically indeed, refused to cede religious authority, even when imprisoned and tortured. They didn't change their views of the religious law to placate their caliph, either. Their resistance, for the sake of knowledge rather than personal gain, is an epic story and one that shaped the development of Islam.

Ultimately, al-Ma'mun failed. His son canceled the Mihna, as the conflict was called. The scholars emerged victorious, wielding the authority to develop the law.

Scholar of comparative religion Reza Aslan writes that, had al-Ma'mun prevailed, Islam might have become a completely different religion. "The Caliphate might have become a Papacy; religious authority could have been centralized within the state, and an orthodox Muslim Church would have developed as a result."[66] But that is not what happened. From the Mihna onward, the authority to make Islamic law resided in the hands of the religious scholars, not the rulers.

The schools of Islamic legal thought arose in the first place, at least partially, because scholars sought power to counterbalance the always-suspect political authorities.[67] (Power has always corrupted.) The private, informal study circles of the muftis lacked political power. But the schools did accord the scholars sufficient authority to counterbalance the ruler, because their unifying doctrine collectivized scholars across geographical areas, increasing their numbers and power.[68]

Thus, throughout Islamic history, those who governed were generally separate from those who developed religious law. Indeed, they were often at odds with each other. Although many rulers sought to portray themselves as religious in order to legitimize themselves, never in Islamic history did clerics actually govern. That would have been a theocracy, and never in over 1,300 years of Islamic rule was Islamic government a theocracy. Not until 1979 and the Iranian Revolution, when a new Shi'i theory of governance by the religious scholars emerged and actualized the first intentional—and experimental—theocracy in Islam.

Separating scholars and rulers in society, each with influence, led naturally to a system of checks and balances. The religious scholars checked the ruler because he needed their approval to be seen as legitimate. Only at the expense of his legitimacy could the ruler break the law or pressure the scholars to change the law. If he did so, he would be seen as breaking *God's law*—no trivial matter.[69] Moreover, the religious scholars enjoyed the loyalty of the people, because they sorted out the daily conflicts and questions in their communities. For the ruler to gain the support of the people, he required the support of the religious scholars. If he failed to acquire it, the religious scholars were nicely situated to foment a rebellion against him, as the people respected and heeded them.

The ruler reciprocatively checked the scholars, too. He wielded the force of the empire, which could discipline or imprison them. The ruler could dismiss his qadis if he perceived insubordination, though the new qadis would most likely also come from the scholar class. (Islamic history has a long tradition of Islamic scholars resisting powerful state-appointed judicial positions because they valued their independence as legal scholars.)[70]

The people also checked the ruler, because they paid taxes, which required the ruler to be responsive to their interests. The people pressured the ruler to ensure a just and orderly society, because they could take their grievances and complaints to the scholars, who could in turn cast doubt on the ruler's legitimacy. This could facilitate the overthrow of the ruler.

Why was legitimacy, bestowed by the scholars, so important to the ruler? The premodern Islamic system didn't designate an automatic successor to the throne, as most European monarchies did. Multiple contenders might claim rights to the throne at any given time.[71] The ruler needed legitimacy and support of the religious scholars not only to attain power but to maintain it.[72]

The scholars usually came from the middle and lower classes of society. (Unsurprisingly, then, fiqh has always tended to favor the middle and lower classes.) Insisting that the ruler comply with shariah as the rule of law didn't enrich the scholars. But it did cement their role in developing the rule of law.[73]

And that's what we're really talking about here: the rule of law. Shariah was the rule of law, the unwritten constitution of Islamic society, by which everyone from the poorest peasant to the caliph agreed to be bound. No one was above the law—neither the caliph nor even the scholars, though they developed the law, prevented as they were from making unfounded laws by the methodologies of legal reasoning.

Of course, no system has ever been perfect or entirely immune to corruption, including our own modern systems. For all pre-twentieth-century legal systems, sexism, too, was a reality. But generally, and in terms of structural integrity, the shariah-based legal system, which operated for over a thousand years until colonialism, worked.

Why did the existence of a class of religious scholars result in a strong rule-of-law system?

The scholars functioned as the judiciary, evaluating the legality of the ruler and of the laws. If the ruler attempted to appropriate private property for his treasury or commit other excesses, the law would prevent him. That meant the ruler would resort to taxing his citizens for revenue, which in turn meant that he would need to consider their interests. Powerful legal scholars also ensured security and predictability, because laws were well-defined; this meant citizens could confidently invest in long-term projects and leave property to their descendants.[74]

Also operating in premodern Islamic lands was the more general concept of the Circle of Justice, which undergirded the Islamic system of law and governance. The Circle of Justice, a four-thousand-year-old Middle Eastern concept originating before the birth of Islam, emphasized *reciprocal* justice. That is, the Circle decreed that all elements of society respect and depend upon one another, so that conflicts of interest could be absorbed without fracturing society.[75]

In Islamic society, the Circle of Justice worked like this: the ruler could only maintain his rule with a military; which military had to be sustained with money; which money came from taxes; which taxes the citizens could pay only if they were prosperous; which prosperity came from public order and justice; which public order and justice came from shariah (developed by the scholars) as rule of law; which shariah had to be enforced and respected as the law of the land by the ruler; which ruler maintained his rule with a military (thus propelling us back to the beginning of the Circle).[76]

The Circle of Justice still informs Middle Eastern politics. Pre-1979 Islamist movements gained credibility because they promised justice. Decades later, the 2011 Arab uprisings again arose on slogans demanding, in essence, reciprocal justice.[77]

The Arab uprisings included Muslims and non-Muslims, all uniting for justice. But what did multireligious justice mean under the shariah-based legal system? That's the subject of the next chapter.

CHAPTER SEVEN

RELIGIOUS MINORITIES WITHIN THE SHARIAH SYSTEM

TOO MANY PEOPLE MISTAKENLY BELIEVE that shariah is something imposed on non-Muslims; that jihad is holy war meant to convert people of other religions to Islam; and that Muslims have always wholeheartedly persecuted religious minorities, whereas non-Muslims have always wholeheartedly embraced diversity (the "myth of persecution"[1]). All these assumptions are theologically and historically untrue, as repeatedly shown by both Muslim and non-Muslim scholars.

During a talk I gave at a highly regarded high school, a student raised his hand and sneered, "Everyone knows that Muslims have to convert people or kill them."

I felt a vast sadness at his statement.

Forced conversion is prohibited in Islam. This prohibition is so well-established and unequivocal that it is not even debatable or arguable. The Qur'an repeatedly prohibits forced conversion, declaring, "There is no compulsion in matters of faith." (2:256)

The Qur'an contains at least seven statements prohibiting forced conversion. That's remarkable for a seventh-century religious text originating in a time and place where not only was warfare the status quo but where two massive empires (Zoroastrian and Christian) had been battling each other for three bloody decades. The first of these verses appears above; six others follow:

- "If your God had willed, everyone on earth would have believed; are you then going to compel the people to become believers?" (10:99)

- "And say, 'The truth is from your Lord, so whoever wills—let him believe; and whoever wills—let him disbelieve.'" (18:29)
- "And so [O Prophet] remind them! You are only a reminder; you cannot compel them [to believe]." (88:22)
- "Your duty is no more than to deliver the message; and the reckoning is Ours." (13:40)
- "[Say] to you your religion, and to me my religion!" (109:5)
- "You are not to compel the people, so remind, by means of the Qur'an, those who take heed." (50:45)

Throughout history, Muslims generally followed these Qur'anic commands and did not implement policies of forced conversion. I'm not saying forced conversion never occurred in 1,400 years or that Muslims were saints. I don't pretend there was never any friction between religious groups, people being who they are. But, in 1,400 years of Muslim history, incidents of forced conversion were rare, as well established by both Muslim and non-Muslim scholars. One of these, Michael Bonner, writes:

> There was no forced conversion, no choice between "Islam and the sword." Islamic law, following a clear Quranic principle, prohibited any such thing: dhimmis [non-Muslims] must be allowed to practice their religion. . . . [I]n fact, although there have been instances of forced conversion in Islamic history, these have been exceptional.[2]

The myth that Muslims advocate forced conversion began when Islam was new. For seventh-century and later European Christians, Islam was naturally a false religion. (How could it not have been?) They knew little of what Muslims believed, but they perceived Muhammad as the anti-Christ. They couldn't conceive how a false religion could spread as fast as it did. It must be, they assumed, that Muslims were converting people at sword-point.

Yet, as historian Juan Cole writes, any conversion, even *voluntary* conversion, was uncommon early in Islamic history:

> During the first decades of Muslim rule [any] conversion appears to have been rare; there is no evidence that the Muslims demanded it of anyone.[3]

It's true that Muslims conquered territories. But, writes Gerald Hawting, a revisionist historian (and not particularly sympathetic toward

Islam), Muslim conquerors did not want the conquered people to convert to Islam:

> The Umayyads and the Arab tribesmen who first conquered the Middle
> East regarded their religion as largely exclusive of the conquered peoples.
> There was no sustained attempt to force or even persuade the conquered
> peoples to accept Islam, and it was assumed that they would remain in
> their own communities paying taxes to support the conquerors.[4]

Moreover, evidence indicates that, in early Islam, the ruling elite actually tried to prevent people from becoming Muslim, because many of the caliphs and governors wanted to retain the idea that Islam was for Arabs as the chosen people.

Islamic studies professor Carl Ernst adds that the "Arabs were not interested in converting non-Muslims to Islam,"[5] and that when non-Muslims under Islamic rule did wish to convert to Islam—because it appealed to them or because of intermarriage or for practical reasons—"it was at first a baffling issue for Muslim authorities."[6]

How the Arabs, with their tiny military force, gained such military victories over both the enormous Persian Sassanian and Roman Byzantine Empires has always been a matter of some puzzlement. Historian Arthur Goldschmidt writes that some Jewish and Christian communities aided the Arabs in their conquests:

> The disgruntled Syrian and Egyptian Christians viewed the Muslim
> Arabs as liberators from the Byzantine yoke and often welcomed them.
> The Copts, for example, turned Egypt over in 640 to Amr's Arab force,
> which, even with reinforcements, numbered fewer than 10,000. Like-
> wise, the Jews, numerous in Palestine and Syria, chose Muslim indiffer-
> ence over Byzantine persecution.[7]

The conquests at times resulted from contractual negotiations rather than warfare. Sometimes, the contractual negotiations took surprising forms:

> So much emphasis did the Arabs place on acquiring other cultures'
> knowledge that Greek manuscripts were obtained from the [Roman]
> Byzantine Empire through peace treaties in return for maintaining the
> status quo.[8]

In other words: "We won't attack you if you give us your books."

When the second caliph of Islam, Umar, conquered Jerusalem in 638, the Muslims left Christians free to practice Christianity and visit the holy places.[9] They didn't touch the churches, instead building their own shrine, the Dome of the Rock, and their own mosque, al-Aqsa. They removed the piles of garbage that had accumulated on Temple Mount[10] and invited the Jews, who had been banished from the city by the former Christian rulers, to return and worship as they wished.[11] Comparative religion scholar Jane Smith notes that the Muslims' appropriation of Jerusalem "was one of the most peaceful of [the city's] long and painful history."[12]

Again, I'm not saying that Muslims throughout history were perfect or that interreligious relations were always harmonious. But neither do Muslims deserve the virulent stereotypes—violent, barbaric, forcibly converting others to Islam. I myself have been battered by these stereotypes quite regularly in my life as a Californian Muslim. (I have never tried to convert anyone.)

My social studies teachers seemed particularly possessed of these views. In eleventh grade, my history teacher instructed his somnolent students that "the Qur'an told Muslims to spread Islam by the sword."

I was shocked. My Sunday school teacher had explicitly devoted an entire Sunday session on the impossibility of forcing belief and how Islam forbade it. Therefore when, years later, my history teacher confidently espoused the opposite, I suffered a fight-or-flight reaction, shaking, face flushed, heart pounding somewhere near my throat. I thought I might vomit. But I raised my hand and spoke for the first time in class that year to tell my teacher that he was wrong. He admitted that he had not read the Qur'an.

To reiterate: the Arab conquests were not a religious enterprise.

Ergo, they were not jihad.

A NOTE ON JIHAD

Jihad means to "struggle" or "strive" in the way of God. My childhood largely featured a jihad to get good grades—not unsurprisingly, as I was the child of immigrants. ("Education," my father told me sternly, "is the only thing no one can ever take away from you.")

In a religious sense, jihad—striving in the way of God—falls into two broad categories: the "greater jihad" and the "lesser jihad." The greater jihad is the internal struggle to make oneself a better person. The lesser jihad is the external struggle to make society a better place.

The internal jihad is about ridding oneself of wicked impulses, such as cheating, lying, jealousy, and backbiting. The Prophet Muhammad once famously remarked, upon returning from battle, that he had returned from the lesser jihad (physical fighting) only to engage in the greater jihad (the struggle to become a better person).

The external jihad is about improving society, and shariah identifies several types:

1. "jihad by the word," which means using verbal persuasion, like writing letters to the editor or to members of Congress, to correct injustice;
2. "jihad by the hand," which means doing good works to correct societal injustice, such as volunteering in a homeless shelter; and
3. "jihad by the sword," which means using force in self-defense or to overthrow direct oppression.

Jihad by the sword, also called military jihad, is *never* aggressive warfare; it is warfare only in self-defense or against direct oppression. The self-defense must be against an *immediate* threat and, according to some Islamic scholars, the oppression must actively prevent Muslims from practicing their religion. In addition, such jihad can be declared only by a publicly recognized leader of the worldwide Muslim community (there's no such person today). Therefore, requirements for a legitimate jihad by the sword can rarely be fulfilled—virtually never in our modern world.

But suppose the requirements for jihad have been fulfilled. Even then, Muslims are constrained by extremely strict rules of engagement. Here are just a few:

- Muslims may not kill non-combatants (civilians).
- Muslims may not kill children or the elderly.
- Muslims may not kill anyone taking refuge in holy buildings.
- Muslims may not arbitrarily destroy property.

- Muslims may not uproot trees.
- Muslims may not commit rape.
- Muslims may not commit terrorism.
- Muslims may not cheat or use treachery.
- Muslims may not poison the water supply.
- Muslims may not torture anyone (including animals).
- Muslims may not commit suicide.
- Muslims may not kill other Muslims.[13]

Note that these rules of engagement—established since very early Islam—are, if anything, more restrictive than our modern international rules of warfare.

Terrorism, which can be defined as the clandestine use of force, has always been forbidden in Islam. Shaykh Abdallah bin Bayyah, one of the most well-respected Islamic scholars in the world, unequivocally prohibits terrorism, which he exhaustively defines as

all violent acts that aim to obliterate, sabotage, and terrorize people, kill the innocent, and destroy property . . . [including] the circulation of illegal drugs, as well as the violence of vigilantes against legitimate authorities, aimed to create sedition and anarchy and strike fear among civilians, or even with the express aim of overthrowing a legitimate government.[14]

Why do al-Qaeda and ISIS wrongly claim that their acts of terror are jihad? To legitimize themselves! According to shariah, al-Qaeda and ISIS are not jihadists but criminal mass murderers.

Our media is at fault for relentlessly using "jihadi" or "jihadist" as synonymous with "terrorist," despite numerous objections to this usage. If it's bad behavior and the perpetrator is a Muslim, it must be jihad, right? Wrong. Terrorism *violates* jihad.

Jihad has never meant "holy war," either. In Islam, war is never "holy"—it is either justified or unjustified.[15] It is justified as jihad only when waged in self-defense or to overthrow oppression.

Indeed, Muhammad would never have accepted the idea of war as holy. He urged us to pursue knowledge, and he never started a war. He famously said, "The ink of the scholar is more sacred than the blood of the martyr."

In Islam, no warfare is allowed except that which qualifies as a jihad. That means no wars for territory, no wars for resources, no wars for oil. The Arabic word for warfare is *harb*, not *jihad*. Significantly, unlike *jihad*, *harb* is never attached to or combined with the phrase "in the way of God."

The restriction on aggressive warfare comes from the Qur'an, which repeatedly forbids Muslims from starting a fight, as in the verse, "But do not attack them . . . unless they attack you first." (2:190) The Qur'an regularly insists that if the other side desists fighting, then Muslims have no choice but to desist, as well: "If they incline to peace, you must incline to peace." (8:61) The verses that do urge Muslims to fight do so only in self-defense and in the particular historical circumstances at the time.

Indeed, for the first two-thirds of his mission, though Muhammad and his followers were persecuted and tortured, they never fought back and instead practiced the jihad of nonviolent resistance, called "the jihad of patient forbearance."[16]

The jihad of patient forbearance can be internal or external. For Muhammad and his followers, the jihad of patient forbearance included

1. preaching their views of God and society;
2. freeing slaves who had converted to Islam;
3. performing other acts of charity;
4. migrating to Abyssinia (now Ethiopia); and
5. migrating to Medina.[17]

The Qur'an praises Muhammad's followers for adhering to the jihad of patient forbearance: "And when they hear abusive talk, they turn away from it and say, 'to us our deeds and to you yours; peace be upon you.'" (28:55)

After the new Muslims fled to Medina, where conflict between the Meccans continued, they practiced the jihad of patient forbearance for another three years. Only then, during the last third of his mission, did the Qur'an give Muhammad permission to fight back.[18]

What changed? In Mecca, Muhammad was a private person preaching a new religion. In Medina, he was the political leader of a city. As such, he was head of the army, not just an individual preacher. For fifteen years he had exercised nonviolent resistance, to no avail. When the Meccans marched on Medina, Muhammad was obligated to defend those under his protection.

The verses in the Qur'an that allow Muslims to fight back against aggressors were revealed in Medina. These verses did not give permission to Muslims to go out and start a war. They gave permission to Muhammad to fight back, not against just any old non-Muslims, but against the specific Meccan pagans who were attacking them in the seventh century.

Although Muhammad fought only in defensive battles, after his death his successors did fight wars for territorial conquest and empire building. Religious scholars in the service of rulers anxious to expand territory interpreted religion to allow them to wage wars. To legitimate this, they had to circumvent the Qur'anic restriction on aggressive warfare. Therefore, some Muslim scholars (but not all and not enough to form a consensus) after Muhammad's death began formulating a theory of military jihad that simply ignored the Qur'anic verses that instructed them not to attack "unless they were attacked first."

This is why Carl Ernst notes that the Arab conquests were not a religious enterprise[19] but one stemming from the pursuit of political power, a quest for survival, and the acquisition of territory. As such, the conquests were comfortably aligned with the customs and practices of the time—but not necessarily aligned with shariah. Muslims themselves recognized this over time and abandoned this theory of self-serving warfare. Modern jihad by the sword has for centuries now been defined as defensive warfare.

Still, the stereotype of Muslims continually salivating to kill non-Muslims persists. Our media covers violent Muslims exhaustively (and as a function of Islam itself) but mostly ignores modern ethnic cleansing campaigns by non-Muslims who victimize Muslims. In the Christian-majority Central African Republic, Muslims have been the victims of a largely unreported ethnic cleansing campaign (carried out by the mainly Christian group, Anti-Balaka) that started in 2014 and has killed or displaced tens of thousands.[20] Rohingya Muslims have been the victims of ethnic cleansing by the Buddhists (including Buddhist monks) in Myanmar.[21] In the worst type of organized persecution since World War II,[22] Serbian and Croatian Christians executed an ethnic cleansing campaign (later formally declared a genocide[23]), with the approval of the Serbian Orthodox Church, against Bosnian and Kosovar Muslims.[24] Russians have carried out various ethnic cleansing operations, which some define as genocide, of (mostly) Muslims in Chechnya and Ingushetia.[25] State-backed violence against Muslims in Gujarat in 2002 resulted in thousands of deaths and expulsions.[26] And, as of this writing, 40 percent of China's Uyghur Muslims have disappeared, one million or more being held in "re-education" camps that the UN likens to "massive internment camps,"[27] where they are made to drink alcohol, eat pork, and suffer torture.

Therefore, let us differentiate between religious rules and human nature.

If the Arab conquests were motivated by empire building, not religion, this raises the next question: why did Muslims treat differently non-Muslims who resided in the lands they ruled?

RELIGIOUS MINORITIES UNDER MUSLIM RULE

People generally view their own philosophy of life, whether religious or not, as the correct universal way of being. Historically, just as Christians and other religionists viewed their religions as the correct universal way of being, so Muslims viewed their religion as the correct universal way of being. In Communist countries, where the absence of religion is the correct universal way of being, such as China and the former Soviet Union, religionists have been and continue to be severely repressed. Similarly, the US has fought wars based on the view that *democracy* is the correct universal way of being, even contradictorily supporting undemocratic dictators with the justification of promoting democracy (by fighting Communism and, later, "Islamism").[28]

Just as Americans take for granted the idea that democracy is the correct, just system of governance, seventh-century Muslims would have taken for granted that the Islamic shariah-based system was the correct,

just system of governance.[29] Even so, Islamic scholars did not force shariah onto non-Muslims.

The structure of the shariah-based legal system, based on legal pluralism, allowed religious minorities to observe their own religious laws and
traditions. Since even Muslims could consult from a variety of muftis,
it was just as easy for Jews and Christians to consult their own religious
authorities. Everybody followed the administrative rules (the siyasa laws)
that the ruler made and the qadi implemented. But personal religious
laws were customized for each religion.

Usually, in return for paying a tax (*jizya*), non-Muslims, called *dhimmis* or "protected people," received certain protections, such as the right
to retain their religion and cultural and personal laws; security of per-
manent residence; no time limits on residency; an exemption from military service; and protection from aggressors, whether these were Muslim
or not.[30]

The jizya was a political device, not a religious one. Although the
Qur'an mentions "jizya," it does so in the specific context of a seventh-
century war with Meccan pagan tribes. Moreover, the Qur'an doesn't treat
the jizya as a general poll tax but as reparation for the pagans' breaking
their treaties.[31] The Qur'an does not mandate poll taxes on non-Muslims.

Nevertheless, the early Muslims eventually (though not initially)
started charging poll taxes on non-Muslims by interpreting the Qur'an
in a way that fit with the culture of their world and their contemporaries.
But this doesn't make the jizya a religious requirement. After all, the
early Muslims also ignored the Qur'an's commands to never start a war.
Cultural norms are often stronger than religion.

Although Muslims didn't pay the jizya, they did pay a tax called the
zakat. Non-Muslims did not pay the zakat tax.

Abundant hateful literature cites the jizya as evidence of Muslim intolerance, perpetuating the myth of persecution. This misses the key point,
that a thousand and more years ago, poll taxes were a standard feature
of life everywhere; conquered people paid taxes to every conqueror—no
matter who it was, Christian or Muslim or Zoroastrian—as a matter of
routine. As Christians in the early Islamic empire remarked, what made
the Muslims different from most was that they *also* allowed people to
believe what they wished and to retain their religious laws and customs.[32]

The jizya and the laws governing non-Muslims were implemented unevenly over the centuries—sometimes more harshly, sometimes more leniently, and sometimes not at all. Umar, the second caliph of Islam (ruled 634–644 CE), under whom Islamic rule spread extensively, banished some non-Muslim tribes from his area; on the other hand, he not only allowed others to stay, he sometimes exempted them from the jizya.[33] Umar allowed members of multiple Christian tribes to pay the (Muslim) zakat tax instead of the jizya.[34] He also granted the request of some Christians to serve in the military (as Muslims did) instead of paying the jizya.[35]

In addition, non-Muslims held "significant government offices throughout Islamic history."[36] A Christian record in the 680s under the Umayyad rulers noted that "some of the Arab ruling class were Christian."[37]

Muslim rulers routinely exempted women, the elderly, the poor, religious clerics, and monks from paying the jizya.[38] At times, state funds (which were replenished by, among other sources, the Muslim zakat and the non-Muslim jizya) were "often disbursed for the maintenance of poor Jews and Christians."[39] As well, "poor residents of Islamic lands, irrespective of religion, could expect to be entitled to a portion of the government's *zakat*-revenues."[40]

Treatment of minority groups varied with rulers, politics, and circumstances on the ground. Some rulers were more tolerant than others. Prejudice toward Christians in Muslim lands probably increased in the wake of the numerous Christian Crusades, just as anti-Japanese prejudice increased after the bombing of Pearl Harbor and anti-Muslim hatred increased after 9/11. Laws in every time and place change frequently and depend upon issues such as survival, security concerns, fear, tribalism, the need for labor and resources, and the particular individuals in power.

Rules regarding minorities—dhimmi rules—both placed restrictions on and required respect for minorities. Although the rules were taken seriously, the restrictions were also flexible and frequently circumvented, depending on personal and societal alliances. People intermarried, formed friendships, and transacted business with those of other religions. Conflicts arose not just between Muslims and dhimmis, but amongst Muslims themselves, dhimmis themselves, and even amongst the various Christian subgroups.[41] The dhimmi rules fluctuated in response.

Muslims did sometimes violate the rules of respect for dhimmis, but as scholar of medieval Islamic history Michael Bonner notes, "On the whole, however, such episodes [of persecution] remained exceptional, like the episodes of forced conversion to Islam."[42]

Bonner adds:

> There is no doubt that the history of the dhimma compares favorably with the treatment of non-Christians in Europe during most of the premodern era.[43]

However tolerant the jizya and the dhimmi rules were for the time, the vast majority of Muslims agree that they have no place in the modern world. And since these rules were located primarily in siyasa regulations, no reason for their modern application exists today. If some Muslim extremist or terrorist groups call for jizya or dhimmi laws in order to garner power for themselves, this is a tiny fraction of Muslims worldwide and is no different from American white supremacist groups who seek to marginalize Muslims, blacks, and Jews.

To try to apply the jizya rules and dhimmi laws to our modern world would be nonsensical—these laws were premodern solutions to the problem of how to reconcile imperialism, empire, religious differences, and diversity.[44] That they were not violent solutions is to be commended, but they were nonetheless discriminatory laws that the vast majority of Muslims now view as historical relics.

In contrast, those who perpetuate the "myth of persecution" to depict Muslims as intolerant are simply taking modern views of diversity and projecting them back to ancient cultures, while simultaneously ignoring (or selectively making excuses for) what everyone else was doing at the time.

What *was* everyone else doing at the time? Historian Michael Goodich writes the following summary of what life was like for a non-Christian in Christian lands in the medieval era:

> [The most marginalized people were] the ideological foes of Christianity, such as Jews, Muslims, heretics, and apostates, who were outside the Christian polity and were denied salvation. They lacked full civil rights, did not share in the dominant religious consensus, could not occupy

public office or take part in the public festivities that were a mark of social and ideological unity, and suffered persecution, expulsion, and sometimes even execution because of their faith.[45]

Even later, in the Renaissance era, it was unenviable to be a Muslim (or a non-Christian) in Christian lands. The Spanish Inquisition of the late fifteenth century led to hundreds of years of the forced conversion, death, and banishment of Spanish Muslims and Jews, as well as the extinguishing of Jewish and Muslim culture and even architecture in Spain.[46] Most Western accounts, both contemporary and modern, fail to hold Ferdinand and Isabella accountable—they ignore their atrocities or give them a pass for conducting such a thorough ethnic cleansing that finding accurate counts of executed or expelled Muslims and Jews is nearly impossible, though it must have been in the millions. Religious scholar Huston Smith is an exception, writing:

> Spain and Anatolia changed hands at about the same time—Christians expelled the Moors from Spain, while Muslims conquered what is now Turkey. Every Muslim was driven from Spain, put to the sword, or forced to convert, whereas the seat of the Eastern Orthodox church remains in Istanbul to this day.[47]

The Portuguese conquered Goa, in India, and in 1511 slaughtered the entire Muslim population there.[48] The Jesuit Portuguese went on to establish an era of forcible conversion to Catholicism, destroying Hindu temples and Muslim mosques.[49] The Goan Inquisition lasted for over two centuries, until 1820.

In contrast to these considerably less-desirable solutions to the management of diversity issues, the Muslim approach of a tax in return for protection, exemption from military service, and relative religious freedom was more lenient than in much of the world at the time. As academic researchers Maria Jesús Rubiera Mata and Mikel de Epalza observe, "We must recognize that in the Middle Ages this tolerance [of Muslim rule in Spain] was in itself quite unusual."[50]

The jizya, already in abeyance, was formally abolished by the Ottomans in the mid-nineteenth century, before slavery was abolished in the United States.

My Google search for "European poll tax" produced masses of vicious material on—not European poll taxes—but Islam and the jizya. That's because the English-language, overwhelmingly non-Muslim internet is a fine vehicle for pointing fingers at other cultures while ignoring the faults of our own.

The reality is that poll taxes were neither unique to Islam nor a Muslim invention. Both the Roman Byzantine (Christian) Empire and the Persian Sassanian (Zoroastrian) Empire levied poll taxes on Jews residing within their territories.[51] After the Goan Inquisition ended, in the nineteenth century, the Portuguese continued to apply poll taxes to Hindus and Muslims. As late as the nineteenth century, the English government levied a poll tax on English Catholics for not belonging to the Church of England.[52] And not until 1962, with the passage of the Twenty-Fourth Amendment to the Constitution, did the US outlaw the poll tax as a condition of voting: at that time five states still maintained the poll tax, a relic of the Jim Crow laws, which aimed to disenfranchise black voters and institute segregation.[53]

In other words, laws vary with context—historical, religious, political, and social-psychological context. The jizya was developed in the seventh century against the backdrop of empire, the desire to protect the strength of Islam as a religion and a rule, and the need to accommodate diverse populations under such rule.[54] As legal scholar Anver Emon writes: "Far from being constitutive of an Islamic ethos, the *dhimmi* rules are symptomatic of the messy business of ordering and regulating a diverse society."[55]

Even in the West, can we truly say that we are beyond this "messy business of regulating a diverse society"? As of this writing, Slovakia has moved to effectively criminalize Islam.[56] In America and Europe, Muslims endeavoring to build mosques have faced numerous legal challenges.[57] European countries have outlawed face veils, though Chicagoans and Germans in winter might be just as covered up as the few Muslim women who wear burqas.[58] Some European countries outlaw headscarves, yet exempt nuns in full habit.[59] Some European countries have outlawed the building of minarets.[60] The US Supreme Court *allowed* the execution of a Muslim prisoner who was denied his request for an imam, though it *halted* the execution of a prisoner who was denied his request for a Buddhist spiritual adviser.[61]

US courts have historically approved government policies, even those of doubtful constitutionality, that disproportionately target Muslims as national security threats."[62] In fact, since the passage of the Patriot Act after 9/11, federal prosecutors have targeted Muslim communities not only to search for criminal behavior but to create and encourage it. They have used the popular conflation of "Muslim" and "terrorist" to convict Muslims under "material support for terrorism" statutes, *even if* these Muslims "have harmed nobody and have taken no real steps toward doing so."[63] In other words, Muslims have been convicted, even recently, for doing nothing but having a "violent state of mind,"[64] and they have been incarcerated in secret prisons known collectively as "Guantanamo North," where most inmates are Muslim.[65] These prisons contain prisoners who were transferred thousands of miles without justification or notice and have among the most extreme restrictions on communication, despite the fact that many have no disciplinary infractions or violent histories.[66]

Fourteen states have enacted "anti-shariah" legislation (discussed later), which aims to target Muslim Americans as suspicious, un-American, and unable to belong in their own country.[67] Our American court system imposes sentences that are four times longer for Muslims than for non-Muslims convicted of similar crimes (and Muslims get seven times more media attention than non-Muslims accused of similar crimes).[68] The US Supreme Court has upheld Donald Trump's travel ban on (mostly) Muslims, thus approving discrimination against Muslims in our immigration policy.[69]

Ongoing calls to ban (relatively new) teaching about Islam as a world religion in our schools are common. Muslim children in American schools are twice as likely to be bullied because of their faith as Jewish children and four times as likely as the general school population. Sadly, a quarter of the bullying involves a teacher or school official.[70]

The point of this recitation—which could apply in similar themes but with different details to other minority groups in Europe and America—is that in the twenty-first century, we're still trying to deal with the messiness of diversity. Today, we have little excuse for prejudice, but it's still firmly embedded in our legal and political systems. Projecting our modern standards of equality onto Muslims of a thousand years ago is hypocritical when we ourselves wrestle with such standards.

To sum up, the jizya and the dhimmi rules were not religiously mandated but man-made historical phenomena that were relatively enlightened and tolerant for the time but today would constitute incongruous discriminatory practices. Most Muslims agree with this view. In a 2016 conference in Morocco, 250 eminent Islamic scholars issued the Marrakesh Declaration, a collective, enormously significant fatwa affirming religious freedom from within the Muslim tradition, affirming the UN's Universal Declaration of Human Rights, prohibiting the use of religion to undermine the rights of religious minorities, and prohibiting all forms of religious bigotry, vilification, and denigration.[71] Should you feel an urge to dismiss this fatwa, consider its implications: jizya is no longer a practical part of modern Islamic law—but this fatwa is.

CHAPTER EIGHT

SHATTERING A MILLENNIUM AND DISRUPTING A CIVILIZATION

IN THE EARLY SIXTEENTH CENTURY, there occurred a singular moment of equipoise: Europe, the Ottoman Empire, Mughal India, and China had all achieved near equality in power and advancement. Any of them could have pulled ahead. Any of them could have colonized the New World.

But it was European countries that colonized the Americas—perhaps because they were geographically closest—and the wealth they accrued therefrom tilted the balance of power in their favor, allowing them to colonize most of the remaining world, including most Muslim lands. Western colonizers managed to subjugate three great Islamic empires— advanced civilizations—sometimes by attacking them directly but more often by first insinuating themselves as traders and advisers, and then accruing their increasing financial and military power to the point that they became controlling powers behind (or beside) the Muslim rulers.[1] Sometimes, they leveraged debt. At other times, they simply took possession of Muslim lands or established themselves as ruling elites.[2] The end result of these varied approaches was the same: subjugation and control of Islamic civilization.

Explaining colonialism's effects on Muslim lands is not about blaming the West for the state of the modern Muslim world. The desire for power is universal; empires decline, they fall to conquerors, their people become subjugated. Rather, an explanation of European colonialism of Islamic lands is necessary to understanding both the demise of the shariah-based system of law and why it's not the law in any Muslim country today.

Carl Ernst remarks that colonialism does not seem to resonate with us Americans, for whom

the word "colonial" conjures up quaint images of reconstructed theme parks like Williamsburg . . . [not the] far more efficient systems of colonial rule that the French and British developed in the nineteenth century, with powerful support in technology, policing, and racial ideology.[3]

I'm guilty of this ignorance! Growing up in the American public school system, I had little understanding of what "colonist" meant beyond the Thirteen Colonies. The American Revolution was, moreover, fought between colonists and the mother country, not between the native people and invading colonizers, which would have been analogous to the situation in Muslim lands.

So, please, envision with me the world where most Muslims lived in the early nineteenth century. The Ottoman Empire ruled the Muslim heartland and, after four centuries of power, was declining. Muslim Mughal emperors had ruled India for three centuries, but the English—having elbowed out the French, Dutch, and Portuguese—had colonized India since approximately the mid-eighteenth century. The Dutch consoled themselves with Indonesia, and the French colonized Algeria. Napoleon invaded Egypt (then a province of the Ottoman Empire) but failed to establish control there; instead, the British acquired Egypt in the late nineteenth century and, from there, Sudan.[4]

Nearly 90 percent of the world's Muslim population was colonized. Just take a minute to imagine what the world would look like if 90 percent of Europe and America had been colonized by Muslims during the Industrial Revolution and had attained independence only in the mid-twentieth century. I listen with incredulity to the present-day fear-mongering of Islamophobes warning of Muslims taking over the West, "creeping sharia," "Eurabia," and the "Islamization of Europe," given that it was Europeans who subjugated nearly the entire global Muslim population for a century or more.

THE EFFECTS OF COLONIALISM IN MUSLIM LANDS

Many Americans and Europeans don't truly understand what happens under colonialism. Most of us haven't experienced it, and we usually learn about it in school from the colonizer's perspective. But colonialism affects all aspects of civilization. In Muslim lands, colonialism destroyed the building blocks of the economy, fractured society, disrupted modernization, and dismantled the legal system.

In terms of economics, European colonial powers used Muslim lands as sources of cheap raw materials, which they acquired and sent back to their home countries for development. Exporting raw materials from Muslim communities destroyed the artisan classes (who had traditionally worked the raw materials) and severed traditional business relationships. Thus, whereas the European industrial sector had developed organically from the European artisan classes, the Muslim industrial sector disintegrated or never developed in the first place. Even after independence, Muslim-majority countries continued to be dependent on the West because they had no industrial sector to develop their resources.[5]

For example, when the French colonized Algeria, they acquired the best and most productive land. They divided villages and dispossessed small landowners. This not only depleted wealth but destroyed traditional rural communities, relationships, and the artisan class. By Algerian independence, French policy had produced "wide-scale pauperization" of Algerian society.[6]

Colonialism also redrew the borders of Muslims lands, not according to the people who lived within them but according to the whims of colonial powers. As a result, for example, the Kurds now reside in five separate countries. (Imagine if Muslims had redrawn Europe so that the French became minority populations in five different countries.) The partition of India—after a century of the British fomenting religious divisions—into what is now India, Pakistan, and Bangladesh caused the greatest migration in human history. Afghanistan was created as "a buffer state" between British India and czarist Russia, which both vied for access to the Indian Ocean.[7]

Local culture, religion, and systems of education were decimated under colonialism. Muslim Algerians were not allowed to attain French citizenship (though Christian and Jewish Algerians could do so) or even participate in French society or government unless they gave up their Islamic culture, laws, and traditions.[8] The French colonialists' sentiment was stated as follows: "There is no longer an Arab people, there are men who talk another language than ours."[9]

Islamic religious education was often forced underground. Educational institutions were dismantled, leaving Muslims undereducated in their religion and lacking scholars to develop fiqh. Whereas Christianity and Judaism modernized in response to the Industrial Revolution, Islam could not likewise modernize, because its people, institutions, and educational systems were subjugated.[10]

General education suffered as well as religious education. In the nineteenth century, Lord Cromer became the British consul general of Egypt and its de facto ruler for a quarter century. He boasted that British occupation had "practically abolished" free education in Egypt, despite the Egyptian demand for education for both girls and boys.[11]

Colonialism had a social impact too. Training some people but not others in the languages and customs of the colonial powers fractured the indigenous population. In Algeria, a whole segment of the population spoke French and not Arabic, which divided society and disconnected generations. In India, English was imposed as the national language.

The colonialists also divided and conquered. Pitting ethnic and religious groups against one another, colonialists even started rumors of atrocities to foment tensions and riots. It's no wonder, then, that such tensions are still smoldering in these countries (though they're often now explained—as you might have guessed—by the ubiquitous "Oh, they've been at each other's throats for centuries"). In India, for example, "communal violence" between Hindus and Muslims was a British construct: professor of South Asian history Cynthia Talbot notes the general consensus "that it is questionable whether a Hindu or Muslim identity existed prior to the nineteenth century in any meaningful sense."[12]

During the entire colonial period, various Christian missionary activity targeting Muslims was lively and continuous. Thomas Kidd, a historian at Baylor University, writes that American Protestant attitudes toward Islam were informed by two notions: that all Muslims had to be brought to Christianity and that Islam was the anti-Christ.[13] In the words of renowned historian Maxime Rodinson: "The degraded state of the Muslim world [under colonialism] made it an obvious target for Christian missionaries. The proselytizing crusade was launched with renewed vigor and quickly spread."[14]

Colonial powers wielded "clash of civilizations" rhetoric more often than did their Muslim opponents. The French in Algeria spoke in terms of "battles between the cross and the crescent," whereas Muslim commanders spoke of war to "defend their liberties and religion."[15] The French archbishop stated that the Church's mission was to convert Arab Muslims to Christianity.[16]

Colonialism extensively impacted the morale of the subjugated population because it was utterly humiliating. Europeans justified violent colonization of Muslim countries on the basis of *racial theory*, which explained that the white man was biologically superior to the nonwhite man, and it was the "white man's burden" to rule (the English version) and impose a "civilizing mission" (the French version) on everyone else.[17] Taken for granted as truth were platitudes such as "accuracy is abhorrent to the Oriental mind"[18] ("Oriental" in this context meaning Muslims and other non-Europeans), and "Orientals are inveterate liars, they are 'lethargic and suspicious,' and in everything oppose the clarity, directness, and nobility of the Anglo-Saxon race."[19]

On a road trip, my husband and children and I listened to Jules Verne's *Around the World in 80 Days*. We were struck by how often the English protagonist in this Victorian novel encountered "savages and fanatics" outside Europe. We eventually realized that *every* non-European was definitionally a savage and fanatic. Verne was a contemporary of colonialist Europeans, who regarded any Muslim opposition to their foreign, political, often violent domination as the product of "religious fanaticism," rather than the natural opposition of a people opposing invasion and domination of their lands.[20]

Degradation of Islam, of Muslims, and of Muslim culture was all part of colonialism. Muslims were routinely accused of oppressing Muslim women. Even those Englishmen who actively opposed women's rights in England—Lord Cromer actually founded the Men's League for Opposing Women's Suffrage in England[21]—denigrated Muslims for being sexist.

Colonial attitudes are normalized today in the West. I'm still asked, "Why have Muslims always been backward?" In fact, recent research has shown that Americans and Europeans commonly believe that Muslims are intellectually inferior: social psychologist Nour Kteily and neuroscientist Emile Bruneau conclude from their study, "On average, samples of British and American participants explicitly rate Muslims as less 'evolved' than their own group."[22]

Few Americans and Europeans apparently realize that for a thousand years Islamic civilization was the intellectual center of the world. Our educational system has largely ignored Islamic scholarship, partly because of colonial attitudes now normalized. Therefore, allow me a brief digression to explain why colonial attitudes—and current ones, by extension—are so inaccurate.

The eighth- and ninth-century Arab Muslims viewed knowledge as a religious duty, and to this end, they established centers of learning and translation. They published tens of thousands of books a year.[23] It is said that the tenth-century Muslim ruler of Córdoba had more books in his library than those in all the other libraries of Europe combined.[24]

You can blame the Arabs for having to learn algebra in school, as they developed it in the ninth century. Computer scientists owe a debt to the ninth-century mathematician al-Khwarizmi, from whose name the word *algorithm* derives.[25] The first writings in statistics appeared in Arabic some 800 years before Pascal and Fermat, and the Arabs used combinatorics 1,200 years ago.[26]

In case you need some coffee to learn all that math, you can thank the Arabs for that, too, as they discovered it in the ninth century, some six or seven centuries before the habit caught on in Europe.[27]

Muslims did not just "preserve" Greek scholarship for Renaissance Europeans, as is grudgingly conceded. They built on it, debunked it when faulty, and advanced their own discoveries. Islamic medicine was based on diagnosis and treatment, not on the earlier Greek reliance on miraculous cures.[28] The ninth-century philosopher and scientist al-Kindi disproved the Greeks' theories about vision and was the first to develop the foundations of modern-day optics; a century later, Ibn Haytham described in detail how vision worked.[29]

The eleventh-century polymath Ibn Sina wrote a medical treatise that was translated eighty-seven times and used in Europe until the seventeenth century. The thirteenth-century Arabs knew blood circulated in the body four centuries before the English physician William Harvey, who gets the entire credit for the discovery. The Arabs developed vaccines as early as the ninth century and were using antiseptics to clean wounds by the year 1000, something that wasn't done in Europe until the 1800s.[30] They performed surgeries, including cataract surgery, and used catgut to stitch wounds. Free government-funded hospitals operated in Muslim lands as early as 707.[31]

Muslim rulers sponsored innovators and artists of all kinds. In the ninth century, seventy-year-old Abbas ibn Firnas—the world's first aviator—climbed into the harness of his glider, launched himself into the air, and flew across the Spanish countryside, surviving the landing.[32] Luster-painted decoration on glass and pottery originated in ninth-century Islamic lands and was transmitted to Europe around the fourteenth century. So intricate and prized were Islamic textiles that they shrouded the bones of Christian saints; the words *taffeta*, *damask*, and *organdy* come from Arabic.[33]

Lady Mary Wortley Montagu was one of the relative few who believed her own eyes over her countrymen's cultural prejudice. Lady Mary traveled to Istanbul in the eighteenth century, saw that women owned large estates and managed their own properties without male interference, and wrote in a letter home that "tis very easy to see that they [Turkish women] have more liberty than we have."[34] She also saw that the Ottomans had developed a smallpox inoculation—the ninth-century Muslim physician al-Razi was the first to scientifically describe the disease[35]—and she labored to persuade the English, upon her return home, to use it, as well. Lady Mary encountered resistance—a woman advocating an "Oriental" process!—but eventually established inoculation in both England and France, nearly half a century before Edward Jenner, who gets all the credit for the smallpox vaccine.[36]

These are just a few examples. A thousand years of a geographically massive and ascendant Islamic civilization was never a secret. It was just ignored whenever possible and characterized as evil when not, even as Europeans learned from Muslim scholars and translated their accomplishments.

We can draw two conclusions from the effects of colonialism, according to Carl Ernst:

1. Muslims got to know Europeans really well, because Europeans imposed their culture on them, "overthrew native dynasties, dismantled traditional systems of education, enforced centralized authoritarian rule, and trained new local elites in the new

languages of power—English, French, Dutch, Italian, Portuguese, and Russian"; and

2. Muslims were subdued through violent conquest, "undertaken by largely Christian powers, yet paradoxically it is the Muslims who are regarded as naturally violent."[37]

Muslim-majority countries have been modern nation-states for only a few decades, their process of self-determination disrupted by colonialism, their autocratic governmental apparatus an inheritance of the colonial state. Arbitrary borders and puppet leaders left in place by colonialists—in addition to the depletion of resources—resulted in weak nations with strongman rulers. This prevented the development of the nongovernmental organizations (NGOs) necessary to supporting democracy, such as trade unions, educational and social services, and professional and human rights groups, as well as political parties and the media.[38] Many of these problems—autocratic rulers, poverty, lack of opportunity—are hardly unique to Muslim-majority countries; non-Muslim-majority countries in Asia, Africa, and Latin America struggle with the same issues.

Because colonial officials had focused on demeaning and marginalizing Islam, anticolonial liberation movements naturally became couched in terms of that very Islam. The notion of "Islam as a religion and a state" only emerged in the twentieth century, a reaction to colonialism. Shariah, too, became a banner for resistance against postcolonial secular dictatorship.

But what was left of shariah after colonialism had dismantled it?

COLONIALISM AND THE SHARIAH SYSTEM

Colonialism both directly and indirectly dismantled the shariah-based legal system via three broad avenues.

First, colonialism crushed the system of Islamic religious education by imposing secular schools on Muslim populations and pressuring them to give up their language, religion, and culture. As a result, Muslims did not receive education in the Islamic scholarly religious tradition. The class of religious scholars diminished.

Second, colonialism (and pressure therefrom) destroyed the waqf system, which supported religious education. Recall that, for centuries, centers of religious education had been founded and supported by waqf charitable endowments, the ongoing income of which paid for teachers, supplies, and dormitories. Because these properties were held in charitable trust, they were not partitioned upon inheritance by multiple heirs, remaining whole for generations. Women managed a substantial number of waqf properties and also benefited from them.

This situation began to change when precolonial Muslim governments increased military spending to fend off encroaching European powers. They needed money. And they cast their hungry eyes upon the waqf properties.

In the Ottoman Empire, during the nineteenth century, waqf charitable endowments supported over *half* of real property. The government, in a radical move, appropriated the income of all major waqf endowments.[39] For the first time in Islamic history, endowments supervised by high-level Islamic scholars came under the aegis of the government.[40]

The waqf system, thus weakened by the Ottomans, deteriorated under colonialism. In Algeria, the French passed legislation so that the waqf trusts were destroyed and the properties could be sold (to the French). Incredibly, the French justified this legislation by arguing that the waqf system was un-Islamic![41]

The state and colonial appropriation of waqf properties, along with their consequent dissociation from their charitable purposes, dismantled the system of Islamic religious education. Madrasas, schools, and centers for religious education had all been supported by waqf trusts; without the trusts, these institutions disintegrated for lack of funding, were intentionally disassembled, or were co-opted by the state.[42] The result: devastation of the population of religious scholars and institutions qualified to develop fiqh, resulting in a momentous disruption of the organic modernization of shariah.

Lack of waqf funding also caused a narrowing of Islamic religious education. Islamic educational institutions traditionally had taught not solely religious law but other subjects that grounded the religious law, like the sciences, logic, and philosophy. Under colonialism and lack of funding, such institutions were reduced to teaching the religious law in isolation, adrift and unanchored in the larger world.[43]

Third, aside from Islamic educational institutions, Islamic *legal* institutions were also dismantled. The establishment of European-style codes and European-style courts in Muslim lands meant that shariah courts and qadis became superfluous and then extinct. When the real-world legal system of shariah was thus undone, when shariah courts and institutions of justice no longer applied the law in real-life situations, the law became abstract.

Since the eighteenth and nineteenth centuries, therefore, with the disintegration of Islamic legal institutions, fiqh has become more abstract and disconnected to the real world:

> Without the institutions of case-by-case adjudication, we are left with texts that contain the abstract doctrine of interpretive communities immersed in a cultural context long gone.[44]

In other words, without its institutions, Islamic law diminished and transformed from a real-world, rule-of-law system, which had operated successfully for more than a thousand years, to an ideology.[45]

COLONIALISM AND TRANSFORMATION OF THE LAW

In addition to the destruction of the Islamic religious education system and the dismantling of Islamic legal institutions, the substantive law itself was changed by colonialism. Law as we think of it today is government-made, fixed, and enforceable. Shariah, as we've seen, was not fixed and didn't come from the state; it was a system of legal pluralism, evolving with time and changing according to circumstance.

Both these systems clashed under colonialism. Muslims were pressured to implement European law codes or had such codes imposed on them, either wholesale or amalgamated with fiqh rules. Why? Colonial governments feared that allowing Islamic legal institutions to operate might foment rebellion against colonial regimes.[46] They had reason to be afraid: the religio-legal scholar class had always scrutinized rulers. Law was a tool of control, and shariah was a potential obstacle to colonial interests.[47]

Colonial powers were not only suspicious of shariah; they were hostile to it and considered it too soft. Yes, *soft*. The British governor Warren Hastings, in eighteenth-century India, complained that Islamic law was too lenient and flexible. Hastings denounced shariah because it was founded on an "abhorrence of bloodshed" and too easily allowed criminals to escape without punishment.[48]

The British legal understanding of crime and punishment, especially in the eighteenth century, differed dramatically from that of Muslims. In England at the time, some two hundred crimes were punishable by death, including minor theft (worth five shillings, which equaled one-fourth of a pound).[49] In contrast, a primary goal of shariah was to avoid zero-sum solutions and provide workable compromises whenever possible.

For example, in homicide cases, shariah encouraged forgiving the murderer or accepting monetary compensation for the loss of the victim (though death was also a possible penalty). The British found monetary compensation downright offensive, because to them it sounded like blood money. They considered death to be the appropriate punishment.

Therefore, the British colonialists set about introducing their own laws into Muslim legal systems. In India, the British amalgamated British law with selected fiqh rules obtained from a few treatises lifted from the vast corpus of centuries of fiqh writings. The British then translated these few treatises, at times inaccurately. And then they *abridged* these inaccurate translations.[50] These inaccurate abridgements they then applied to Muslims as fixed laws.

In other words, the British transformed shariah—a flexible and adaptable case-based law dependent upon myriad cultural and social circumstances spanning centuries and on which there were few matters of agreement—into a fixed, text-based law[51] coming from the state, divorced from its cultural and social context.

Amazingly enough, if qualified Muslim fiqh judges did try to consult additional relevant untranslated Arabic texts, rather than relying exclusively on the coded British versions, their decisions were overturned as being *outside the law*.[52]

It's hard to overstate how catastrophic codification was for shariah. First, Islamic law became rigidified and fixed and monolithic, the opposite of its historical character. Instead of multiple fiqh opinions that could vary and contradict each other, one fiqh rule was chosen from many and incorporated into a statute, thereby setting it in stone; the rest were lost. Whereas the conclusion of one scholar had never been binding upon another, codification caused one scholar's opinion to become the law for everyone. Instead of the many legal opinions Muslims could choose from, suddenly they were ruled by one law. Disagreement on legal issues, once an integral part of the law, was no longer acceptable. Throughout its history, shariah had adapted to circumstances according to culture, custom, hardship, and the public interest; as a result of colonialism, however, the law became inflexible, unchangeable, and unadaptable.

Codification of Islamic law also eliminated the need for Islamic scholars. With a statutory version of fiqh, anyone could apply Islamic law (even British colonials). Whereas Islamic religious scholars had checked and constrained rulers since the beginning of Islam, suddenly the scholars no longer wielded power. They were no longer needed to interpret the law or make the law, because the code was the law. The system of checks and balances crumbled.

With the shariah-based legal system dismantled, fiqh scholars had fewer vocational opportunities. Studying Western law abruptly made more sense than studying Islamic law. Consequently, the breadth and depth of the community of Islamic legal scholars dwindled. Few scholars were left to develop fiqh. As a result, according to American law professor and shaykh Khaled Abou El Fadl, many of those "speaking for Islamic law today have never received any systematic training in the methodologies of legal analysis and thought."[53]

After codifying Islamic law so they could use it and control it, colonial judges could then apply what they thought was Islamic law to cases involving Muslims. British and French colonial judges, themselves not Muslims or Islamic scholars and with no understanding of the vastness of the legal tradition, interpreted Islamic law for Muslims "as if they were unable to see the truth of their own tradition."[54] Imagine if the United States' judiciary were overpowered by foreigners, unqualified, condescending, and culturally hostile, who reduced our case law into a few rules and then started telling us what those rules meant.

The codification and abridgement of the vast scope of fiqh also eliminated the differences between the Islamic schools of law. The differences between the Sunni schools, as well as the differences between Shi'i law and Sunni law generally, were glossed over, neglected, and subsumed into the one British codified version of Islamic law. This monolithic amalgamation completely erased the diversity, adaptability, and plurality of Islamic law and "reduced the scope of Islamic legal analysis."[55]

Finally, the common-law principle of *stare decisis* contributed to the rigidification of Islamic law. Stare decisis requires judges to follow previous legal precedents. This differed from the shariah system, in which qadis were not bound by prior legal court precedent but rather could look to an entire corpus of fatwas. The qadis were not bound to even one school of legal thought; this gave them a great deal of discretion. When the British applied stare decisis to fiqh, this flexibility was lost.

Codification, stare decisis, abridgement—the convergence of these produced an unchanging and inflexible version of shariah, which colonial officials then regularly denigrated for being unchanging and inflexible. (How circular! How unjust!) They could then marginalize shariah as "contrary and incompatible with modernity."[56]

Even lands that escaped direct colonization, such as Iran, attempted codification under pressure from colonial powers. The Ottoman Empire, too, was pressured into Western-style reforms. In the 1850s, the Ottomans, relying heavily on Western legal codes as models, codified fiqh rules into an enormous code called the Majalla.

As a result, shariah in the Ottoman Empire, as in India, became rigid and inflexible. It didn't matter that the Ottomans were Muslim themselves, codifying the law with the help of Islamic scholars. Codification means you extricate a few legal rules from a vast corpus, leaving out most and inflexibly enforcing the rest. But who decides what's left out?

Because it was nineteenth-century men deciding which few fiqh rules to adopt and which multitudes to disregard, provisions that would have benefited women were inevitably excluded from the code. Under the traditional Islamic legal system, a woman could use the fatwas of any of the schools to support her case, and the qadi could look at a plurality of opinions to choose the best one for the circumstances. But codification eliminated all this choice. When the Ottomans codified family law in 1917, for example, they included all the husband's rights to unilateral divorce but left out the numerous discourses on ways a woman could obtain a divorce.[57]

In addition to being politically, socially, and legally colonized, Muslims were, like other colonized populations, "colonized in our minds."[58] British court decisions in India fundamentally affected the way that Muslims *themselves* conceptualized and understood shariah and fiqh[59]—namely, as backward, inflexible, and misogynistic. Too many Muslims today, well into the twenty-first century, still conceptualize shariah in this way.

How could this heartbreak have happened? Indian Muslims bought into the British version of Islamic law. They relied on cases that British judges had adjudicated. They accepted the codification of fiqh as appropriate, accepted the idea of Islamic law as fixed and unchanging. They even argued *against* pluralistic legal thinking, the hallmark of the Islamic legal tradition. Even now, Muslims as a whole have generally internalized and accepted the versions and views of shariah that were presented to them by their colonial overlords.[60]

We Muslims are still, as a worldwide community, colonized in our own minds. Many Muslim fundamentalists now focus on the sensational bits of Islamic law they've heard about and that seem uniquely Islamic (stoning! amputation!), and they promote those in opposition to the West, never perceiving that this understanding of Islam as rigid was given to them by Western colonialists in the first place. Many Muslim progressives equally focus on the sensational bits of Islamic law they hear about in the news and reject shariah as backward, never comprehending that colonial powers originally gave them this very understanding of shariah. Not enough Muslims understand that extracting isolated rules from an extinct social context is not necessarily shariah.

Let me give you one example of being colonized in our own minds. Nineteenth-century Orientalists aired the idea that the "gate of ijtihad" had "closed" around the tenth century. (Ijtihad, you will recall, is independent reasoning used to interpret the religious texts.) This meant, the Orientalists declared, that Muslims had decided that all Islamic religious questions had been answered, eliminating the need for ijtihad, and thus development of shariah ceased over a thousand years ago.

That an entire civilization could halt independent reasoning for nearly a thousand years is a mind-boggling idea. It's hard for me to see how any system of law could fail to change in a thousand years, much less a system that contained built-in mechanisms for change.

Although the phrase "closure of the gate of ijtihad" did appear in Islamic texts, the context was not law but theology: that is, Islamic scholars asked themselves, "What would happen if *mujtahids*—those who were qualified to exercise ijtihad—ever became extinct?"[61] This was a philosophical question, not a practical one. Mujtahids continued to exist after the tenth century, and the Islamic scholars never unanimously decided to eliminate all ijtihad;[62] indeed, it's difficult to imagine how they could have done so.

Nevertheless, this narrative of the "closure of the gate of ijtihad" fit neatly into nineteenth-century racial theory as justification for "civilizing missions" to Islamic lands. A standard justification in colonizing a people is their portrayal as inferior, backward, or evil. An Orientalist, with probably little or no expertise in Arabic, coming across this phrase in Islamic literature, might very well have misunderstood it and celebrated its discovery as proof of a stagnant civilization.

It is only in the last thirty years or so that this idea has been mostly debunked in scholarship,[63] though not in everyday discourse. Anti-Muslim propagandists perpetuate this idea to show the backwardness of Islam, but Muslims buy into this, as well. At dinner with Muslim friends a few years ago, my host not only matter-of-factly referred to "closure of the gate of ijtihad" as if it were an obvious truth but also insisted on it. As one scholar writes:

> Although Orientalist scholars might have invented and exploited this myth, the fact remains that Muslim intellectuals from all over the Muslim world accepted this fiction as a settled historical fact.[64]

This is how Muslims, intellectuals as well as laypeople, are colonized in our own minds.

One of the best practical illustrations of how colonialism affected shariah on the ground concerns women's rights.

MUSLIM WOMEN AND COLONIALISM

European colonial officials arrived in Muslim lands in the eighteenth and nineteenth centuries and began criticizing the treatment of Muslim women there. Many of these officials had decried feminism in their own countries, actively opposing women's suffrage; some, in fact, claimed that the smaller circumference of women's skulls proved their intellectual inferiority.[65] That didn't stop colonialists from virtuously wielding women's rights as a weapon in Muslim lands.

Yet, colonialism *damaged* Muslim women's rights, at least with respect to the law. Here's how Noah Feldman describes it:

> When the British applied their law to Muslims in place of shariah, as they did in some colonies, the result was to strip married women of the property that Islamic law had always granted them—hardly progress toward equality of the sexes.[66]

Recall Lady Mary Wortley Montagu's comment that it was easy to see that Turkish women had more freedom than Englishwomen. English common law denied wives not only their own property but also their very legal personhood,[67] something that Muslim women had had since the seventh century.

In England, a woman had virtually no right to divorce until the mid-nineteenth century.[68] Yet, by the time the British colonized Muslim lands, Muslim women had had the right to divorce for a thousand years. They had open access to courts under the Ottoman Empire, and divorce was never considered the absolute right of the husband.[69] A man could certainly divorce his wife more easily than a wife could divorce her husband—also the case in England until the twentieth century—but Muslim wife-initiated divorces were not rare.

Records show instances of women in the eighteenth century granting *themselves* divorces, sometimes simply by leaving the marital home, in front of witnesses, while announcing that they were no longer married to their spouses.[70] Or, sometimes, women would claim to the court, with two witnesses, that their husbands had divorced them while drunk and simply didn't remember![71] These cases were upheld by the qadis, who confirmed the divorces.

But under colonialism, wife-initiated divorce became much harder to achieve in Muslim lands. European rule limited access to the courts. Women complaining to the court of domestic violence or rape—complaints that had been commonly heard in Ottoman courts[72]—found they suddenly had fewer rights under their Western colonizers.[73] After all, under eighteenth-century British law, a man could legally beat his wife with impunity, including with whips and clubs, as long as he didn't endanger her life.[74]

None of this European sexism prevented colonialists from deriding, as evidence of oppression, Muslim women's head coverings. Before colonialism, Muslims, Christians, Hindus, and Jews in Islamic lands had all dressed pretty much the same way within any given region; differences in dress related to regional differences rather than religious differences. Arab Christian and Jewish women wore head coverings,[75] as did Hindu women in India. Even today, pictures of older Greek women frequently show them wearing headscarves.

But the colonial Europeans pointed to the headscarves and veils of Muslim women and said, "Look at you, with your backward religion, oppressing your women by making them cover their heads." As a result, some non-Muslim women began removing their head coverings, and some Muslim women began donning them in defiance. In Egypt, not until the early twentieth century did veiling become associated uniquely with Islam, after colonialism framed it that way.[76]

"White men saving brown women from brown men," in the famous words of Gayatri Spivak, was and still is one of the great justifications for colonizing or invading Muslim countries. But when white men set out to save brown women from brown men, what happens? A catch-22.[77] Colonialists informed Muslim women that becoming modern (or civilized or free or whatever) necessitated discarding their head coverings, thus leaving them with two choices: they could agree with the white men and become "traitors" to their own culture and religion, or they could disagree with the white men and be dismissed as oppressed and "brainwashed."

These tropes still plague us. Recently, a psychologist acquaintance argued to me that even unpressured Muslim women who freely chose to wear head coverings had been "brainwashed" into doing so. I responded that she herself chose to wear jeans because she had been brainwashed into approving of them as acceptable clothing. (Jeans would have been immodest a hundred years ago.) What does immodesty have to do with freedom, or modesty with its lack?

Leila Ahmed, a professor of women's studies and Islam at Harvard University, writes that the "Western legacy of androcentrism and misogyny" was no better than in any other culture, and yet no one told Western women that their only recourse for equal rights was the wholesale adoption of some other completely foreign culture.[78] They would have been offended at the very notion, just as Muslim women were. Western feminists didn't abandon their religion and culture; they engaged with it.

But Muslim women could not similarly engage with their religion and culture to increase their rights, because both were already being attacked as backward, both by colonizers and by the secular modernists the colonizers left behind. Any attempts to change religion and culture to increase women's rights were seen as caving to Western denigration.

Once Muslim lands were free of colonization, however, Muslim women should have been able to get on with equal rights, correct?

Before answering this question, let's note that it presumes that Muslim women didn't have rights and still don't. Let's also note that—despite the relentless framing of Islam as misogynist—as of 2017, the United States had fewer women in its legislature than the following Muslim-majority countries: Senegal, Tunisia, Sudan, Albania, Afghanistan, Kazakhstan, Algeria, Iraq, Mauritania, Turkmenistan, Somalia, United Arab Emirates, Bosnia-Herzegovina, Pakistan, Morocco, Bangladesh, Saudi Arabia, and Indonesia.[79] That's in addition to the thirteen Muslim women who have been prime ministers or presidents in recent decades.

It's true that some Muslim women in the world lack the same opportunities as men, but why assume the reason is Islam? Plenty of non-Muslim Asian, African, and Latin American women struggle for equal opportunities, as well, but their struggles are rarely characterized as problems of religion. The examples of oppressed Muslim women usually presented to us by our media are often neither representative of Muslim women nor even religious examples—rather, they stem from other factors, including poverty (which leads to, among other things, lack of educational opportunities); sexist culture (such as prohibitions on driving); cultural interpretations of religion (such as prohibiting a woman to lead a mixed-gender prayer); and the same kinds of sexism that permeate all countries but especially developing countries and traditional societies (whether they are Muslim or not).

It's easy to forget that Western feminist attitudes are of recent origin. American women lacked the right to vote until 1920; Swiss women didn't get the equal right to vote until 1971. The age of consent for girls in the US was mostly ten or twelve (in Delaware it was *seven*) until 1920.[80] Children fifteen and younger can still marry in some US states.[81] Western women throughout the twentieth century struggled for their rights and even today often do not receive equal pay for equal work.

But let's get back to the question I posed above: why couldn't Muslim women's rights movements easily progress after colonialism? As always, the reasons are myriad.

First, Muslim feminists continued to be perceived as "caving in" to the West. European powers might have left Muslim lands, but Muslims were smarting from centuries of vilification. They still are: even today, Islamic scholars who issue fatwas on women's issues are vulnerable to criticisms of being "too feminist," because some Muslims see any feminist result—even one mandated by Islam!—as betraying traditional culture and aping the West.

Second, Muslim women's rights movements were impeded by traditional interpretations of fiqh. Yes, I've argued that the Qur'an and the spirit of Islam are both feminist; much of fiqh, too, was feminist when developed. But fiqh rules that were feminist for premodern times—and even for much later Victorian times—would not necessarily be considered feminist today.

But fiqh can evolve, right? Why could Islamic scholars not simply reinterpret fiqh rules in light of modern circumstances, as they always had?

The answer is the third reason early twentieth-century Muslim women's movements were stonewalled: they collided with the colonized minds of Muslims. Because so many Muslims had accepted the colonial rhetoric that Islam was sexist, they defended the sexism. Or they believed fiqh was rigid and unchangeable. In the early twentieth century, these attitudes unfairly and unnecessarily cornered Muslim women into either rejecting Islam if they wanted equal rights or rejecting equal rights if they wanted Islam.[82]

Some Muslims have forgotten that Muhammad and the Qur'an aimed to raise the status of women and that the Qur'an treats men and women equally in numerous verses (in, essentially, the ones not tied to historical contexts). Historically, in Muslim civilization, women were not hidden. They argued with the Prophet, they were scholars and judges and rulers and queens, they led armies, and—under shariah—they had legal rights. Given that Islam was so concerned with raising the status of women fourteen centuries ago, when women's rights were an incomprehensible concept, using Islam today to impose sexism is a perversion.

When Islamic civilization was ascendant, religious legal scholars were proud and secure in their legal tradition, debating each other, critiquing hadith literature, and entertaining various methods of interpretation. They were too confident in the overall form of Islam to be shaken by variances in the minutiae of religion, as Jonathan Brown writes:

> Whether in law or theology, Muslim scholars accepted that the religion they taught the believers was at best an imposing thicket of probabilities built around a core of certainties.[83]

Scholars were therefore tolerant of debating those probabilities. But these days, Muslims feel besieged by ubiquitous attacks on the very foundations of Islam, and so we cling to traditional interpretations with greater tenacity, and a challenge to any detail feels like a threat to our entire religion. When threatened, we—like all people—tend toward conservatism, doubling back to the attitudes of bygone days when we felt secure and unthreatened. We become unwilling to entertain innovative ways of thinking. Unfortunately, this reaction often disproportionately affects women, and it hampered early Muslim women's rights movements.

These factors, though troublesome, did not completely obstruct feminists, though it hampered them. In the 1970s, however, Muslim feminists found a particularly effective way to barrel past these obstacles. The vehicle for change? The Islamist movement.

Sometimes, the Islamists strove toward the same goals as feminist movements, such as when the Islamists encouraged girls' education as a religious duty. But sometimes, Islamists unwittingly helped feminist movements—such as when they tried to *take away* women's rights. For example, before Ayatollah Khomeini, feminists in Iran had been condemned as imitating the West, but when Khomeini began eliminating women's rights, women challenged him: "How dare you curtail my rights!" they said. "Islam gives me rights!"[84]

Iranian women framed their discussions of women's rights as responses to Khomeini's policies, rather than as imitations of Western culture. This opened a new window of discourse, eliminating colonizers from the equation entirely. Eventually, Khomeini had to quietly reinstate many of the rights he had initially eliminated.[85]

Once the discourse shifted in this way, Muslims in Iran and elsewhere began contesting the idea that Islam restricted women's rights. It wasn't God's law that limited women's rights, they argued, but the centuries-old male interpretation of God's law. Increasingly, women began to reread and reinterpret the Islamic sacred texts. And they began to promote women's rights from an Islamic perspective.

Many Muslim women fighting for rights don't necessarily want to be called "feminists" or "reformers," because those terms originated outside their cultures and come laden with condescending colonial baggage. Some Muslim women's movements are faith-based movements, and some are secular. I myself belong to an organization that promotes women's rights from an Islamic perspective.

My parents came from India, and I practice Islam the way my parents practice it and the way my grandmothers practiced it. I'm just as much a representative of Islam as any other Muslim woman.

Yet, all my life, those around me have assumed that I have broken the chains of Islam to become a corporate lawyer—even though what my parents always wanted most for me was financial independence above all else. I was raised on stories of the Prophet's strong female contemporaries and took for granted that Islam gave me equal rights. When my non-Muslim American peers assumed that the restrictions on my social life—not drinking, not dating—were imposed on me because I was a girl, I thought, surprised, "How sexist."

POSTCOLONIAL MUSLIM NATION-STATES

In a nutshell, then, by the time most Muslim lands became independent in the twentieth century, Muslims were suffering from widespread humiliation, lack of confidence, an identity crisis, and a sense of inferiority—not to mention the mess of their newly decolonized countries. The cultural and political question for newly independent Muslim lands became this: how should Muslims cope with the decline of Islamic power, the wealth and military superiority of European civilization, and the changed (and changing) role of Islam in modern public life?

Answers fell into three broad categories. *Secularists* agreed with the colonialists and relegated Islam to personal life, if anywhere. *Islamists* rejected the Western cultural and political model, instead advocating modernization in terms of Islamic values, asking: What would an Islamic state look like? Islamic economics? Islamic democracy? (The Qur'an and Sunna do not have explicit answers to these questions.) *Modernists* took a middle ground between the two. They accepted the Western cultural and political model as superior, but they argued for reconciling that with Islam.

What's interesting is that those in all three categories accepted the colonialist view of Western cultural superiority and Muslim cultural inferiority. Even the Islamists' need to reject the Western model was *itself* the mark of colonialism and the need to address the problem of Western superiority.[86] Once experienced, colonialism could not be unexperienced.

When Muslim-majority countries attained independence from their Western colonizers, most adopted the secularist/colonialist approach. Their leaders had been members of local elites and had been trained, educated, employed, and left in power by the colonial administrations.[87] Many spoke only the European languages of their colonizers and not the local languages. They had participated in a colonial order that had assumed, without question, the inferiority of Islamic law and culture.

That is why, when these local elites came to power after independence, they didn't take Islam into consideration when nation building. Rather, they sought to mold their new nation-states in the image of the West. Political scientist S. V. R. Nasr writes:

> They targeted Islam, its values, institutions, and role in public life, blaming it for the ills of society and promising that secularization would pave the way for modernization.[88]

Most new leaders changed the laws of their new nation-states to reflect the Western models, opting for the French civil-law system rather than the English common-law system. Most of them became dictators, too, because sudden power without an established system of checks and balances does often result in dictatorship. And most postcolonial Muslim secular states tried to control Islam or even excise Islam from the new social order:

> The postcolonial Muslim state therefore emerged in the mold of the colonial one—development-oriented in aim, hostile to Islam, and modernizing and westernizing in practice.[89]

By sidelining Islam and rejecting it as a mainstream democratic concept, postcolonial states left shariah in the hands of the extremists.[90]

Like states that had been directly colonized, Turkey epitomized this new hostility to Islam. By 1923, Turkey was all that remained of the Ottoman Empire, which had been declining for centuries, superseded by European countries in power and wealth. As head of the new Turkish state, Mustafa Kemal Ataturk abolished the caliphate; completely demolished the (already diminished) scholar class by subsuming all religious, educational, and social institutions under the control of the government; removed Islam as an official religion; dismantled the shariah courts; closed down the Sufi orders (which are still banned today); and implemented new laws based on European codes, continuing the process that had begun in the nineteenth century. Astoundingly, he converted the entire country from Arabic script to Roman script in about six months. He introduced Western dress codes and abolished the fez, requiring men to wear European hats.[91] In the twentieth century, generations of Turkish women were unable to go to school or work in the public sector because they wore headscarves, which were banned.

Postcolonial Muslim countries couldn't develop organically, as European nation-states had; instead, Muslim-majority states were continuations of the colonial state (not to be confused with the European state), complete with colonial machinery, institutions, and mission of domination.[92] Heads of the new Muslim-majority countries used the colonial governing apparatus that was already in place. Often, this apparatus contributed to a lack of transparency, ethnic and religious divisions, and autocratic state governments.

For example, colonial rulers had divided and conquered along ethnic, religious, and class lines. They exercised favoritism between groups and encouraged tensions. When the colonizers left, these tensions remained.[93] That's why so many post-independence political factions formed around *identity politics*—along racial, ethnic, and religious divisions—because the colonizers had deliberately inflamed these divisions and because the new borders maximized these festering tensions.[94]

I asked a friend in Pakistan once about politics. Pakistan was formed as a democratic republic, but it's been a military dictatorship for much of its life. Even now, under a civilian government, its electoral system is not truly free. Why? Because, my friend answered, the same few families exercise a stranglehold on politics, which outsiders cannot pierce.

This also is an inheritance of the colonial state. Colonizers bolstered local (native) elites in return for their support. These local elites thus wielded considerable power over the peasantry.[95] And they still do, long after the colonizers have left. Local elites control politics and power at every level and have resisted land reform.[96]

The reason it's so important to understand colonialism is that it explains the situation of Muslim-majority countries today. It also explains (a) how the development of fiqh and the shariah-based legal system were disrupted; (b) how the idea that Islamic law is rigid and inflexible came from the colonizers, even though they themselves had changed its implementation to become rigid and inflexible; (c) how colonial attitudes about Islam and Muslims are culturally normalized in American and European societies even now; (d) why Muslims might be sensitive about Christians trying to convert them, given the Christianizing missions that came alongside colonialism; and (e) why postcolonial Muslim-majority countries continue to struggle.

Oh, and one more: colonialism explains how secular Muslim postcolonial governments repressed Islam enough that it was only a matter of time before it came roaring back.

CHAPTER NINE

SHARIAH IN POSTCOLONIAL MUSLIM-MAJORITY COUNTRIES

SHARIAH IS GONE. Not shariah as the way of God, no, of course not. But the shariah-based legal system that flourished for over a thousand years? *That's* gone.

The question now is whether and in what form it can ever come back. The fundamental difference between the old shariah legal system and today's legal systems is a matter of who makes the law. Today, law comes from the top, from the nation-state. Shariah, in contrast, was developed by those on the ground, the scholars.

Since the independence struggles of the twentieth century, Muslims have debated who is qualified to develop fiqh and why modern Islamic scholars—who have lost political power, as well as their religious educational and legal systems—have not yet been able to adequately adapt fiqh to modern circumstances. From independence until the 1970s, most modern Muslim-majority countries were secular, though nationalist resistance movements often flew the banner of Islam. But, inspired by the Iranian revolution and the concurrent rise in conservatism throughout all religions—not to mention dissatisfaction with postcolonial secular governments—calls for Islam in government began increasing. Complicating these debates was a new, twentieth-century notion of an "Islamic state."

Although some countries claim to base their governments on Islam, no country today is ruled by shariah as it used to be. Muslim-majority countries are all constitutional states, most with civil codes based on the European system. The countries that claim to be based on shariah actually combine modern, Western-style law with varying degrees of Islamic-sounding provisions. In other words, for a variety of reasons, such as satisfying demands for shariah and legitimizing themselves, Muslim-majority governments simply select decontextualized, isolated fiqh rules—or even *bits* of isolated fiqh rules, or even just laws that "sound Islamic"—and graft them onto modern, European-style civil codes. That's not shariah.

A few countries maintain separate shariah courts, but these courts are not like the shariah courts of old. They're primarily relegated to family law, and they generally interpret "shariah legislation" that comes from the government, not from a wide variety of fiqh. Even where they do apply traditional fiqh rules, these are in the context of the modern state, where the apparatus of the shariah-based legal system has disappeared. Unlike the qadis, who used a contemporary, variable, dynamic, flexible tradition, these modern-day shariah courts look to ancient fiqh rules from sometimes thousand-year-old contexts, sometimes without regard to developments on the ground.[1]

Even Iran and Saudi Arabia, which most people think of as Islamic states, are not ruled by shariah as it operated throughout history.

IRAN AND SAUDI ARABIA

By 1979, most Iranians hated their shah, Muhammad Reza Pahlavi, a repressive dictator whose policies had benefited mostly the upper classes and had increased national poverty and dependence upon imports. A wide array of groups achieved the shah's overthrow in the Iranian Revolution,[2] but in the consequent power void, Ayatollah Khomeini emerged with control of the country.

Khomeini had developed a theory of *wilayat al-faqih*, or "governance by the religious legal scholars." Never in 1,400 years of Islamic history had the Islamic religious scholars ever governed; Islamic lands had never been ruled by theocracies. But in 1979, for the first time in Islamic history, religious scholars assumed the governing power of the nation-state.

Despite its theocratic nature, though, Iran is not ruled by shariah. It's a modern nation-state with a constitution and a civil code. Iran has grafted Islamic-sounding provisions and selected, isolated fiqh rules onto its civil code, making such provisions rigid and enforceable. That's not shariah.

Whereas Iran's regime is a Shi'i theocratic democracy, Saudi Arabia's official religion is Wahhabi Islam, and it's a theocratic absolute monarchy. It's also the only country in the world where shariah seems to be the law of the land. The Saudis certainly tell us that it is; they tell us that the Qur'an and the Sunna are the constitution. The Grand Mufti of Saudi Arabia issues fatwas that are considered nearly laws, and courts consult Hanbali (the school from which Wahhabism developed) fiqh books.[3]

However, looks can be deceiving. As the renowned scholar of Islam Rudolph Peters remarks:

> It is tempting to describe the Saudi legal system as traditional and very similar to the pre-modern Islamic legal system. This, however, is not the case. In spite of its traditional outward appearance, the judicial system has been subjected to an intense process of rationalisation and bureaucratisation, implemented through statute law.[4]

I still remember my Islamic law professor, a Lebanese Christian, casually telling my class, "Saudi Arabia would be a freer country if it actually *applied* Islamic law."

He meant, he went on to say, that much of what is applied in Saudi Arabia is cultural tribal law. Moreover, most of what we understand as characteristics of the Saudi state—segregation, the bans on women voting and driving, lack of political and journalistic freedom—are cultural practices, not religious ones. Certainly, practices like jailing activists without a trial and assassinating resident American journalists, of which the Saudi government is accused, violate shariah in any form.

Corporal punishments are common in Saudi Arabia, which is why most people associate them with Islam. However, shariah punishments were always subject to strict procedural limitations (discussed in the next chapter), rendering them extremely difficult to implement. It's hard to imagine how the Saudi judges could possibly be applying the required shariah limitations when corporal punishments occur with such frequency.

In fact, the Wahhabi version of shariah often contravenes shariah as understood by the other schools of Islam. So extreme is Wahhabi Islam on the Islamic spectrum that, in 2016, an international gathering of prominent Islamic scholars at a UAE-funded conference excluded Wahhabism and its progeny, like Salafism and Deobandism, from a definition of Islam.[5] (This is unusual, though, and other definitions have included it.) Wahhabism does not allow for the pluralism of fiqh, and Wahhabis have a history of declaring other Muslims heretics. The Saudi regime has historically discriminated against its Shi'i and Sufi populations.[6]

This brings us to the main problem with deeming Saudi Arabia an Islamic state run by shariah. Throughout history, shariah was represented by competing schools of legal thought, with autonomous, pluralistic, and diverse legal institutions that often challenged the ruling powers and prevented the establishment of a theocracy.[7] Historically, Muslim lands were not theocracies—the institutions that governed were separate from the institutions that developed religious law. But in Saudi Arabia, one (extreme) school of religious thought, considered God's law, is represented and enforced by the government, which closely controls the scholars and religious institutions.[8] Such a theocratic state is, in the words of one shaykh, "anathema to Islamic history and theology."[9]

The balance of power that was so integral to the premodern shariah-based legal system does not operate in Saudi Arabia. The government has little incentive to respond to its citizens, as its oil wealth eliminates its dependency upon taxes.[10] The scholars don't check the government; rather than adversaries, they are partners, having formed the Saudi state together. Historically, even if the ruler managed to control some scholars, the class of scholars was traditionally independent.[11]

As in the case of Iran, the establishment of a theocratic state such as Saudi Arabia is a new development in Islamic history.[12] Furthermore, most Islamic scholars would not consider a dynastic, absolute monarchy to be a legitimately Islamic form of government. Shariah requires that Muslims be allowed to select their leaders.[13]

If neither Iran nor Saudi Arabia is an Islamic state, then what is? Before answering that, however, we should wonder whether Muslims even *want* an Islamic state.

DO ALL MUSLIMS DESIRE AN ISLAMIC STATE?

The Qur'an has no prescription for an Islamic state or any political system. Historically, Islamic lands were no more or less "religious" than other lands. Yet, the puzzling, predominant assumption is that all Muslims must want an Islamic state.

Modern "neo-orientalists" have recently used ancient, long-defunct, and questionable Islamic concepts to argue that Islam is a "political system" and therefore destined to "clash with our civilization."[14] Even scholars without anti-Islam agendas take for granted that Christians want to separate religion and state, whereas Muslims do not.

Steven Fish, a political scientist, has conducted extensive studies, using empirical statistical evidence, to test whether these clichés are true. Fish concludes:

> On balance, the empirical evidence suggests that Islam does not incline its adherents to extraordinary religiosity or enthusiasm for the fusion of religious and political authority.[15]

Fish found that Muslims are in line with a "global consensus in favor of dividing political and religious power."[16] He found that Muslims are not even inclined to require that their political leaders be religious or especially devout.[17]

In other words, Muslims as a whole aren't any different from anyone else regarding this issue.

What adds to the scary myth that Muslims must live in an Islamic state is the contrasting, popular belief that religion and state are completely separate in the West. But many countries combine religion and politics, including some Latin American countries and Israel. Great Britain, Germany, and Norway have state religions or provide funding to religious institutions that are officially recognized.[18]

In the US, thriving religious movements consistently seek to combine Christianity with government. "Project Blitz," a project of the Congressional Prayer Caucus Foundation, seeks to overwhelm state legislatures with bills that erode the separation of church and state, with the ultimate goal of transforming the US into an officially Christian country.[19] The movement's potential legislation includes spreading Christian symbolism, the teaching and persuasion of Christianity, and discrimination against entire communities of people, such as the LGBTQI community.[20] Although this group represents a small minority, as recently as 2007, a whopping 55 percent of Americans polled believed that the Bible should be either *a* source of legislation in the United States or the *only* source of legislation in the United States;[21] that's similar to the percentage of

Iranians who want shariah as a source of law (though "shariah" is a much more amorphous concept than "the Bible").

According to polls, most Muslims worldwide do not want shariah to be the *only* source of legislation in their countries.[22] Although most Muslims do want shariah to be *one* of the sources of legislation in their countries, most do not want religious leaders making laws or writing their constitutions.[23] Most Muslims also want neither a theocracy nor a secular democracy.[24] Nor do they see any conflict between Islam and democracy.[25] The polls also showed widespread desire for democracy, freedom of speech, and equal rights for women.[26]

The problem with polls is that "caliphate" and "Islamic state" and "shariah" are terms with multilayered and even elusive meanings. They conjure nostalgic, vague images of a time when Islamic civilization was erudite and powerful and rulers were not above the law. For Muslims feeling berated and besieged by the West, as well as repressed by their own governments, longing for the golden age of Islam may well influence polls, not to mention politics.

Yet, a clearer picture of Muslim beliefs emerges when the questions asked are more specific. For example, some Muslims may yearn in the abstract for a caliphate, but Muslims overwhelmingly reject ISIS, which claims to be a caliphate. In fact, most Muslims worldwide do not want their religious leaders to govern directly.[27]

If I lived in a Muslim-majority country and were asked if I wanted shariah to be a source of legislation in my country, my answer would depend on how I conceived of shariah. If I thought of shariah as the Maqasid al-Shariah (giving me the right to life, family, religion, intellect, human dignity, and resources), then I would say yes. Who wouldn't want these rights?

But if I thought of shariah as the whole system of Islamic law, which includes the divine sources and fiqh, then I would say no. I wouldn't want someone in government interpreting fiqh for me and imposing it through the law. Why? First, fiqh was meant to be flexible and adaptable, not fixed in a code and imposed by the government. Second, legislating religion sounds like a theocracy to me. Third, much of the fiqh literature is ancient, and I don't want someone else selectively pulling out thousand-year-old outdated religious statements for me to follow. Besides (fourth), fiqh was primarily designed for private lives, not for public policing. And fifth, fiqh rules were not meant to be taken out of their contexts and enforced in a void, without the shariah legal landscape of institutions and checks and balances.

As a Muslim American, I do personally feel that no one can be trusted to legislate or impose religious law. I also personally feel that the United States is a perfectly valid Islamic state. A secular state that allows the free practice of religion is, in my opinion, a valid Islamic model.

I am not alone in my thinking. Even centuries ago, some Islamic scholars argued that a country is an "abode of Islam" if Muslims can live there and practice their religion in safety. Some still take this position today.[28] And although the majority of Islamic scholars may not describe secular democracies as "Islamic countries" or "abodes of Islam," they do describe them as "abodes of peace" or "abodes of covenant."[29]

Muslims have always been allowed, under shariah, to live in lands that were governed by some other law, as long as they were free to practice their religion. When Muhammad's followers were tortured and perse-cuted in early seventh-century Mecca, some of them fled to Abyssinia, where the Christian king welcomed them. This raised the question of whether Muslims had to follow the law of the land in which they were living, even if that law were not Islamic.

The answer was yes, they did. Muslim jurists assumed that Muslims residing in or entering non-Muslim territories entered into an agreement with the host country and were therefore obligated to follow the law of that country. This agreement could be explicit, like applying for a visa today. Or it could be implied: for Muslim citizens born in non-Muslim countries, the mere act of citizenship constitutes an "implied by law" agreement.[30]

Therefore, *shariah itself* required seventh-century Muslims emigrat-ing to Abyssinia to follow Abyssinian laws. Today, *shariah itself* requires Muslims to follow the laws of the country in which they reside, whether that country is Islamic or not, whether it's American or European or something else.

What if the law of my country prevents me from practicing Islam? Historically, in such situations, some scholars advised Muslims to immi-grate to a place where they could practice their religion freely. Others said the Muslims could stay and adjust their practices. (Adjust their Is-lamic practices!) But *no* scholars decreed that Muslims could overthrow or fight the government, either by violence or nonviolence.[31] In fact, Khaled Abou El Fadl writes:

> Under an implied by law agreement, a Muslim may not commit hostile acts against the host state and may not commit acts of treachery, deceit, fraud, betrayal, or usurpation.[32]

In sum, Muslims need not live in an "Islamic state." But, then, why do Islamist political parties do consistently well in the polls? Is it because they promise a "return to shariah"? Or because they promise justice?

WHAT ISLAMISTS WANT

The Qur'an sets out no prescription for a political state. In fact, shariah generally contains no specific required model for an Islamic state. However, Muslims do have the example of the Prophet. When he governed Medina, Muhammad's religious and political power could have transformed him into an authoritarian ruler, but it didn't. His well-documented consultations included both men and women, both Muslims and non-Muslims, and he aimed for consensus among his people regarding important decisions. The Constitution of Medina united the city for the public good and for political security but allowed for personal choice of religion within that framework.[33] Based on this example of governance, most scholars do not consider absolute monarchies and other authoritarian forms of government to be valid forms of Islamic government. But neither do they agree on what does constitute a valid Islamic state.

Islamist parties—those who mix Islam and politics—have been successful partly because of their commitment to social justice. Before coming to power, Ayatollah Khomeini and Islamic scholars in Iran had helped the urban poor by implementing support networks for them.[34] Hamas had provided desperately needed social services in the Palestinian territories. The Muslim Brotherhood was originally founded as a movement for peaceful social change, and for most of its nearly century-old existence, it has remained that way, except for a marginalized violent minority of Brothers that operated between the 1950s and the 1970s.[35] Islamist activists throughout the Middle East and North Africa gained popularity because they provided health clinics, youth programs, daycare, schools, and other social services.[36]

Islamists have often used the language of the Circle of Justice, which, as discussed, informed the Middle East for over four thousand years. Although it disintegrated somewhat during the colonial and postcolonial periods in the Middle East, Islamists have again begun to use the social justice language of the Circle to oppose dictators and autocratic governments. As historian Linda T. Darling notes:

When Islamist groups presented themselves as the carriers of a justice opposed to state policies, many people supported them as much or more for their promise of justice, interpreted in the light of the Circle, as for their Islam, or saw them as part and parcel of the same message.[37]

The Circle of Justice stresses reciprocal justice, which is not necessarily the same as democracy. Middle East politics may have been misunderstood partly because Western politicians failed to take the Circle of Justice into account.[38] Much of the rhetoric in the Arab uprisings of 2011 stemmed from the Circle of Justice concepts of freedom from tyranny, a social contract between ruler and ruled, and rights to food and medical care.[39] Demonstrations often began at mosques not because they were religious or extremist in nature, but because mosques were the only venue where people could legally congregate—in some cases, Christian Syrians and atheists came to Friday prayers at the mosque, as well, to participate in the uprising.[40]

Therefore, the call for shariah is not just about religion and state. It's about justice. The phrase "Islam is a religion and a state" arose as a twentieth-century slogan in opposition to secular repression.

But equally, the call for shariah is about the rule of law. One of the most remarkable achievements of the Islamic legal system was that, over a thousand years ago, everyone from the poorest peasant to the caliph was bound by the law.

Today, though, Muslim populations are subject to dictators who act *above* the law. They limit opposition, cancel elections, dissolve parliament, order summary executions, and declare states of emergency. Is it any wonder that Muslims long for shariah? Or that Islam has been a banner around which everyone can rally? It's only natural that opposition to secular dictators would frequently take the form of an Islamic opposition.

Islamists who advocate an "Islamic state" are generally not the religious scholars. They are usually engineers and doctors and others, advocating a state governed by "Islamic values." That means they're often not knowledgeable about shariah.

This lack of a deep understanding of shariah, plus the fact that Islamic religious educational institutions have deteriorated in the last two centuries,[41] results in an Islamist rhetoric that is unschooled in the rich Islamic legal tradition. Islamic studies scholar Frank Griffel writes that Islamists such as

> Hasan al-Banna, Sayyid Qutb, and Abu l-A'la [sic] Mawdudi (1904–79), who were self-trained in their competence of Islamic law, led the call for the implementation of a shari'a that in this form had never existed in premodern times.[42]

In other words, in their ignorance of the Islamic legal tradition, Islamists have arrived at simplistic, literalist, and mistaken interpretations that would never have been accepted in Islamic history.[43] Many Islamists mistakenly do not historically contextualize the Qur'an, hadith, and fiqh, as they must for accurate understanding. (How can you know whether a Qur'anic verse still applies if you don't know the reason for revelation?) Or they assign modern meanings to 1,400-year-old Qur'anic words. (It's possible, for example, though not generally accepted, that a word commonly translated as "virgin" originally meant "golden raisin.")[44] Or they completely disregard fiqh, which—though admittedly outdated in parts, because of ancient attitudes and mores—explains and elucidates the hadith and the Qur'an.[45]

Islamists generally haven't explained precisely how they will "bring back" shariah.[46] They have rarely been given a chance to try. (Some of these groups are called *post-Islamist*, to indicate their willingness to adopt political Islam that accommodates modern democracy,[47] but for this book I'm going to call them all Islamists.) However, the Islamists committed to working within the system, which is most of them, have adopted a variety of approaches.

Sometimes, for instance, Islamists advocate including a statement that Islam or "shariah" will be a source of legislation. This is vague enough that it doesn't necessarily affect the substantive content of the law much, if at all. The Qur'an, the Sunna, and fiqh can all be interpreted in a way that is compatible with our modern notions of fairness and justice and with international conventions.

Islamists usually don't seek to regulate every Islamic fiqh rule. They understand that most Muslims do not want Islamic practices to be enforced by the state.[48] For example, though drinking alcohol is clearly prohibited in Islam, some Islamists wouldn't make it illegal. Currently, some Muslim-majority countries allow the sale of alcohol, some limit it, and some ban it.[49]

Let's contrast this with the premodern shariah system, though. Historically, siyasa laws (those made by the ruler for the public good) didn't ban alcohol for everyone in Islamic lands.[50] Non-Muslims could drink alcohol and even cultivate and sell it. Fiqh prohibited Muslims from drinking alcohol, but even then, this was a private matter, usually not intrusively policed by the state. Therefore, modern states that ban alcohol for both Muslims and non-Muslims are not acting Islamically!

The most flexible Islamist movements are willing to leave the parliamentary processes in place and simply require consultation with Islamic authorities in the making of laws. They require not that laws derive exclusively from Islam but that Islamic sources be incorporated into the debate. Some groups in Morocco and Egypt take this position.[51] In the past few decades, Islamist platforms have added demands for the following: accountability; an end to political repression; and human rights, democracy, and uncorrupt government.[52]

The vast majority of Islamists are peaceful and advocate their views through participation in the political system. Banning Islamists from the political process—or repressing them or jailing them—tends to radicalize them. Allowing them to participate in the political process tends to result in more moderation and flexibility, as their views become tempered with the necessity of coalition building and pragmatism.[53]

Tunisia is a case in point. Since the uprisings of 2011, the Islamist Ennahda Party has become more flexible, showing itself to be more inclusive than the secular party. Ennahda selected a Jewish candidate for municipal elections in 2018,[54] as well as Tunis's first female mayor, whose aim, she says, is the freedom of all women.[55] Ennahda has had to work with a variety of partners—its Shura Council, grassroots activists, and other parties—and, consequently, has deleted the word "shariah" from its constitution. Ennahda has instead looked to Islamic principles, focusing on "social justice, equality, and good governance."[56] Essentially, that's the Maqasid!

Recently browsing a website featuring cruises to Tunisia, I came across the statement that the country was "very [socially] liberal by Islamic standards." Many countries, not just Muslim-majority ones, are socially conservative, but that's not because of their religious standards. Tunisia has an *Islamist* party in power! Yet, the website sentence frames Tunisia's liberality as emerging not from Islam but despite it.

It is no exaggeration to say that Islamic principles were some of the most liberal in the world for a thousand years. If that's changed now, the reason must obviously not be religion. Tunisia has had the only peaceful and successful post-uprising transition to democracy, and partly it's because of the Islamist party's willingness to include various groups within the political process.

Unquestionably, some Islamist groups are conservative. Some are even misogynistic. Some are fundamentalist. I myself would not like to live within the governance of every Islamist group. But that doesn't mean "Islamist" is simply a synonym for "fundamentalist" or even "terrorist."

American and European policy has often operated as if these terms are indeed synonymous, however. This has sometimes led to the hampering of Islamist democrats, as in Algeria. After Algeria won its independence from France, a 1965 coup resulted in an autocratic military regime with no real elections. After the 1988 protests led to a new constitution, the first multiparty elections were held, in 1990. In the first round of the 1991 national elections, the Islamic democratic party (FIS) won by a landslide. A second round of elections was required under the constitution, and it looked like the Islamic party would again win by a landslide. But then the military government canceled the elections, banned the party, and jailed its leaders and activists.[57]

It's not clear how "Islamist" the FIS would have been. It never got a chance. The French assisted the autocratic Algerian government in a "preemptive coup d'etat" against the FIS, and the US went along with the French.[58] The result of canceling the elections was a decade-long civil war.

Historians William Cleveland and Martin Bunton remark:

There could be little doubt that the United States was uncomfortable with political Islam. In part this was because few US officials acknowledged that the intrusive US presence in the Middle East and US support for oppressive and unpopular regimes were primary causes that nurtured many Islamist movements.[59]

In their reference to "many Islamist movements" above, Cleveland and Bunton include violent movements like al-Qaeda and ISIS, as well as the far more numerous nonviolent movements.[60]

If Western NGOs, media, and governments have been hostile toward Islamist groups, they've largely ignored Muslim women's rights activists within these groups. But women are changing the social dynamics of Islamist groups, rejecting the Western path to feminism and forging their own.[61] Islam*ic* feminism as well as Islam*ist* feminism both are often ignored, buried under the Islam-is-sexist trope. I've never heard that it's impossible to be a devout Jew or Christian or Hindu and still be a feminist, yet all these religions have traditionally contained downright sexist practices. If we can have Jewish and Christian and Hindu feminists, why not Muslim feminists?

Here's one example. In Lebanon, shariah courts deal with family laws: secularists want to abolish them, and religionists consider them necessary. Because of these rigid ideological positions, investigations into what the courts actually do have been minimal and opaque. But Muslim women started demanding transparency: they said, we want the religious courts, but we want to know if they're protecting our rights. Their approach presumed that shariah was just but that unjust legal results could stem from human error and the wrongful application of shariah. That's why, these women concluded, Muslims had a duty to "intervene, question, and reform" these human errors.[62]

Although some Islamists undoubtedly resist "women's rights," we should be wary of assuming that they conceptualize or define them the way Western people do. Morocco elected the first-ever Islamist government in 2011, and of the four coalition parties (Islamist, nationalist, socialist, and royalist), only the Islamist party appointed a woman minister.[63] The Muslim Brotherhood's party resisted "women's rights," but it also provided assistance for seven million female heads of household.[64] Decades ago in Turkey, Islamist women encouraged women's political participation by arguing that women were liable only to God and shouldn't be ruled by their husbands—that is, they shouldn't put their husbands on pedestals reserved for God.[65]

In addition to women's rights, Islamist treatment of religious minorities has, quite rightly, come under close scrutiny. Virtually no mainstream Islamist groups "dispute the need for an Islamic paradigm of civil society in which religious pluralism generates principles of coexistence among different religious and ethnic communities."[66] In other words, virtually no mainstream Islamists aim to grant inferior status to non-Muslims. (Note, however, that the issue of religious minorities is not solely pertinent to Muslim-majority countries; quite a few non-Muslim-majority countries also officially or unofficially favor certain religious groups over others or discriminate against them.)[67]

Finally, not only do Islamists vary enormously; they can evolve over time, as Ennahda has. It's easy to fling slogans around when your party is banned and your slogans have no actual effect. Not so easy when you have to govern a country. Today, virtually no Islamist groups assert that the state should be governed solely by shariah, and the vast majority do not aim to overturn the political structures of their countries to establish caliphates.

But, hang on—what about ISIS? Isn't that exactly what ISIS is trying to do?

ISIS, ISIL, OR DAESH?

It's hard to know what to call these people, besides "murdering criminals." I'm going to call them ISIS, because that's more specific than ISIL and more recognizable than Daesh,* which is what I really wish to call them. The worst thing to call them is "the Islamic State"—it's like calling the KKK "the Christian State."

---

* *Daesh* is the acronym for this group in Arabic. But the word *daesh* also approximately means "bullies" or "people who crush you" in Arabic, which is why Arabic-speaking Muslims like calling these criminals "Daesh."

ISIS terrorists are perceived as Islamists, but they are not motivated by the desire for shariah. They're motivated by politics and power. Like al-Qaeda and all other Muslim terrorists, they're not jihadists, under shariah, but mass murderers.

Are these terrorists self-described Muslims? Yes. Do they claim to base their acts on Islam? Yes. Are they "Islamic," which means do they adhere to the tenets of Islam? No, because they violate numerous established rules of Islam, including severe prohibitions on terrorism. There's nothing Islamic about setting up a terrorist entity that rules by violence and intimidation.

Islamic scholars have overwhelmingly condemned ISIS as un-Islamic, and Muslims worldwide have nearly unanimously rejected ISIS.[68]

Islam and ISIS can be analogized to Christianity and the Lord's Resistance Army in Africa. The Lord's Army members are Christian and claim to act in accordance with Christianity. But most Christians would say their violence and brutality—every bit as horrific as that of ISIS—is not Christian.

Though ISIS frames its endeavors in religious language in order to recruit Muslims, it's a modern political project, not a religious one, aiming to conquer property and amass power. It grew from the US' 2003 invasion of Iraq, which disenfranchised Sunni Muslims and ousted high-level officials from Saddam Hussein's secular government—over a hundred of whom joined ISIS.[69]

ISIS also resembles the Ku Klux Klan, which bases its hatred of blacks and Jews (and others) on the Bible. The KKK originated in 1860s America and achieved considerable political power in the early twentieth century.[70] The only reason ISIS has succeeded more spectacularly than the KKK is because ISIS operates in *failed states*.

ISIS and al-Qaeda constitute a fractionally tiny minority of Muslims. Indeed, sociologist Charles Kurzman says the real question is why there aren't more Muslim terrorists.[71] Over the last quarter century, he estimates, terrorists have recruited less than seven hundred-thousandths (that's 7/100,000 or 0.00007) of the Muslim population worldwide.[72] This frustrates ISIS and al-Qaeda, who constantly bemoan their lack of success and upbraid Muslims for not joining them.[73]

Most ISIS and al-Qaeda fighters have little interest in religion. When asked, Muslim terrorists cite political grievances, not religion. The aim of terrorist groups is not to proselytize Islam; in fact, most victims of Muslim terrorism are Muslim themselves.[74] Journalist Didier Francois, who was held captive by ISIS for over ten months, told CNN that his captors didn't discuss religion with him; they discussed politics.

"It has nothing to do with the Quran," said Francois. "They didn't want even to give us a Quran."[75]

Though ISIS recruits tend to be committed to their Muslim identities, most only tenuously grasp Islam. An Associated Press analysis of leaked ISIS documents showed that the huge majority of ISIS recruits had little or no knowledge of Islam.[76] ISIS fighters who have been captured have commonly told judges that they have no idea whether ISIS practices conformed to shariah. Indeed, two young British men who set off to join ISIS in Syria had ordered these books from Amazon to prepare for their journey: *Islam for Dummies* and *The Koran for Dummies*.[77]

Muslims generally join ISIS (and other extremist organizations) for reasons other than religion. ISIS gives them jobs at a time of rampant youth unemployment.[78] ISIS offers humiliated and enraged young men a way to defend their families and tribes.[79] ISIS represents a politically powerful way to act upon a perpetual sense of injustice.[80]

Criminologist Andrew Silke says that the reason for Muslim terrorists' involvement has to do with what's happening in their "personal lives, employment discrimination, [and] yearnings for revenge for the death toll of Muslims."[81] He remarks that governments prefer to blame "Islamicist ideology," because that's simpler and that way "we can leave all of the messy, complicated behavioural stuff alone."[82]

Marc Sageman, former CIA officer, forensic psychiatrist, and terrorism consultant, has studied violence since childhood, inspired by his parents' survival of the Holocaust. His work shows that the motivation for the "radicalization" of Muslims is not religion but a confluence of the following factors, occurring in the following order: "moral outrage at recent political events" particularly at the treatment of Muslims; belief that the West is at war with Islam, which is confirmed repeatedly by American and European politicians and pundits; personal hurtful experiences; and the joining of existing militant networks, which persuade them to act on their grievances.[83]

In addition to political grievances, shortages regarding basic needs spawn militant groups. In 2015, British scientists at the Global Sustainability Institute at Anglia Ruskin University found that regional food insecurity and scarcity of water were significant factors in violent unrest—including the rise of ISIS, al-Qaeda, Boko Haram, and al-Shabab. Of the seventeen countries most at risk for food and water insecurity, fourteen were Muslim-majority countries, and at least ten were subject to ongoing American counterterrorism operations.[84]

In sum, ISIS and al-Qaeda violate myriad rules of shariah, including the prohibition on killing civilians, destroying property, committing suicide, and terrorism. Such groups justify their acts and recruit members by using religious language, but that doesn't make them "Islamist," any more than quoting the Bible makes the KKK "Christianist" (a word Western news media never ever uses).

Another related misconception is that shariah allows suicide attacks. However, suicide attacks are neither sanctioned by nor unique to Islam, which prohibits suicide and killing civilians. The clandestine use of force is also prohibited.

Suicide attacks have been a strategy since antiquity—yes, even against the Romans and ancient Persians! In modern times, nearly four thousand Japanese Kamikaze pilots killed over twelve thousand American servicemen during World War II.[85] The group with the most suicide attacks in recorded history is the Sri Lankan Tamil Tigers, a Hindu Marxist-Leninist group.

Political scientist Robert Pape of the University of Chicago conducted a quarter-century study on suicide terrorism. He found "little connection between suicide terrorism and Islamic fundamentalism, or any one of the world's religions."[86] Pape concludes:

> The root cause of suicide terrorism is foreign occupation and the threat that foreign military presence poses to the local community's way of life.[87]

Attacking Muslim countries will not curb suicide terrorism, because the reason for suicide terrorism is foreign occupation.[88] Before the 2003 US invasion of Iraq, how many suicide attacks had occurred in Iraqi history? Zero.

Pape notes that if suicide terrorism were due to Islam, then suicide terrorism should not have subsided, as it did, when American, French, and Israeli combat forces withdrew from Lebanon.[89] Similarly, Palestinian suicide attacks should not have dramatically declined, as they did, when Israel withdrew from Gaza in 2004 and 2005.[90] They declined because suicide terrorism is caused by foreign occupation.

In sum: terrorism violates shariah, and the vast majority of Islamists eschew violence and work within the political system. But what are they working to achieve?

A FEW MODERN MUSLIM SCHOLARS ON WHAT AN ISLAMIC GOVERNMENT MIGHT LOOK LIKE

Steve Bannon, President Trump's former chief strategist, believes that Muslims are innately opposed to democratic values; he has described the Syrian refugees thus: "These are not people with thousands of years of democracy in their DNA."[91]

Aside from uttering the very definition of a racist statement, this guy clearly never took a biology class.

Nevertheless, I contest his meaning; if anyone has democracy in their (cultural) DNA, it's Muslims. Only one historical governmental system is recognized by all Muslims as legitimate, and that was the multireligious city of Medina under Muhammad's leadership. Records from this period indicate clearly that all residents, whatever their religion, worked together for the common good of the city, while individual religious freedom was guaranteed. After the rule of the first four caliphs, who were elected—democratically, mind you—Muslim rule devolved into dynasties, which have never been universally accepted as valid Islamic government.

The frequent questioning of whether "Islam and democracy are compatible" is frankly insulting. No one questions whether Christianity and democracy are compatible, even though democracy in the West didn't come *from* Christianity—on the contrary, democracy in the West came from a *distancing* of Christianity and government.[92]

Shariah contains multiple democratic principles. The Prophet said that the best form of jihad was to speak truth to an oppressive ruler. *Aqd* signifies a contract between the governor and the governed (like a constitution). *Maslaha* means the public interest (the basis of siyasa laws). The Qur'anic concept of *shura*, or mutual consultation between a leader of a community and its citizens, can predicate a consultative governmental body, such as a parliament. Some Muslims argue that, since the Qur'an does not specify a model of government, shariah requires only that the people be allowed to select their leaders, whatever the process.[93]

Most Muslim-majority countries have constitutions that already require a democratic system of government. What's needed is unclenching the grip of autocratic rulers and forcing them to comply with their own constitutions.[94] It's not shariah that's preventing democracy or supporting dictators.

According to a 2007 worldwide Gallup poll, Muslims fall into four general categories regarding democracy. Most Muslims want democracy and see no conflict with Islam; some want democracy but not necessarily Western-style democracy; some reject democracy completely as a Western construct; and some want only secular democracy, with Islam relegated to private life.[95]

Most Islamist platforms in Muslim-majority countries demand shariah as well as democracy. But what would a democratic "Islamic state" look like?

According to some Islamic scholars, such as Wael Hallaq, an "Islamic state" is inherently self-contradictory and impossible.[96] He believes that the modern nation-state and the traditional shariah-based system of Islamic governance are irreconcilable. In the former, law descends from the top, from the government; in the latter, law arose from the bottom up, from the middle-to-lower-class religious scholars.[97] We cannot import the old system into the new nation-state system, Hallaq insists, because the old system is now "institutionally defunct (including its hermeneutics, courts, discursive practices, educational systems, and the entire range of its sociology of knowledge)."[98]

Law professor Abdullah An-Na'im would agree with Hallaq, but he views a secular state as an Islamic state. To rephrase, an-Na'im argues that an Islamic state *must* be a secular state. Why? Because shariah requires willing belief, and once a state imposes shariah on its citizens, willing belief disappears.[99]

An-Na'im notes that because religion and governance were separate in Islamic history, they should be separate today. The hallmark of the shariah-based legal system was freedom to dissent and debate, and the best space for dissent and debate is a secular state with constitutional democratic governance and protection of human rights.[100] An-Na'im allows for shariah to be accommodated through the democratic process just as any other value system would be accommodated; that is, just as we do in the US, citizens would propose, lobby, and vote on laws according to their moral codes or religions.[101]

Law professor and Islamic scholar Anver Emon proposes another Islamic model. He first observes that shariah has been used recently in two problematic and opposing ways, both stemming from subaltern positions—that is, from positions of colonial subjugation. On the one hand, fundamentalists reject modernity because they associate it with Western colonialists. On the other hand, secular Muslims adopt the colonialist view that Islam is backward and therefore an obstacle to modernity.[102] Both positions erroneously assume that shariah is a rigid code of rules that can be severed from their historical context and applied to the modern world.

Emon solves this problem by returning *context* to shariah. How? Through institutions. Retain the secular state, he says, but bring back religio-legal institutions to develop fiqh, check each other, provide legal pluralism, and offer advice, mediation, or arbitration for anyone who wants it—but not for those who don't. These institutions would offer a variety of qualified interpretations of shariah in temporal, geographical, political, and cultural contexts.[103] Thus, we'd have a "marketplace" of Islamic legal ideas.[104]

A "marketplace" of organizations interpreting shariah would necessarily interact with one another, debate one another, develop new interpretations, and educate Muslim citizens about different interpretations of shariah.[105] Muslims in such a state could choose between organizations that interpreted and developed fiqh with various approaches: conservative, liberal, traditional, modernist, and everything in between.

Scholar of constitutional and Islamic law Asifa Quraishi-Landes agrees that it's structural reform, not religious reform, that Muslims need. Her goal is legal pluralism. She proposes a two-tiered system of law, in which people could choose either secular law or religious law to resolve disputes.[106]

The government would make secular laws in the first tier. These would be laws for the public order, based on the public good—like the siyasa laws issued by the ruler in the premodern shariah system. The second tier would be a legally independent, but officially recognized, realm of religious law, whether shariah or halakha or other religious law. Citizens could voluntarily choose this option if they wanted religious, rather than secular, answers to their problems. They could have their disputes resolved according to the fiqh school of their choice (or the church or synagogue or temple of their choice).[107]

Secularists could avoid the religious law realm altogether and resolve their legal issues under secular law in the first tier. Religious people would have to follow *some* of the secular laws—like those on taxation and speed limits and building codes—but could opt for the religious rules whenever relevant.

Here's the key: both realms, secular and religious, would comprise the shariah system, just as they had in premodern times.

But wait! In such a system, how could religionists ensure that the government's secular siyasa laws were in keeping with shariah? Conversely, how could secularists ensure that the government didn't start legislating religious law in the guise of siyasa laws?

These are legitimate concerns. Muslims in some countries, like Turkey, have been oppressed by secularism. Secularists and non-Sunni Muslims in some countries, like Saudi Arabia, have been oppressed by religionists.

Quraishi-Landes's solution would be a "shariah-check" system. The government's siyasa rules would be checked to ensure that they both didn't violate shariah and were also fair to non-Muslims. How? By ensuring that the laws were based on the public good, as encapsulated in the Maqasid al-Shariah.

Who would perform the shariah check? An entity that the people would agree upon—perhaps a review council or a supreme court.

Enacting a law that doesn't violate shariah is not equivalent to *imposing* shariah. Taxation doesn't violate shariah, yet American tax laws do not "impose shariah" on anyone. Laws allowing Jews to produce wine and Christians to raise pigs to sell likewise do not violate shariah, which allows for non-Muslims to follow their own religious laws—but that doesn't mean they *impose* shariah on such Jews and Christians.

Today, many Muslims (and more non-Muslims) misunderstand the concepts of shariah, fiqh, and siyasa, mistakenly believing that all three kinds of laws are unchangeable and mandated by God. This can thwart re-interpretations of fiqh. Instead, Muslims should conceptualize a shariah-based legal system as an adaptive rule-of-law system of legal pluralism (a system in which multiple valid legal results are possible and law comes from multiple sources, not just the government), encompassing both fiqh and siyasa.[108] This is the basis for Quraishi-Landes's model of Islamic constitutionalism: shariah as pluralist rule of law.[109]

Although An-Na'im, Emon, and Quraishi-Landes offer differing visions of structure and politics, they all base them on Islamic concepts. They all provide religious rules only for those who want them and provide secular pathways for those who do not. And yet all models are Islamic models.

Muslims vary as widely as any other community of people. Yet, Americans and Europeans routinely dismiss liberal and mainstream Muslim thinkers, portraying only the fundamentalists as true Muslims, writing long articles to prove ISIS is authentically "Islamic" (despite worldwide Muslim condemnation of ISIS).

I encounter such sentiments quite regularly in a personal context too. I'm continually dumbfounded at the number of people who assume that my perspective is a "liberal" or "Westernized" version of Islam (though I consider myself a mainstream and observant Muslim), simply because I look and sound like a normal person. This raises three significant issues that apply to me personally and to Muslims generally.

First, why do these people assume I'm liberal (I admit to being Western) simply because of the way I look and sound? How can they possibly assume themselves to be expert in the rich, immense variety of worldwide Islamic thought? The obvious answer is that they've been conditioned to think of the Saudis and the Taliban and even terrorist groups as the Muslim norm.

Second, even if I were liberal on this worldwide spectrum, why would that render my Islam inauthentic?

Third, if my Islam is indeed liberal, why should its liberality necessarily be the result of "Westernization"? The West is not the sole source of democracy and liberal thinking.

Islamic government can adhere in numerous ways to the Islamic legal tradition and be authentically Islamic—even if, ironically, the result comes out looking scarcely different from Western models of government.

FREEDOM OF CONSCIENCE IN AN "ISLAMIC STATE"

As I discussed previously, historical Islamic empires were multiracial and multireligious empires. Historian William Dalrymple writes:

> As late as the eighteenth century, European visitors to the Moghul and Ottoman Empires were astounded by the degree of religious tolerance that they found there. . . . If that coexistence was not always harmonious, it was at least a kind of pluralist equilibrium which simply has no parallel in European history.[110]

Similarly, Norman Daniel noted, "In the long run only Islam effectively tolerated other religions within itself."[111]

These statements might come as a surprise. Western public opinion routinely assumes Islam is violent toward people of other religions. The well-publicized cases of reprehensible discrimination against non-Muslims in Muslim-majority countries contributes to this view (though it's quite common to ignore discrimination against Muslims by non-Muslims in various countries). Therefore, I want to discuss here the Qur'anic and shariah views of how non-Muslims and apostates should be treated, as these impact all models of government in which Islam plays a direct or indirect role.

The Qur'an repeatedly forbids forced conversion, as discussed, and commands respect toward those of other religions. The Qur'an also firmly establishes that you don't have to be Muslim to go to heaven. It treats Muslims as neither solely destined for salvation, nor a chosen people:

- "The believers, the Jews, the Christians, and the Sabians, *all* who believe in God and the Last Day and do good deeds, have their reward with their Lord. And no fear need they have, and neither shall they grieve." (2:62)

- "Surely anyone who surrenders his whole being to God and is a doer of good, shall have his reward with his Lord; and all such need have no fear, and neither shall they grieve." (2:112)

Monotheists are never called infidels in the Qur'an, contrary to what most of those in the West and some Muslims, too, believe. *Kafir* in the Qur'an doesn't mean "infidel" or "unbeliever" or even "atheist," though it's sometimes translated to mean these things. *Kafir* in the Qur'an means someone who worships an entity *in addition* to God.[112] (Remember "There is no god but God"?)

The Qur'an particularly respects Jews and Christians, as in the above verse. They are usually called "People of the Book," a term I find confusing. I prefer "People of an Earlier Revelation."[113] In other words, Jews and Christians are among those who received the word of God before Muhammad. Indeed, the Qur'an does not use the words *Muslim* and *Islam* to mean the religion of only Muhammad; rather, the Qur'an uses these terms to mean "believer," someone who believes in God.[114]

Initially, "People of an Earlier Revelation" included only Muslims, Jews, Christians, and Sabians. But as Islam spread and Muslims encountered other religious communities, they gathered Zoroastrians, Hindus, and Buddhists into their definition, as well—even if such communities were not monotheistic. In fact, some Muslims regard *all* people as "People of an Earlier Revelation," because the Qur'an says that every community has been sent a prophet.[115]

When the Qur'an gave Muhammad permission to fight back against the Meccans, it also gave Muslims permission to defend churches and synagogues:

> *Had God not granted people the ability to defend themselves against others, it would have resulted in the destruction of churches, synagogues, monasteries, and mosques.* (22:39–40)

The Qur'an admonishes Jews and Christians for not respecting each other and for tearing down each other's religious houses. (2:113–14)

Muhammad not only tolerated people of other faiths but also actively engaged them in pluralism. He invited Christians to worship in his mosque and instructed Muslims to repair churches that had fallen into disrepair. Muhammad's legal covenants with Christians and Jews have survived: they show that, for example, he instructed Muslims not to fight against their Christian brothers and sisters, and he assured Jews, in the Treaty of Maqnah, that they could "be in peace," without "suppression or violence."[116]

Well, okay, you might be thinking, but doesn't Islam require the killing of people who *leave* Islam?

The Islamic law of apostasy is an ancient one, stemming from a time when other religions also punished people for apostasy. It was in abeyance for centuries and has been revived only in recent decades by fundamentalists and Ayatollah Khomeini's fatwa on Salman Rushdie.

The Qur'an does not specify any earthly punishment for apostasy. The Islamic punishment for the crime of apostasy comes from fiqh. As you know by now, fiqh interpretations have everything to do with the time, place, and culture of those doing the interpreting.

Classical fiqh of over a thousand years ago did decree the death penalty for apostasy. The accused was usually given three days to repent and recant. Some schools prescribed, as penalty for apostasy, imprisonment for women but death for men, because men would be in a position to wage war against Islam.[117]

These classical fiqh rules are based on a hadith in which Muhammad allegedly instructed the killing of those who left Islam—but Muhammad's own example contradicts this purported hadith. Muhammad never once ordered the execution of anyone for ceasing to be Muslim. Muhammad himself let apostates leave his community without pursuing or punishing them, reiterating on more than one occasion (including in a formal treaty with the Meccans)[118] that people could leave the Muslim community without punishment.[119]

How could early Islamic scholars have specified the death penalty for apostasy, despite Muhammad's example? And despite the Qur'anic verses forbidding forced conversion?

The answer: the early scholars didn't define apostasy as simple cessation of personal belief.

Rather, the scholars defined apostasy as both ceasing to believe in Islam *and* waging war or insurrection on Islam and Muslims. To them, apostasy meant rejecting the "legislation, authority, public order, and governance"[120] of Islamic lands. (We might call that treason.) That's why many fiqh books include apostasy in the section on warfare, not in the section on crimes.[121]

Muhammad's hadith, then, makes sense in light of his conduct. Even if the hadith is a true one, Muhammad was speaking of those not simply leaving Islam but leaving Islam *plus* waging war on Muslims or engaging in some other political rejection of the public order.[122]

Even early Islamic scholars agreed that only "external expressions of apostasy" could be punished, not the private religious beliefs and practices of individuals.[123] This attitude makes sense, as a cornerstone of the Islamic legal tradition is that "the law does not seek to know what is in people's hearts."[124]

Practically speaking, as well, punishments for apostasy were rarely imposed in Islamic history, even when apostates publicly criticized Islam, and only when they caused some societal upheaval.[125] Frank Griffel writes that Muslim jurists developed a law that almost entirely circumvented the punishment:

> [Jurists developed] a legal loophole that prevented the application of the harsh law of apostasy in all but the most manifest cases, namely, when someone was intentionally provoking the Muslim community and its judges.[126]

Islamic apostasy laws were typical of the time. Religion was an integral part of public law and order, as well as citizenship, not only in Islamic lands but in Christian and Zoroastrian lands. (England didn't abolish the death penalty for blasphemy until the seventeenth century; blasphemy as a crime was only abolished in 2008.)[127] Historians Louise Nyholm Kallestrup and Raisa Maria Toivo describe Europe thus: "In the medieval and early modern periods, religion, politics and economics were each part of the other."[128]

Rejecting religion publicly, inciting others to do the same, and taking up arms against the religious community meant a rejection of all the law and order stemming from those religions. As an-Na'im explains, apostasy rules

> were in fact concessions to the social and economic realities of the time, and not the message Islam intended for humanity at large into the indefinite future.[129]

The early Islamic scholars interpreted the Qur'an in light of their own sociopolitical reality. Fiqh develops as sociopolitical reality changes. Just as we don't assume Jews will kill apostates because the Old Testament tells them to,[130] or that Christians will kill apostates because canon law required execution (usually by fire) for them,[131] we shouldn't assume Muslims must apply apostasy laws coming from fiqh rules of over a thousand years ago. Most modern Muslim scholars agree that classical apostasy laws are a relic of the past, in line with ancient times but not with modern times.

Many high-level modern Islamic scholars have confirmed that the Islamic crime of apostasy in Islam does not apply to cessation of personal belief. Grand Mufti Ali Gomaa, Grand Mufti Sayyid Tantawi, and Shaykh Yusuf al-Qaradawi have all stressed that people have the right to change what they believe without punishment. Shaykh Khaled Abou El Fadl argues that the classical punishment on apostasy must be rejected, because an isolated hadith cannot overrule the many verses of religious tolerance in the Qur'an.[132]

That's why it's especially tragic that some Muslim-majority countries have indeed prosecuted people for apostasy in the modern era, even in the absence of treason. Although these cases are rare, *any* prosecution at all for apostasy is too many. I am ashamed to say that, of the fifty-four or so Muslim-majority countries in the world, eight list apostasy as a capital offense.[133]

Such laws must be eliminated. They do not accord with modern interpretations of shariah. In fact, they violate the spirit, and often the letter, of even *classical* fiqh.

The Qur'an itself gives no earthly penalty for apostasy, yet contains more than a hundred verses affirming freedom of religion, freedom of conscience, and the truth of other religions.[134] In fact, beyond simply urging religious tolerance, the Qur'an advocates respectful engagement of diversity, as in this verse:

> *O humankind, We created you from a male and a female, and We made you into different races and tribes so you could learn from one another. The noblest of you in the sight of God are those of you who are most conscientious."* (49:13)

This verse doesn't tell Muslims to go convert people from different races and tribes; it urges us all to learn from one another. The Qur'an also considers diversity as a sign of God:

> *And among the signs of God is the constitution of the heavens and the earth, and the diversity of your languages and complexions [colors] . . .* (30:22)

The Qur'an says God could have made everyone into believers, but instead it made us diverse; instead of competing in our diversity, we should compete to do good:

> *For each of them, We have established a law and a revealed way. And if God had wished, God would have made you a single nation; but the intent is to test you in what God has given you. So compete with one another in good works.* (5:48)

Islam and Islamic history contain the building blocks for inclusive democracy, which may or may not look like Western democracy. Developing strong democratic governments will take time, too, because Muslim-majority countries are newly independent and wrestling with competing visions of future governance. After all, Western countries took four hundred years and multiple revolutions to become democratic—and they hadn't even been colonized.

CHAPTER TEN

THE SCARY STUFF

Punishments

APOSTASY IS JUST one of the Islamic punishments to achieve notoriety in the West today. By the time I was thirteen, my classmates in California public schools somehow knew that Muslims chopped the hands off of thieves, though they knew no Muslims except me, and I didn't chop off any hands. This, as well as other stereotypes, was confirmed by television and films, not least Disney's *Aladdin*, which nearly suffered Princess Jasmine to lose her hand to a merchant's knife, added racism to its lyrics (describing Arabia as a "barbaric" place where they routinely cut off ears) and to its characters (giving the good ones American accents with fair skin and small noses and giving the villains dark skin and big hooked noses).

Under shariah, no one would *ever* have sanctioned the merchant's amputation of Jasmine's hand for theft. Where was her requisite trial? Where did they evaluate whether amputation as a penalty applied to the theft (it didn't) or whether she'd made a mistake (she had) or whether she had stolen from hunger (she had indeed), thus rendering amputation inapplicable and even conviction unlikely? Shariah has never *ever* given license to anyone, much less fruit-stand merchants, to take the law into their own hands.

Shariah rules on offenses and punishments form a tiny part of shariah—only about 2 percent of any jurisprudential text.[1] Such rules were designed to limit the violence of the time and deter reprehensible conduct.

Harsh punishments were the norm in premodern times, before police forces existed. Death by stoning constitutes most of the penalties for violating the Ten Commandments.[2] Until the nineteenth century,

English common law punished hundreds of crimes, even misdemeanors, with death.[3]

Harsh punishments everywhere were meant as deterrents, because the chances of being caught committing a crime were low. In some cases, these punishments were *homiletic*, demonstrating the moral severity of an offense but not necessarily intended to be implemented.

In Islamic lands, the chances of being caught were low, not only because of a lack of police and other enforcement agencies but also because of shariah itself. Shariah prohibits "searching out transgressions (*tajassus*)" and requires "turning a blind eye to private misconduct (*satr*)."[4] Therefore, you couldn't spy on someone in order to catch them at a crime. And, even if you knew someone who drank alcohol in the privacy of his house, you weren't allowed to burst in on him to prove it. (Yes! A prohibition on unreasonable searches and seizures!)

One of Muhammad's companions, Umar, later the second caliph, stars in a famous story illustrating these principles. Walking in Medina one evening, Umar heard raucous noises emanating from one of the houses. He climbed over the wall of the house and found inside a man not only drinking wine but cavorting with a woman who was not his wife. Umar accused the man of sinning, and the man retorted that, whereas he himself may have indeed sinned, Umar had committed *three* Qur'anic sins: seeking out faults in others (49:12), climbing over the wall of the house (2:189), and entering a home without permission (24:27). Umar, by all accounts a hard-headed individual, shamefacedly admitted his fault and departed.[5]

These principles of not searching out offenses and turning a blind eye to private misconduct were not simply anomalous cultural approaches: they were rules of legal procedure. In other words, shariah guarantees a right to privacy.[6]

Shariah regards as punishable offenses only those forbidden actions that also impinge on the rights of other people or violate the public order. Shariah forbids lying and backbiting, too, but doesn't necessarily regulate them as crimes.

Criminal offenses were categorized into "determined" offenses, those mentioned in the Qur'an and Sunna, and "discretionary" offenses (*ta'zir*), those developed by the Islamic scholars. By far, most offenses were categorized as discretionary. These were developed, as all Islamic law is, within the framework of the Maqasid al-Shariah. Only a handful of offenses were categorized as "determined," and these were categorized as two types: *qisas* crimes and *hudud* crimes.

Qisas crimes include homicide and bodily injury. The traditional possible outcomes for these crimes were retaliation to the same degree, compensation, or forgiveness by the victim. For example, if a family member were murdered, the family could demand retaliation in the form of the death of the murderer (as in our death penalty) or monetary compensation for their loss (as in our wrongful-death civil suits). Retaliation was discouraged, and compensation was considered more commendable. Most commendable, though, was forgiving the murderer.

The hudud (sing. *hadd*) offenses are the "limits prescribed by God," because they are mentioned, along with their penalties, in the Qur'an. All scholars agreed that these five offenses constitute hudud: illicit sex, wrongful accusation of illicit sex, *sariqa* (a certain type of theft), consumption of intoxicants, and armed robbery or banditry. They disagreed about whether to include apostasy, discussed in the last chapter.

THE HUDUD OFFENSES

Hudud offenses are generally considered fixed and mandatory because the Qur'an mentions them. The categories, definitions, and punishments for the crimes come primarily from fiqh, though, and not scripture. The hudud are not necessarily considered the most reprehensible crimes. On the contrary, in ancient fiqh texts, illicit sex is always ranked in importance below the sin of "associating others with God" and often below the sin of "disrespectfulness toward one's parents."[7]

Although most people of all backgrounds would agree that defamation, theft, and armed robbery should be considered crimes (or torts) even today, most people, including most Muslims, would not agree that the state should punish either consumption of intoxicants (of alcohol, at least) or extramarital sex. These punishments made more sense in ancient times, when extramarital sex was punished across cultures and religions, often with death. In the West, we still punish consumption of some intoxicants, though, like cocaine and even alcohol in certain situations.

Early Muslims understood the Qur'anic rationale behind forbidding drunkenness and illicit sex, because these sins caused harm or violated the public order, as did the other hudud crimes. Illicit sex could result in illegitimate children, which negatively impacted the family and disrupted the system of inheritance; this in turn affected the predictable distribution of property, which was necessary for the stability of society. Intoxication—*public* intoxication is the true offense here—increased the likelihood of public disorder, damage to property and people, and assault.[8] Drunk driving and "drunk and disorderly conduct" are still punishable offenses today, for the same reasons.

It's always the hudud punishments—death or flogging or amputation—that are publicized today as evidence of the harshness of shariah. But it is no exaggeration to say that, in virtually every case that hudud penalties are applied today, they *never* should have been applied.

Let me reiterate: *under shariah itself*, for multiple reasons, hudud punishments should never be applied. I'll discuss the reasons why in detail below, but let me first summarize generally. First, several Islamic principles significantly impede charging anyone with any hadd crime, rendering such charges extremely rare. Second, even if someone is charged, the proof required to convict him or her of a hadd crime is stupendously unattainable. And third, even if someone is convicted, shariah judges have multiple fiqh tools they can use to set aside punishments. That's why the hudud punishments, *from an Islamic perspective*, should never be imposed today.

Most Muslims in the world understand this. Indeed, before the founding of Saudi Arabia in the early twentieth century, hudud punishments were nearly extinct and certainly in abeyance. Even now, only a tiny minority of the Muslim-majority countries in the world maintain hudud punishments on their books. Many of the so-called punishments you hear about—stoning, honor killings—are extrajudicial, un-Islamic, and committed by people taking what they think is the law into their own hands.

Finally, as you read, note the lack of sexism in the laws of the following hudud offenses. They may seem harsh, but they apply equally to everyone.

HOW TO PROVE A HUDUD OFFENSE

Although the Qur'an sets out some punishments, it also repeatedly stresses God's vast mercy and forgiveness. All but one chapter of the Qur'an begins with the words, "God is most compassionate, most merciful."* This command for mercy, in addition to the following widely attested hadith, has been a cornerstone of shariah:

> Ward off the *hudud* from the Muslims as much as you all can, and if you find a way out for the person, then let them go. For it is better for the authority to err in mercy than to err in punishment.[9]

This hadith gave birth to several legal principles. First, it is *always* better to forgive than punish. Second, because punishment is tempered with God's mercy, repentance is generally enough to avert a hudud penalty.[10] (Repentance! Who can't bring themselves to repent?) Third, people are innocent until proven guilty: "the fundamental principle is freedom of liability."[11] And fourth, *any doubt whatsoever* must be construed in favor of the accused to prevent a conviction.[12]

Any doubt whatsoever! That means that, for the hudud offenses, shariah requires 100 percent certainty that the accused is guilty. That's 0 percent doubt. And that's why it's so hard to convict anyone in a hudud crime.

One hundred percent certainty is a remarkably high standard of proof. Our Anglo-American common law assumes that it is impossible to achieve absolute certainty of guilt. Hence, in American law, only a preponderance of the evidence—a likelihood of over 50 percent—is enough for liability in most civil cases. That means you can have 49 percent doubt! For criminal convictions, the standard is somewhat higher: the jury must be convinced only of guilt "beyond a reasonable doubt." The jury can still conclude the presence of doubt—just not *reasonable* doubt.

Shariah, however, requires that in hudud cases there can be absolutely no doubt whatsoever of any kind, reasonable or unreasonable.

In addition to the 100 percent certainty requirement, all sorts of procedural restrictions apply to hudud cases, as well. The aforementioned principles of not prying into private affairs and turning a blind eye to private misconduct apply to hudud offenses. Witnesses to hudud crimes are also not legally or morally obligated to testify (no subpoenas!) and, at least in the case of illicit sex, are encouraged *not* to testify.[13]

---

*Why not this one? We can't be certain, but it was probably originally a part or continuation of a previous chapter.

Circumstantial evidence is not admissible for the hudud, as it is under common law. If you saw someone staggering down the street, swinging an open wine bottle, reeking of alcohol, and singing slurred ditties, this would be insufficient for a hadd punishment.

Shariah does not admit hearsay, either, in hudud cases. That is, you cannot testify that someone else had said something pertaining to the case.[14] You heard someone say that the accused had drunk alcohol? Not admissible as evidence.

Shariah gives Muslims the right not to incriminate themselves. (Yes, like our Fifth Amendment.) The first two caliphs of Islam, Abu Bakr and Umar, rulers and lawgivers though they were, would advise accused people to *not confess* in hudud cases. They are recorded as routinely advising the accused, "Have you stolen? Say no."[15]

Even someone who confesses to a hadd crime cannot be subject to the punishment if he or she retracts the confession. In the case of illicit sex, for example, to be convicted, a person must confess to the crime on four independent occasions, without coercion. But if someone confesses four times independently and then later says, "Never mind, I take my confession back," then the hadd punishment cannot be applied.[16]

A famous incident in Islamic history illustrates the difficulty of receiving a hadd punishment even if you want it. A man repeatedly tried to confess his adultery to the Prophet Muhammad, who, having learned of his intent, fled whenever he heard the man approach. When the man did corner him, the Prophet repeatedly suggested that the man had actually not committed adultery ("Perhaps you simply kissed her?").[17]

Shariah imposes stringent requirements on confessions, since early Islam. Confessions must follow exact required legal wording. The judge must advise the accused that he may retract the confession at any time. Only confessions made in court are valid.[18] Confessions cannot be accepted from minors, mentally ill persons, or persons who were tortured or otherwise coerced. (Until the eighteenth century, torture was officially sanctioned by the criminal laws of most European countries.)[19]

In addition to all the above procedural restrictions, Muslims devised further limitations on hudud penalties. First, hudud penalties were suspended completely at various times throughout Islamic history, on the authority of Prophet Muhammad or the early caliphs—for example, the second caliph, Umar, suspended the amputation penalty for theft in times of famine. Second, the hudud offenses were deliberately so narrowly defined that only a rare transgression fell within the definition. Third and most importantly, the evidentiary requirements were virtually unachievable.

To illustrate the procedural, definitional, and evidentiary rules around the hudud offenses, I'll discuss them in the context of two examples: illicit sexual intercourse and theft.

ILLICIT SEXUAL INTERCOURSE

In Islam, illicit or "unlawful" sexual intercourse, *zina*, means any sexual intercourse outside marriage.[20] The Qur'anic punishment for this is the same for a man as for a woman—there's no sexism here—and it's not execution. It's a hundred lashes.

The stoning punishment for zina probably came into fiqh from Judaic law. Jews in Medina at the time of the Prophet punished adulterers by stoning them. Early Islamic scholars unquestionably used and were influenced by the laws of other cultures, including Judaic law and Roman law, in developing fiqh.

The political and cultural environment was a factor, as well. Constantine (fourth century) had also prescribed death for adultery; Justinian (sixth century) had retained it, but also prescribed corporal punishment, depending on the situation.[21] Stoning, therefore, was a common punishment at the time and would have made sense to early Muslims (seventh century) to add to their own laws.

But let me tell you what you need in Islam to convict anyone—man or woman—of the hadd offense of illicit sexual intercourse: you must bring *four eyewitnesses to the act of intercourse itself.*

That means you must show that the eyewitnesses—all four of them!— saw every bit of sexual penetration with their own eyes. It is not enough to see two naked people in bed together. All four witnesses must have seen the penis go all the way into the vagina "like an eyeliner applier entering into its container."[22]

Wow.

They had eyeliner back then? (Yes, they did.)

There's more. You must prove that the witnesses are all reliable and trustworthy. The testimony of all four must be technically accurate as to the wording. Each witness's testimony must be completely consistent with the others in every particular. If one witness doesn't see the penetration but the other three do, then all four are liable for false accusation of illicit sexual intercourse, which is in itself a *hadd* crime. Finally, any witness may retract a testimony at any time up to implementation of the sentence, which throws out the penalty.[23]

I don't know of any lawyer who would wish for this kind of impossible burden of proof.

In traditional fiqh, only men could testify as witnesses for hudud crimes, because in antiquity most women did not have nearly as much education or power as men and would consequently be more vulnerable to coercion than men. In case you're thinking, "Aha! Muslim women *are* oppressed!" note that Muslim women could testify in other, non-hudud cases, and that European women couldn't testify in court at all before at least the eighteenth century and in some places the nineteenth century. Restricting testimony to men in hudud cases arose from a concern for the accused; given the severe penalties, uncoerced truth was crucial. The modern view is that women are no longer in such a vulnerable position today and therefore can testify in all courtroom proceedings.

Suppose, though, that you *can* bring four trustworthy male eyewitnesses, all shown to be trustworthy, who have all seen the penetration (as intimately as seeing a "bucket go into a well"![24]) with their own eyes and can each testify consistently with one another in every particular. Even then, the accused can invoke all sorts of defenses, including duress, coercion, lack of intent, mistake, and repentance.

More than that, even if, by some cosmic convergence, the prosecution can bring four eyewitnesses *and* they have satisfied all their requirements *and* the accused has absolutely no defenses, the court can even then decide—for any reason!—that there's more than 0 percent doubt and thus conclude that the hudud punishment doesn't apply.

You might quite reasonably be wondering how there could ever be four eyewitnesses to the actual penetration in sexual intercourse when such witnesses shouldn't have been prying into people's private affairs and should have been turning a blind eye to personal sinning. The answer is: there *never* can. (Not unless two people are fornicating in public.) That was the point.

THEFT

Shariah treats most types of theft like torts, not crimes, requiring the return of the property or payment of damages.[25] In only a narrow, specific kind of theft, called sariqa, can amputation ever be imposed. Amputation comes from a Qur'anic verse decreeing that, for a man or woman who steals, "cut his hand," though immediately following is a verse that says, "But those who repent after a crime and reform shall be forgiven by God." (5:38–39)

Arguably, the Qur'an never actually meant amputation in this verse. The Arabic word for "cut" can have many meanings, most relating to "stopping," as in "cut off someone's conversation." Even within the Qur'an itself, "cut" has multiple meanings. Reading the verse this way makes sense: for a man or woman who steals, "stop their hands from theft."[26] This interpretation is also consistent with the historical penalty for theft in Islamic lands, which was flogging and not amputation.[27]

Whatever the punishment, repentance and reform should be a defense, as the Qur'anic verse decrees.

Still, some kinds of theft did qualify for amputation under traditional fiqh, but—like illicit sex—the punishment of amputation was always so circumscribed and limited that it was rarely implemented. The conditions that must be met for sariqa are too numerous to include, but here are just a few:

- The hadd penalty doesn't apply to any thief compelled by hunger.
- Two eyewitnesses must have seen, with their own eyes, the thief steal the property.
- The theft must have been surreptitious (which makes eyewitnesses difficult to produce! If you can produce them, how can the theft have been surreptitious?).
- The thief cannot have had the goods at his disposal (like if he worked in a shop where they were sold).
- The thief must be Muslim, of sound mind, and of age.
- The property cannot have been in an unlocked, unsecured, or unguarded place.
- The property cannot have been in an inappropriate place (like jewelry in the barn).

- The property must be of a particular value.
- A month cannot have passed since the theft occurred.
- The property cannot have been meat or anything edible or potable or fowl or game or a dog or a cat or animal dung or dirt or arsenic or pebbles or stones or glass or coals or firewood or fruit of a donkey or a grazing animal or a plant pulled up from its roots or a tree or produce from a walled garden.
- Embezzlement doesn't qualify.
- Stealing a thing found in a public bath doesn't qualify.
- The thief could not have stolen from his spouse, son, parents, debtor, or maternal relatives.[28]

Even if the prosecution can satisfy this steep burden of proof, the penalty for sariqa can be avoided in a number of additional ways. For example, the thief can return the property before judgment.[29] Or the thief can repent.[30] Or the thief can pay damages to the victim in recompense. Or the victim can donate the property to the thief.[31]

In addition, as in the other hudud offenses, any doubt whatsoever will prevent imposition of the penalty. But what exactly does "any doubt whatsoever" mean?

ANY DOUBT WHATSOEVER (AMBIGUITY)

Defenses to crimes generally, including the hudud, included mistake (such as if the thief took something accidentally), duress (as in rape), lack of intent (like accidentally ingesting alcohol), capacity (not being of sound mind or of age or Muslim), self-defense, and repentance.[32] Therefore, even if the prosecution could meet that insurmountable burden of proof in hudud crimes, the accused could still claim one of these defenses.

Suppose, though, that the accused couldn't think of any defenses, not even "I'm really sorry and I won't do it again." *Even then*, the court could, for almost any reason, decide there was less than 100 percent certainty and not impose the punishment.

Recall the Prophet's command to "ward off the hudud" and search for a way out for the accused. Combine this with the requirement of 100 percent certainty. What do you get? The command to search for any possible uncertainty, doubt, or ambiguity in a hadd case.

Traditional Islamic jurists did just that. They developed the legal principle of "warding off the hudud by ambiguities (*shubuhat*)."[33] They went out of their way to search for ambiguities that could cast the slightest doubt on the accused's guilt.

They didn't do this because they were "soft on crime." Islamic judges simply followed the Prophet's dictates, as well as the Qur'an's exhortations to repentance, reform, and mercy. They turned all of these into rules of legal procedure.

Shariah courts accepted even inconceivably preposterous claims, from both men and women, as evidence of ambiguity in hudud cases. For example, a thief caught stealing could simply claim that the allegedly stolen item belonged to her; this caused enough doubt to negate the penalty.[34] Someone who was obviously drunk and even vomiting wine could acceptably claim that he had drunk the alcohol accidentally, and this provided sufficient doubt to negate a hadd penalty.[35]

Someone accused of illicit sex could claim, "Oops, I thought I was having sex with my spouse because it was dark."[36] Or he could claim, even without proof, that he had married the woman with whom he had had intercourse.[37] It was not uncommon for accused women to claim that they had been drugged with sweets and raped while unconscious.[38] Anyone could claim that there hadn't been any actual sexual penetration and therefore no illicit sex.[39]

Even pregnancy, for a majority of the jurists, didn't constitute proof of unlawful sexual intercourse, for a multitude of reasons. A woman could have been raped or impregnated in her sleep.[40] A woman could legally claim she conceived from kissing or other "heavy petting" without sexual intercourse.[41] A woman could claim that a long-absent husband had been miraculously transported back to sleep with her.[42] (Yes, she could!) A widow found pregnant could claim that she had been impregnated by her husband—even up to, according to the Maliki school, five years after his death.

Jonathan Brown relates a truly wonderful example of an ambiguity accepted by the shariah judges:

> A Muslim woman in India in the late 1500s, whose husband had died in battle, was suddenly found to be pregnant and was accused of fornication. She claimed that her husband had been miraculously brought

back to life every Friday night, when he would visit her. Jurists of India's predominant Hanafi school of law were consulted on the case and replied that it was indeed technically possible for such a miracle to have occurred.[43]

Were the jurists simply stupid? Didn't they know dead husbands couldn't impregnate their wives? Or that pregnancy couldn't last five years or result from kissing? Of course they knew. But they accepted all these reasons as legal defenses because they were warding off the hudud.

After all, the hudud penalties are the "claims of God." But Muslim jurists considered that God was sublime and did not *need* anything, not even satisfaction of God's claims.[44] Thus, the jurists perceived no contradiction in both accepting the hudud as offenses and simultaneously striving to avoid implementing them.

TA'ZIR

Shariah judges may have warded off the hudud, but they didn't necessarily let criminals go scot-free. Suppose a thief got caught red-handed by two eyewitnesses *and* satisfied the pages-long list of conditions required by the hudud, but then avoided amputation by claiming that the property was his (thereby introducing ambiguity). He wouldn't be guilty of a hadd crime, which requires absolute certainty, but he could be given a ta'zir punishment.

Ta'zir punishments were discretionary and required to be less severe than the hudud punishments. The most common punishments in Islamic history were lashings or *bastinado* (smacking someone on the soles of the feet),[45] which were the only allowable corporal punishments,[46] but also public rebuke, exposure to public scorn, banishment, and imprisonment until repentance.[47] Imprisonment did not necessarily mean "jail" but rather restrictions on movement, such as house arrest. Imprisoned people were entitled to certain rights, including food, medical care, conjugal visits, freedom of opinion, and integrity of person, body, and mind.[48]

Lashings were quite strictly circumscribed. The whip holder was not allowed to raise the whip high enough to show his armpit. The lashes couldn't land all in one place. Sensitive areas such as the head, groin, neck, and chest had to be avoided. The convicted person could not be tied up, women could be lashed with their clothes on, and men had to take off their heavy clothing.[49] Lashings were usually implemented in public to effect shame, reform and deter criminals, and inspire repentance.

Lashings did not aim to inflict lasting damage, nor were they inflexible as to application. For example, if the convicted person were considered too weak to receive a hundred lashes, then he could be hit once with a tied-together bunch of a hundred twigs.[50] Or maybe twice with a bunch of fifty twigs.

I realize that even a lashing for theft might sound offensive and uncivilized. These laws were developed centuries ago, though, and were relatively humane for the time. Consider, too, that in the US, thousands of people serve life sentences without possibility of parole for nonviolent crimes.[47] I cannot speak for anyone else, but were I a thief, I would personally prefer a public lashing to living my entire life in prison, separated from my family and children, without hope of release.

ISLAMIC CRIMINAL LAW TODAY

Given the radically different circumstances of ancient times, what is remarkable is not that the Qur'an specifies corporal punishments, but that it does so for only four crimes and that the Islamic scholars made those punishments nearly impossible to apply. This changed when colonialism dismantled the shariah-based legal system. When the British colonized India,

> British officials were baffled by the leniency of Islamic criminal law and by the loopholes that often precluded the infliction of what they saw as adequate punishment for serious criminals.[52]

The transformation of Islamic criminal law under colonialism resulted in injustice. The punishments were codified—or in some cases made harsher by the colonialists—and the strict procedural restrictions disregarded. The evidentiary requirements were not taken seriously. The entire system of "warding off the hudud" and finding a way out for the accused collided with the goals of colonial justice.

In other words, the punishments remained but without the original safeguards.

In the roughly six hundred years of the Ottoman Empire, execution for illicit sex occurred only once. Once. In six hundred years. Even that instance was political and surrounded by controversy and debate.[53]

Until the twentieth century, the hudud were in abeyance almost everywhere, unheard of except in texts of ancient Islamic history.[54] In some places, they hadn't been applied at all for over a thousand years.[55]

That is why, in the early twentieth century, when the Wahhabis first stoned someone for adultery, disbelief and shock reverberated throughout the Muslim world.[56] Worse, since 1980, Muslim-majority countries have vied with one another to apply the hudud punishments in an effort to portray themselves as Islamically legitimate. But this is not shariah; it's a shameful scramble for power.

A friend of mine asked me why some countries now applied harsh Islamic punishments if they were never meant to be applied. It's a legitimate question, and a painful one for me (and for many Muslims). Shariah aimed to limit violence and harsh punishments; to see shariah now used to accomplish the opposite makes me heartsick.

The first part of the answer is that harsh punishments reported as "shariah law" are usually extrajudicial and not shariah. Sometimes, in various places around the world, Muslim individuals, village tribunals, village elders, family members, or criminals (such as ISIS, al-Shabab, and the Taliban) have taken the law into their own hands to summarily execute those accused of wrongdoing, usually the powerless.[57] But this is murder under shariah.

Second, we do get the impression from our media that hudud punishments are more common than they are. Fifty-two of the fifty-seven Muslim-majority countries that belong to the Organization of Islamic Cooperation (OIC) do not allow stoning or amputation.[58]

Third, nearly all Islamic scholars agree that the hudud are wrongly applied in the few countries that claim to adopt them.[59] The stringent rules of procedure and evidence are ignored. The punishments disproportionately victimize women. The offenses themselves are not understood.

It sounds like a paradox, but it is truth: you cannot be applying the hudud properly because they are virtually impossible to apply.

Therefore, I ask myself in frustration, Why do the few governments that purport to implement shariah fixate on the hudud? Why ignore so much of shariah and concentrate just on the fractional percentage that constitutes punishments? The answer I give myself is this: It's symbolic.

Broadly speaking, shariah isn't significantly different from modern Western law. Where it arguably looks most different from modern Western law (though not necessarily ancient Western law) is in the area of criminal law. Therefore, adopting ancient Islamic punishments serves as an Islamic-identifying, anti-Western, self-legitimizing statement for Muslim governments.

In other words, hudud punishments bolster political legitimacy. Islamists jockeying for power adopt them to show their fidelity to an "Islamic state." Incumbent governments adopt them because they want to "take the wind out of the sails" of their Islamist opponents.[60]

In addition, harsh punishments provide effective tools of control and repression.[61] Public corporal punishments—such as public floggings—are vivid to behold and morbidly fascinating, just like public hangings in Europe were always popular spectacles for the whole family. They spread fear and despair of ever challenging the government. Horribly, a few countries have far exceeded classical Islamic law with respect to corporal punishments, instituting harsh penalties under the guise of ta'zir (discretionary punishments) for numerous crimes that historically never incurred such punishments.[62]

Proponents of hudud punishments also promise a safer society because of the deterrent value of such punishments.[63] Muslim populations—generally ignorant of shariah complexities—can easily be convinced that corporal punishments are required for piety and safety. The blind lead the blind toward their goal of political power.

Groups reinstating hudud punishments have turned upside down the entire purpose of Islamic criminal law as understood for over a thousand years—namely, avoiding harsh punishments while simultaneously deterring people from criminal behavior. In countries with governments seeking to establish or scaffold their legitimacy by imposing harsh penalties, "state-appointed judges and prosecutors are political appointees seeking convictions rather than Islamic legal experts trying to ensure justice."[64]

Political appointees are *seeking convictions* to assert power! Rather than warding off the hudud! In frank violation of the foundational principles of shariah!

The great majority of qualified Muslim religious scholars agree that the conditions required for application of hudud punishments are not extant in the world and perhaps never will be.[65] The early caliphs suspended the penalty for theft in times or famine and drought. Similarly, some Islamic scholars assert that applying any penalty for zina in a world "where everything invites and encourages unlawful sexual relationships" is nonsensical.[66] The Egyptian Muslim Brotherhood, though routinely portrayed as villainous fundamentalists (despite eschewing violence forty years ago), argued as early as the 1940s that the hudud should be suspended until there was no more poverty or want left in the world:

> They [the Muslim Brothers] argued that it is unfair to punish a thief with amputation if he has been driven to his crime by poverty and hunger or to apply the fixed penalty for unlawful intercourse if people lack the financial means to enter into marriage.[67]

Applying hudud punishments today defeats the purpose of shariah and its overarching goals of justice and mercy. Fourteen hundred years ago, the Qur'an repeatedly limited punishments with exhortations to mercy. Fiqh limited the violence of the time. To instead use ancient punishments to suppress human rights and produce *more* violence tragically defiles the purpose of fiqh, the Qur'an, the Sunna, and the Maqasid.

CHAPTER ELEVEN

SHARIAH IN EVERYDAY LIFE

Only a minuscule fraction of shariah is about offenses and punishments; by far the largest part is about personal religious observance and conduct. The divine purpose of shariah (as the way of God), regarding human beings on earth, is to enjoin the good, forbid the evil, do good deeds, promote forgiveness, and always be conscious of God. The daily guides for behavior in the fiqh literature are all efforts to help Muslims accomplish this purpose.

Islam is built upon these five foundations, called "pillars": the belief in one God and Muhammad as the messenger of God; prayer to God; fasting during Ramadan; donation to charity; and pilgrimage to Mecca once in a lifetime if possible. These are what we learn, growing up Muslim.

Childhood memories are imperfect, but I don't recall learning the words "shariah" and "fiqh" until I began my graduate course in Islamic law. My religious upbringing stressed rules of behavior rather than abstract religion. To me as a Muslim child, "Islam" was about behaving in such a way as to please God and my parents.

My experience must have been typical, because many average Muslims today would be hard-pressed to offer a detailed definition of shariah.[1] It would be funny, were it not so depressing, that people who are not Muslim and who have never studied Islam claim to know the meaning of an Islamic term of art that most Muslims do not grow up studying.

While navigating adolescence in California, every difference between my non-Muslim friends and me seemed excruciating and exaggerated. Now, looking back, the differences seem less colossal than they did then, seen through adolescent angst. I was more sheltered than my friends, but that resulted as much from my Indian-immigrant parents as anything else; my Hindu friends were just as sheltered. I prayed at home, fasted during Ramadan, didn't have a boyfriend, and didn't eat pork . . . but are those truly such huge differences? Most of the time, I did what everyone else around me did—homework, orchestra rehearsals, tennis team practices, frozen yogurt breaks, and movie nights. Many of my non-Muslim friends didn't date, either. I grew up with the same rules commonly instructing children of all backgrounds: don't lie, don't cheat, don't steal, obey your parents, and do your homework.

As a parent myself now, I'm struck by how easily others conclude that any differences they perceive in the behavior of Muslims must always result from religion. A friend who attended one of my book talks began a conversation with the man sitting next to her. The man remarked, "My daughter goes to school with hers. There's a lot her daughter can't do because she's Muslim."

My daughter at the time was eleven years old, and the Muslim stuff she couldn't do was eat pork, drink alcohol, or date. Were other eleven-year-olds drinking alcohol and dating? I wondered. As for pork, so many people are vegetarian or even vegan now that I cannot comprehend why that would be a defining factor.

A Muslim college student once related to me how, while playing video games, his friend asked him if he wanted a Coke. When he declined, his friend asked, "Oh, is that because you're Muslim?" No, it's because he wasn't thirsty.

In a similar vein, I'm often asked, "What happens if you don't do what you're supposed to do?"

Nothing happens. What happens when other religious people don't do what they're supposed to do?

Using the word "law" to describe a set of religious beliefs, rules, and principles erroneously implies enforceability. It implies that Muslims are encased in a rigid set of laws, with religious scholars ready to pounce on their personal religious behavior and drag them to prison.

I once explained to a Jewish friend that Islamic law (fiqh) was like Judaic law (halakha): man-made interpretations of the religious texts. She replied, "Yes, but Jewish law isn't enforced—I mean no one tells me that I can't eat pork—except in Israel."[2]

No one tells me, either. Personal devotional behavior that doesn't impact anyone else is not enforced in shariah.

Even in Iran and Saudi Arabia, where the power and intrusiveness of the "religious police" far exceeds that which was historically granted to religious inspectors (*muhtasib*), only select and easily identified aspects of Islam get enforced. After all, how do you punish lies and enforce truthfulness? Or prevent gossiping and backbiting? Or require mercy and forgiveness? All these are just as much a part of shariah as any other easily identifiable prohibitions, such as eating pork. Islamic history, like any human history, is replete with unpunished Muslims who drank alcohol and engaged in other private illicit activities.

I have glanced upon two points here: religious doctrine is different from what people do; and every religion, including Islam, encompasses an enormous diversity of interpretation. These two issues tend to be obvious where one's own religion is concerned but completely befuddling in the context of another's.

Regarding the first: Muslims don't act always from religious motivations. In fact, like other religious people, Muslims don't always follow their religious rules. Islam prohibits the drinking of alcohol, but history brims with even devout Muslims who have drunk, nay, *adored* wine. Traditionally, Jews aren't supposed to eat pork and Catholics aren't supposed to have premarital sex, either, but it's ridiculous to think that all Jews and all Catholics have always complied with these requirements. Conversely, all religions prohibit murder, but people of all religions have committed it.

Regarding the second: all religions are a diverse set of practices around a core set of beliefs. Picture three concentric circles that represent Islam. Within the innermost circle is the core—that which all Muslims agree is Islam, such as the Five Pillars. The middle circle from the center contains beliefs and practices that are definitely Islamic but that are variably interpreted or practiced, such as whether you pray with your hands to your sides or folded on your chest. The outermost circle contains practices that some Muslims believe Islam requires and some don't, such as covering the hair. And completely outside these circles is what everyone agrees is *not* Islamic, like murder and theft.

Many of the same people who have accused me of "picking and choosing" (if I take some Qur'anic verses literally and historically contextualize others) or "ignoring the dictates of my religion" (because of my uncovered head) would not think twice of ignoring parts of the Bible—which, after all, orders disobedient children to be stoned to death (Old Testament)[3] and slaves to be obedient to their masters (New Testament).[4] Such accusers are not limited to religionists, either; many Western non-religionists are equally conditioned to believe that, whereas Jews and Christians contextualize and engage with their texts, Muslims must take every word of their text literally (or else they're "picking and choosing").

I also encounter misunderstandings regarding the difference between an absolute prohibition in Islam and an acceptable difference in interpretation. Some Islamic requirements, like prayer, are not open to interpretation. But details around the requirements may be more fluid, such as exactly *how* you pray; this is evidenced by the slight differences in Sunni and Shi'i prayer format.

Here's an example of such confusion. I have stressed that ISIS and other terrorists violate the rules of engagement for a valid jihad, which absolutely prohibit, among other things, killing civilians and committing suicide. But sometimes people have perceived my statement on ISIS as contradicting my explanation of Islam as open to different interpretations. Can't terrorists, they ask, just reinterpret the Qur'an to make their actions Islamic? If terrorists take the fighting verses out of context, ignore the verses prohibiting nondefensive warfare, and justify violence against civilians because they've been complicit with their governments, why isn't that Islam?

It isn't Islam because religion is a diverse group of practices around a core set of beliefs. One of the core beliefs in Islam is the sanctity of life, which means that taking a life is prohibited except in legitimate warfare (which is very strictly defined) or as a death penalty after a fair trial. Are the murders of abortion-clinic doctors a valid interpretation of Christianity? Is the rape and murder of Rohingya Muslims by Buddhists (including monks) a valid interpretation of Buddhism? Are the bombings and arson attacks of the Jewish Defense League[5] a valid interpretation of Judaism? If the answer to these questions is no, then it should be easy to understand that terrorism is not valid in Islam, no matter the diversity in interpretation.

Too often, we compare our own virtues with others' faults. We compare our ideals with others' realities. We compare our culture when it is ascendant with other cultures when they are descendant. We compare mainstream members of our group with extremist members of other groups.

In the end, in every religion, it's all about the numbers. What's normative? What do all, or at least most, people agree are the parameters of acceptable behavior? The following sections discuss diversity and norms within Islam as manifested in issues that come up in quotidian life.

APPLYING SHARIAH TO MUSLIM LIFE

Although shariah includes "public law," which constitutes regulations on societal behavior, the great majority of shariah is about private law, or how to regulate your private Islamic life. Transactions (*mu'amalat*) are interactions and obligations between people, such as entering into contracts, family law, criminal offenses, and financial transactions; these are usually considered public law. Devotional obligations ('ibadat) are those that humans undertake as part of their relationship to God, such as praying, fasting, and other ritual matters; these are usually considered private law. But these categories sometimes overlap.

The Islamic legal system usually enforced only human interactions that affected the public sphere. Qadis did not generally enforce private shariah rules unless they related to a dispute or some public consequence. Religious police did not come into homes, searching for bottles of wine hidden in the cellar; however, public drunkenness that caused disruption or damage or a dispute would be cause for discipline or adjudication.

In fact, shariah does not seek to enforce private matters. The Prophet said, "I have not been commanded to search in the hearts of men or to open them up."[6] Another legal maxim of shariah is this: "The rulings of the shariah concern the evident and outward, and God concerns Himself with what is in the heart."[7] In other words, for your heart and your private life, you are answerable to God but not to the qadi or the caliph. In addition, as discussed earlier, Muslims must avoid digging up private offenses that don't hurt others (*tajassus*) and turn a blind eye to private misconduct (*satr*).[8]

Most of my Islamic life, during my childhood, related to private behavior and belief. Wariness of lurking pork products constituted the only regularly occurring intrusion on my life outside the home. As I grew older, though, I had to think about leaving my friends to perform my prayers, dressing modestly, fasting during school days, and negotiating male-female boundaries.

The rules on male-female relations are murkier than those on pork, particularly for those navigating the confusing miasma of adolescence.

My parents made adolescence simple for me: don't be alone with a boy and only engage in minor touching, like a handshake. But other observant Muslims had different interpretations. Some Muslim girls dated but drew various lines regarding touching. Others avoided even handshakes and talking to boys.

Islam, like most traditional religions, disapproves of and disallows physical relations between unmarried people. Muslims should avoid situations that lead to such relations. Accordingly, unmarried and unrelated men and women must not retire behind closed doors together (leaving aside, for the moment, LGBTQI and gender fluidity issues).

Until the last century, young men and women in Western countries also did not retreat privately behind closed doors alone. Or they had chaperones. We still impose chaperones in certain circumstances, such as middle school dances, irrelevant of religion. The reasoning behind these and Islamic rules is essentially the same: to prevent difficult and dangerous situations.

Religious practice is often largely a cultural practice, and interpretation is a matter of custom, social norms, and other factors. If you live in a country where modest dress is the norm, you'll dress more modestly too. In a country where men and women are more segregated as a matter of course, gender segregation might seem more natural to you.

A Catholic friend once asked me to explain the source of these rules. "Do you have a pope?" she asked. I tried to explain the fiqh system, but soon she burst out in frustration, "But how do you know what to *do*?"

As a Muslim child, I asked my parents what to do. How do I pray? My parents could answer that. If they couldn't, I could ask a shaykh or someone learned in shariah. Islamic scholars were scarce though; even now, relatively few mosques are within driving distance of me, though I live in a densely populated area. I know someone who must drive five hours to reach her nearest mosque.

I once asked my parents why they hadn't raised me to cover my hair. (Neither did my mother or her Muslim friends cover their hair.) My father explained that, because concerns of modesty and protection had motivated the wearing of head coverings, he reasoned that a headscarf would, in American society, draw more attention to me than less and defeat the religious purpose. Some people thought differently, he said, and that was their choice, but he didn't think Islam required it.

Sounds reasonable. But what if someone else told me that Islam did require it? How would I know who was right? The answer is a good example of how shariah works.

"ISLAMIC" DRESS (OR, FIQH IN ACTION)

Early Muslims wondered, "Is there an Islamic way to dress?"

For answers, they first consulted the Qur'an. The word *hijab* doesn't mean "headscarf" in the Qur'an. It means "screen," and it appears in verse 33:53, which advises screening off the Prophet's wives for their privacy. Whether this verse applies literally, figuratively, or to anyone besides the Prophet's wives has always been debated.

Of the 6,236 verses of the Qur'an, only three specifically relate to clothing. (Obviously the Qur'an does not consider this a great priority.) One verse urges women to draw their outer garments more closely around them to protect them from molestation. (33:59) Another states:

> *Tell the believing men to lower their gaze and to be mindful of their chastity: this will be most conducive to their purity—and verily, God is aware of all that they do. And tell the believing women to lower their gaze and be mindful of their chastity, and to not display their charms in public beyond what would ordinarily appear.* (4:30–31)

The Qur'an commands *both* men and women to lower their gazes in modesty. That means refraining from ogling others ("lowering your gaze") and dressing modestly (not "displaying your charms" beyond what you'd ordinarily show). Muslims have discouraged wearing ostentatious gold and jewels, too, in the interests of modesty; this tends to apply more to men than women.

The above verse raises this big question: what are the "charms"—that is, body parts—of women that would "ordinarily appear"? Those are the parts we can show. Hands ordinarily appear, for example, and thus may be shown.

Clearly, too, what charms ordinarily appear is not an objective measure but a subjective one. What "ordinarily" appears in one culture might be indecent in another: in traditional Indian culture, short blouses baring midriffs "ordinarily appeared," but miniskirts would have been shocking;

in twentieth-century American street dress, bare legs more "ordinarily appeared" than bare midriffs. Circumstance also dictates modesty: someone who might wear a bikini at the beach would probably not wear one to a funeral. And modesty norms fluctuate over time too: in Turkey and Indonesia, the latter of which has the largest population of Muslims in the world, many women didn't start wearing headscarves until thirty years ago.[9]

The vast majority of classical Islamic scholars agreed that the interpretation of "what would ordinarily appear" depended upon at least two elements: custom (*'urf*) and hardship (*haraj*),[10] which can both change over time and geography, thus changing the interpretation. When, after the Prophet's death, Arab armies extended their rule over the former Persian Sassanian Empire and Roman Byzantine Empire, the Arabs absorbed the customs of veiling and seclusion of women in those areas.[11] For example, wealthy Persian women veiled as a sign of high social status, but for a woman working in the fields, covering up completely might have constituted a hardship. Eventually, these cultural practices of veiling and seclusion came to be associated with Islam. But veiling and even covering of the hair were contested in Islamic jurisprudential discourse until at least two or three centuries after Muhammad.[12]

Given these factors, early Islamic scholars debated what body parts could "ordinarily appear." They all agreed that women should be covered from the chest down to their knees and that men should be covered from their knees to their navels. But beyond these parameters, they disagreed.[13]

Most scholars said that women's hands, face, and feet could be visible, because it would be a hardship to cover them and because social norms didn't require it.[14] But then they disagreed on the definitions of hands, face, and feet. Did "hands" mean hands up to the wrist or the elbow? If "feet" could be visible, did that mean feet to the ankle? To the calf? Or even to the knees? Did the face include the neck? Where did the covering for the chest begin—at the base of the neck or the cleavage? Did all the hair have to be covered or only hair from the crown?[15]

Some early jurists, despite viewing uncovered hair with disfavor, maintained that the Qur'an did not explicitly require the covering of hair.[16] The Prophet never forced a woman to cover her hair. In fact, Muslim women as late as the ninth century—two centuries after the Prophet—even prayed with their heads uncovered.[17] Obviously, this couldn't have trans-pired if the Qur'an had been clear about head covering.

Very few Islamic scholars advised covering the face. In fact, most scholars consider that the face veil (*niqab*) predates Islam. These Qur'anic verses nowhere mention the word *niqab*.[18] Significantly, the face veil is disallowed on the Hajj (the Muslim pilgrimage to Mecca) and in vari-ous Muslim institutions, including that bastion of Islamic fiqh, Al-Azhar University, in Cairo.

The two Qur'anic modesty verses above continue with the words, "Hence, let them draw their head coverings [*khumur*] over their bo-soms." (24:31)

Aha, we come to head coverings in the Qur'an! This reference to khu-mur (pl.) also sometimes translates as "scarves." A *khimar* (sing.) means any of various types of cloth worn on the head or neck, such as a woman's scarf or a man's turban.[19] In seventh-century Arabia, women wore an or-namental piece of cloth that trailed down the back of the head, and their tunics opened widely at the chest, showing their bare breasts.[20] There-fore, at the very least, this verse instructed women to cover their breasts with what they were already wearing.

Was this verse *also* instructing women to cover their heads if they were not already doing so? In other words, suppose women commonly wore jackets and the verse read, "Let them draw their jackets over their bosoms"? Would this verse require every woman to wear a jacket?

In the 1990s, two high-level Islamic scholars in Egypt publicly de-bated at length, over weeks, whether Muslim women had a duty to cover their hair. They argued according to respected methodology and their extensive knowledge of shariah, arriving at passionately well-reasoned but opposing fatwas. Muhammad Said Ashmawi, a justice of the Supreme Court of Egypt and a renowned shariah specialist, maintained that head coverings originated as a regional custom and were not obligatory. The Grand Mufti of Al-Azhar University, Sayyid Tantawi, asserted that head coverings were indeed obligatory.[21] But they accepted that God knew best who was correct.

This is fiqh in action! As far as the qualifications of Islamic scholars, you couldn't get much higher than these two. And they reached well-reasoned (though opposing) fatwas. Therefore, they were *both* correct. That means, as a Muslim woman, I can choose whose opinion to follow.

Once, during a question-and-answer session I was conducting, a woman told me that, in her Jesuit tradition, if two qualified religious scholars disagreed, then to designate one as correct and the other as incorrect was a "sin of presumption"—because only God could judge which of them was correct. We smiled at each other in perfect accord. Because this is the Islamic view too.

If the Qur'an had been perfectly clear on matters of dress, then scholars wouldn't have spent fourteen centuries debating it, usually in terms far deeper and more complex than I'm presenting here. The early Islamic scholars' discussions about head covering for women took place in the context of social norms, hardship, class status, history, and women's safety, not oppression or patriarchy (though it must be said that these premodern religious analyses and fatwas and debates did not, by and large, include women). The more covered women were, the safer they were.[22] In a perfect world, safety shouldn't depend upon personal clothing choices, but it was the reality of the time.

To some extent, it's the reality now. Even in the West, we've not yet eradicated the idea that immodestly dressed women are asking for sexual assault. As recently as 1998, the Italian Supreme Court overturned a rapist's conviction on the grounds that the eighteen-year-old victim had worn tight jeans![23]

Safety still pertains to development of fiqh. Headscarf-wearing Muslim women in the US and Europe suffer frequent assaults, and their visibility as Muslims puts them at risk.[24] According to the Bridge Initiative at Georgetown University, in 2015 an attack against Muslims occurred, on average, every forty-eight hours in the US.[25] In early Islam, the headscarf protected women; today, if the headscarf makes women *less* safe, then it defeats the purpose and needn't be worn, at least according to some scholars.[26]

Most Muslim women who wear head coverings cite religious duty as their reason. The headscarf isn't necessarily a religious symbol, like a cross; rather, it's a way to be modest, like wearing long sleeves instead of short sleeves. Or, for some, the headscarf is a Qur'anic edict. Styles of headscarves vary considerably, illustrating differing ideas of modesty. But some women wear headscarves for reasons other than religion.

For some, it's cultural. A friend of mine who spent a year in Yemen said that most women with whom she discussed head covering wore burqas (with only their eyes showing) or chadors (with their faces showing) because of their culture, not religion. Some women who wear headscarves were simply brought up to wear them, as I was brought up to not wear one.

Some women wear the headscarf as an expression of identity. When colonialists disparaged headscarves, Muslim women began wearing them to assert their national identity and opposition to their colonizers.[27] After 9/11, some Muslim American women started wearing their headscarves to show their fellow Americans that Muslims were normal, upstanding citizens. In France, a disproportionate one-third of women who wear burqas—the total number of whom is less than 1 percent of French Muslim women—are converts to Islam,[28] perhaps desirous of tangible signs of their new religious identity.

I have a friend who believes the headscarf is optional, but she wears it because it reminds her to do good deeds. Another friend wears a headscarf when she travels to Muslim-majority countries, to show that she's Muslim. And I know some Muslim women who wear it when they feel like it and not when they don't.

In the mid-twentieth century, few Egyptian women wore headscarves. But, starting in the 1980s, increasing numbers of Egyptian women began wearing headscarves. Why? Because more women had entered the workforce and begun commuting. They found themselves treated more respectfully when they wore headscarves, which emitted a "hands-off" message and caused their coworkers to evaluate them in terms of their abilities rather than appearance. Headscarves gave them the opposite of oppression: freedom and independence.[29]

Wait! Shouldn't women be evaluated for their abilities rather than their appearance, whatever they wear? Yes! But it's an imperfect world, and practical considerations override idealistic ones—even in Western countries.

Why might Muslim women elect to not cover their hair? They might believe Islam doesn't require it. Or that wearing a headscarf in Western countries, where headscarves have provoked attacks and bigotry, defeats the original purpose of protection and might constitute a hardship. Or that, in today's world, modest dress is achievable without a headscarf.

I once heard a high school teacher on the radio. She related how she had displayed a picture of a nun and asked her students to jot down the words that sprung into their minds. They produced words like "pure," "faithful to God," "chaste," and "religious." The teacher then replaced the picture with one of a Middle-Eastern woman wearing a headscarf, but this time the words that her students wrote in response were "backward," "stupid," and "oppressed."

In addition to nuns, non-Muslim women of various backgrounds cover their hair for religious or other reasons. The New Testament instructs women to cover their hair.[30] Many Hindu, Sikh, Rastafarian, and Orthodox Jewish women cover their hair. A small group of women in Israel wear the *sal*, a garment similar to the burqa.[31] Headscarves are worn by Native Americans, Japanese, Eastern Europeans (including Greeks), Filipinos, and African-Americans such as Aretha Franklin.[32] Jennifer Lopez wears a headscarf sometimes, and she's applauded for her style; nobody calls her a rag-head.

Muslim dress is a perfect example of how fiqh works. Scholars started with the Qur'an, examined numerous factors, both "religious" and not, and reached multitudinous opinions, all of which they accepted as valid. Imagine such discussions and debates on every issue within Islam and you get some idea of the diversity of the Islamic legal tradition.

FREE SPEECH

Diversity in Islamic interpretation and Islamic everyday practice is possible explicitly because of the acceptance of free expression in Islam. Shariah accepts a variety of contradictory interpretations, because scholars have always had the freedom to voice them.

When I began writing my first book on Islam, several friends advised me to "be careful." I ascertained their thoughts as clearly as if they'd spoken them: Muslims will kill you if they don't like what you write. How ironic that the only death threats I have received have been from Islam *haters*.

I blame Ayatollah Khomeini for this prevalent view. His well-publicized "fatwa," in which he issued a death sentence against Salman Rushdie for writing *The Satanic Verses*, catapulted the word "fatwa" into Western discourse. The Danish cartoon controversy, discussed below, cemented the image of intolerant Muslims against free expression.

Several distinct issues—not just "free speech"—pertain to one or both of these two incidents: apostasy and blasphemy laws; Khomeini's death sentence against Salman Rushdie; demands to ban Rushdie's book and the Danish cartoons; and the failure to contextualize the protests in the same way that non-Muslim protests would have been contextualized.

Although Khomeini's fatwa was widely publicized, opposition to it was not. Most Muslim governments did not support Khomeini's fatwa. The foreign ministers of forty-six Muslim-majority countries met at the Organization of the Islamic Conference, and, though they approved of banning the book, they did not endorse the death decree.

Most Islamic scholars did not agree with Khomeini either. Many Muslim scholars in Western countries, including fifty Iranian scholars living outside Iran, not only disagreed with Khomeini's fatwa but vehemently condemned it.[33] The scholars at Al-Azhar University, the aforementioned bastion of fiqh, disagreed with the fatwa and maintained that Rushdie was at least entitled to a fair trial.[34]

A fair trial for what? you might ask. Khomeini based his fatwa on the ancient crime of apostasy, condemning Rushdie for renouncing Islam. Apostasy, as I discussed earlier, was defined by classical Islamic scholars as leaving Islam *plus* waging war against the Muslim community. Before Khomeini, criminal charges of apostasy had been in abeyance, like the other hudud. Most modern Islamic scholars reject the crime of apostasy as a historical relic.

Even under the medieval law of apostasy, though, Khomeini's fatwa against Rushdie was wrong for several reasons:

- Khomeini had no jurisdiction outside of his state.
- Under shariah, the accused must be allowed to defend himself in a fair trial before he can be punished.
- Rushdie recanted and apologized, which should have acquitted him from a charge of apostasy.[35]
- Writing a book, vicious and offensive as it was, does not constitute waging war or insurrection against the Muslim community.

Khomeini rejected Rushdie's apology, insisting that even if Rushdie repented and recanted his insults, he should still be killed.[36] This attitude violates even medieval fiqh! And it shows that Khomeini disregarded shariah in favor of dividing Muslims from the West, revenging himself upon Rushdie (who had caricatured Khomeini in his book), and establishing Iran as a leading "Islamic" political power.

Rushdie's crime wasn't blasphemy, either, because blasphemy isn't a crime in Islam. Most Islamic religious scholars, both Sunni and Shiʻa, "refused to classify even intentional jabs at the Prophet as criminally blasphemous."[37] The Prophet himself never retaliated against personal physical or verbal attacks. The second caliph and Prophet's companion, Umar, once asked the Prophet if he could kill someone who insulted the Prophet, and the Prophet said *no*.

Why, then, are there anti-blasphemy laws in Pakistan, Egypt, and other Muslim-majority countries? Because the British inserted blasphemy laws into the laws of their colonized countries. (Ireland, for example, as of 2018, still had a blasphemy law.)[38] Sometimes, blasphemy is erroneously conflated with apostasy.

In other words, Rushdie ran afoul of a political move by a power-corrupted dictator—not shariah. Islamic history is peppered with people like Rushdie, who not only recanted Islam but publicly criticized it and were never punished.[39] Americans commonly believe that Islam forbids free speech and that Khomeini's fatwa was a "law" that most Muslims accepted; neither is true.

Lest we point fingers, we should recognize that attempts to ban speech in America occur with regularity. Books with "anti-Christian" content are often objects of attempted bans[40] (including attempts not only to ban the Qur'an but books *about* the Qur'an[41]). Then mayor and later vice presidential nominee Sarah Palin repeatedly endeavored to censor and remove books from her local library,[42] and DC Comics gave up rights to a series featuring Jesus Christ as a superhero's peace-loving sidekick after receiving heated backlash from conservative Christians.[43] Nevertheless, Christianity is generally not commonly assumed to be against free speech, as is Islam.

Similarly, some Jews protested Mel Gibson's film *The Passion of the Christ*, even causing him to delete scenes.[44] Some Jews and members of Congress have been active in trying to outlaw any boycott of Israel,[45] though boycotts are a form of free expression protected under the First

Amendment.[46] Nevertheless, Judaism is not commonly assumed to be against free speech, as is Islam.

The 1970s musical *Jesus Christ Superstar* was protested by some Jews, Catholics, and Protestants.[47] The musical was banned in India, Belarus, Russia, South Africa, and Hungary and even, briefly, by the BBC.[48] Yet, anti–free speech events by Muslims continue to be seen as proof of the repressive tendencies of Islam, whereas anti–free speech events by non-Muslims are dismissed as inconsequential or even received with compassion.

Those who accuse Muslims of suppressing free speech should understand that, at any given time, numerous best-selling English-language books, written by non-Muslim authors without qualifications or credentials in Islam, vilify Islam with little or no factual basis. Books vilifying Islam sell far more widely than fact-based ones. In fact, I regularly encounter vicious stereotypes of Muslims in books of *all* kinds of genres, fiction and nonfiction—even books ostensibly unrelated to Islam, such as mysteries and cookbooks. (I have begun reading science fiction in self-defense.)

In other words, anti-Muslim hatred in English-language reading material is the norm, yet Muslims do not routinely burn down bookshops and attack publishers. This fact is ignored. Instead, repeatedly resurrected are the two Islam-related incidents that occurred in forty years: Khomeini's fatwa and the Danish cartoon controversy.

When Muslims protested a Danish publisher's cartoons portraying the Prophet Muhammad as a terrorist, a bomb nestling in his turban, these protests were framed in American and European media as "the liberal West versus intolerant Muslims who hate free speech." Peter Gottschalk and Gabriel Greenberg ask:

Why the sudden amnesia about the vicious depictions of Jews in political cartoons from Nazi Germany? Why the rarity of comparison to global Christian outrage regarding . . . Martin Scorsese's *The Last Temptation of Christ* in 1989 or similar protest against the satiric critique of Christianity in *Monty Python's Life of Brian* in 1979?[49]

The authors note that Scorsese's film was banned in many nations and that it led to several bomb threats.[50]

Gottschalk and Greenberg also observe that no one insisted on free speech when the Danish publisher of the Muhammad cartoons refused to publish Iranian cartoons about the Holocaust.[51] The publisher had further refused to publish similar cartoons of Jesus, on the grounds that it would offend Christians.[52] No outcry there, either.

It's hard to imagine that there wouldn't be widespread outrage if the vicious depictions of Jews in Nazi cartoons, referenced in the above quotation, were to be published; it's doubtful that anyone would publish them to begin with, especially since at least nine European nations outlaw denial of the Holocaust or "diminishment of its actuality."[53] Gallup reports that over 75 percent of British and French respondents opine that cartoons "making light of the Holocaust should not be allowed under protection of free speech."[54]

The Danish cartoons of Muhammad were similarly vicious depictions of an entire religious community—so why weren't they similarly contextualized? They didn't portray Osama bin Laden as a terrorist but *Prophet Muhammad*, recognized by both Westerners and Muslims as the representative of Islam and Muslims.[55] The cartoons were understood by both Westerners and Muslims as attacking Islam, its Prophet, and all his followers. These cartoons didn't simply poke fun at terrorists. They stereotyped an entire community of people as terrorists and an entire religion as allowing terrorism.

Yet, any Muslims who objected to the cartoons were characterized as intolerant examples of the Islamic opposition to free expression.

Uncoincidentally, since the cartoons were published, references to Muhammad as a terrorist have increased, despite the Islamic prohibition against terrorism. Muhammad was never a terrorist.

Gottschalk and Greenberg note that when Muslims protested the Danish cartoons, many commentators declared (erroneously) that the protests were

> further evidence that Muslims—if not Islam itself—sought to stifle "freedom of expression," in this case because of prohibitions against depicting the religion's founder.[56]

Islamic views vary on whether and how to depict Muhammad, just as Christian views on images vary (sixteenth-century Protestant reformers stripped churches of their images). Besides, this wasn't about depiction of the Prophet. It was about Muhammad being portrayed as a murderer.

When the *New Yorker* published a cartoon of Barack and Michelle Obama as closet terrorists with Islamist ties, the ensuing protests didn't worry anyone that "condemnations of the Obama cartoon would imperil freedom of expression."[57] The protests were never portrayed as a clash of civilizations or an affront to liberty.

If freedom of expression is so valued in Europe and the US, why are Muslim women not allowed to wear headscarves to school or burkinis to the beach in France? Why did British laws against blasphemy apply only to Christianity and not to Islam, and why could Christian and Jewish schools in England—but not Muslim ones—be established and supported by public funds?[58]

Muslim resentment, therefore, has nothing to do with "opposing our Western freedom of expression." It has to do with the hypocrisy in Western discourse, which allows the routine demonization of Muslims but not others. When the Danish cartoons' publisher's refusal to publish similar cartoons of Jesus came to light, a profusion of Western media articles immediately protested that the cases were different.

Vituperative cartoons portraying Muhammad as a terrorist and murderer (though he and his religion forbade terrorism and murder) are not "criticism" of Islam, that cowardly mask behind which so many Islamophobes hide, any more than Nazi cartoons of Jews were "criticism" of Judaism. Vilifying over a billion and a half people as innately violent and inferior is just bigotry. If this is "criticism," then any demonization, dehumanization, stereotyping of, and prejudice against an entire community of people can always be absolved under "criticism."

The physical attacks on the Danish cartoons' publisher, as well as Khomeini's death sentence against Rushdie, were reprehensible and a different matter from protests or bans. But these were few. As sociologist Charles Kurzman writes, Americans and Europeans have a zero-tolerance policy toward Muslim crimes; any time an unhinged individual commits a crime, it's a national crisis, an ISIS conspiracy, or confirmation of the violent tendencies of Islam.[59] Yet we tolerate hundreds of mass shootings and thousands of murders committed by white men, who have always been portrayed as fringe lunatics (though this has finally been changing recently). Therefore, yes, a few Muslims attacked the cartoon publisher;

but to hold all Muslims responsible for every crime any Muslim commits when we cannot even control the crime in Chicago is ridiculous.

Most Muslims in the world opposed violence against Rushdie and the publisher. Significantly, Muslims often oppose violence *because* of Islam. According to Gallup, although Indonesian Muslims cited Islamic justifications when condemning terrorism, not one respondent who condoned terrorist attacks cited the Qur'an as justification.[60]

WOMEN'S RIGHTS AND SHARIAH

The widespread calumny that Islam oppresses women is so entrenched that it remains profoundly unquestioned even by those confronted by the contrary evidence of their own eyes. The first time I was informed—by a white, male, non-Muslim senior partner—that I was an oppressed Muslim woman, I was in my twenties and a corporate lawyer. I couldn't have been more astonished.

Similarly surprised would have been the thousands of Muslim women scholars peppering history, Muslim women rulers and judges present and past, and the numerous Muslim women in high-level government positions in government today. Religion journalist Tom Verde writes,

> From Indonesia to Pakistan, Kyrgyzstan to Nigeria, Senegal to Turkey, it is not particularly rare in our own times for women in Muslim-majority countries to be appointed and elected to high offices—including heads of state. Nor has it ever been.[61]

I've discussed how Islam unquestionably improved the status of women, one of the main themes of the Qur'an. I've discussed how seventh-century Muslim women had more rights than eighteenth-century Englishwomen. Any religion that treated women as spiritual equals with men and was so concerned with raising their earthly rights *definitionally* could not have been misogynistic and could only have been radically feminist for its time.

All ancient religions were sexist to some degree. They were products of their time. The assumption, even among educated people, that Islam is patriarchal and misogynistic—whereas other religions are not—usually results from relentless conditioning through our educational systems, our media, our arts and literature, and our entertainment industry. Ignorance of Islam, which is then conflated with poverty, cultural practices, political power struggles, and lack of access to education, leads to the assumption that any oppression of Muslim women comes from Islam itself.

Undoubtedly, some Muslim women in the world suffer from misogynistic cultural circumstances. But so do many women in non-Muslim countries in Latin America, Asia, and Africa. These women are not portrayed in our media as oppressed because of Christianity, Buddhism, or Hinduism.

All traditional world cultures were sexist throughout history. Most still are to some degree. Muslims live primarily in developing countries, where—just as in the rest of the developing world—sexist culture holds greater sway than in wealthy industrialized countries. Even in the West, remember, we have not finished fighting for equal rights.

The Islam-oppresses-women trope confirms our biases regarding the superiority of the West. That's why it's easy to believe. That's why we are incessantly brainwashed by the lionizing of women claiming to have escaped from Muslim regimes or Muslim families, the repeated media images of oppressed Muslim women, and the hyperattention given books that promulgate these stereotypes.

We highlight the oppression of women and ignore information that doesn't support it. Why else would my educated audiences evince shock that Iran educates more women than men in its universities? Or that Turkey appointed the world's first female Supreme Court justice in 1954?[62] Or that eighteen Muslim-majority countries have more women in their legislatures than has the United States?

If they're not shocked, they're dismissive. CNN's Don Lemon interviewed the comparative religion scholar Reza Aslan in 2014, and when Aslan mentioned the female heads of states of Muslim-majority countries, Lemon admonished him, "Be honest!" and continued, "For the most part it is not a free and open society for women in those states."[63]

Socioeconomic and cultural factors, not religion, prevent Muslim women from attaining equal rights. We've discussed how colonialism often stripped women of their rights and disrupted modernization of Islam (and thus modernization of Muslim women's rights). Cultural norms also hinder women, as they have throughout history in all traditional and pre-industrialized cultures.

But by far the biggest factor against women's equal rights is poverty. One 2018 study shows that education of Muslim women is limited by economic conditions, not religion.[64] The study found that a country's wealth, not its laws or culture or religion, is the most important factor in determining the education of its women. The researchers even tested whether Islam was a factor in whether Muslim women got educated. They found that it wasn't.[65]

To truly evaluate whether Islam oppresses women, we must compare apples and apples, not apples and oranges. Don't compare non-Muslim American women with Muslim women "over there," overseas, somewhere else. Instead, compare non-Muslim American women with Muslim American women. Then you'll eliminate the red-herring factors of culture, poverty, and postcolonial struggles.

When you do, you'll find that Muslim American women are doing very well. They are the second-most-educated female faith group in the United States.[66] Muslim Americans as a group have the most economic gender parity of any faith group in the United States—that is, the incomes of Muslim American women and Muslim American men are virtually the same, whereas there's more difference of income between men and women in other faith groups.[67] As of this writing, four Muslim Americans (two men and two women) have been elected to the US Congress.

Gallup found that in Muslim-majority countries, most Muslims—both men and women—want equal rights for women.[68] Moreover, whether men wanted equal rights for women had nothing to do with how "religious" or "secular" they were; in fact, in Iran, Lebanon, and Morocco, Muslim men who supported women's rights were *more religious* than the men who did not support women's rights.[69]

That's because shariah is feminist. As Shirin Ebadi, Iranian women's rights activist and the 2003 Nobel Peace Prize winner, stressed in an interview, "By fighting for equal status, we [Muslim women] are doing what God *wants* us to do."[70]

HONOR KILLINGS ARE NOT SHARIAH

Despite evidence regarding women's rights in Islam, a variety of bad behaviors, such as honor killings, are regularly attributed to Muslims as proof that Islam is sexist. But I truly don't understand why "honor killings" are associated with Islam. Honor killings are neither allowed by shariah nor unique to Muslims. "Honor killing" is what murder is called when perpetuated by a male against a female whom he perceives has in some way impugned his honor or shamed his family. Honor killings have occurred throughout history, across religions and cultures, wherever a woman's actions (usually regarding her chastity) are connected to perceptions of family honor and shame.

The notion of "honor killing" is alien to shariah. There's no concept of it. Murder of any kind, for any reason, is absolutely prohibited in Islam.

Even if a man catches his wife or relative in bed with a man, he may not take the law into his own hands and kill them.[71] He would be charged with murder.[72] As Jonathan Brown writes, shariah

> has a clear [prohibition] on honor killing, drawing directly on rulings made by the Prophet Muhammad: a husband who kills his wife and/or her lover has committed homicide like any other case, even if the husband caught the two in the act.[73]

Modern Islamic scholars of the highest levels have affirmed that honor killings are not Islamically legal. Consensus is rare in Islamic law, but we have one in this case: a man is not permitted, under shariah, to summarily kill his wife or female relative for impugning his or his family's honor.[74]

Modern laws in Muslim-majority countries that extend leniency to murderers who commit honor killings—which laws must be eliminated *right now*—were introduced into those countries by British and French colonizers. In India and Pakistan, the notion of an "honor killing" was legally unknown until the British started overturning, on grounds of "provocation," shariah-court sentences of the death penalty for homicide.[75] In Nigeria, as late as 1947, an Islamic court convicted a perpetrator of murder, only to have the British appeals court commute the conviction from murder to the lesser "wilful homicide" on the grounds that the accused had acted from "provocation."[76] Most modern Arab countries based their laws on the Ottoman Criminal Code of 1858, which was drafted almost wholesale from the French Code of 1832, from which the honor-killings provision was copied verbatim.[77]

Honor killings occur in cultures where a woman's obedience or chastity is perceived as impacting the family's honor. Such killings have occurred all over the world, including Asia and Europe—even recently in Italy and Greece.[78] Indeed, until 1981, the Italian penal code mandated extreme leniency to perpetrators of honor killings.[79] Latin America, as well, has a long tradition of leniency toward and even acquittal of men who justify their murders of women by claiming their honor was besmirched. Until 1991, in Brazil, a man could be acquitted of the murder of his wife on the ground of "legitimate defense of honor."[80] In Haiti, until 2005, the Criminal Code mandated that a man be pardoned if he killed his wife upon catching her in the act of committing adultery.[81]

In Europe, honor killings are called "crimes of passion," but they are identical. Honor killings are associated with Muslims; crimes of passion are associated with non-Muslims. This is significant, because—in polls of French, British, and German respondents—some of the same people who found "honor killings" morally unacceptable found "crimes of passion" to be morally acceptable![82]

Eliminating honor killings (or crimes of passion) requires several steps. First, eliminate the laws that allow murderers to use honor or passion as an excuse. Second, at least with respect to Muslims, clarify that shariah does not permit such killings. Increasingly, imams and religious leaders worldwide are conveying this message to their congregations. Third, non-Muslims who insist honor killings are Islamic must stop saying so. Insisting wrongly that Islam permits honor killings itself victimizes women by sending the false message to Muslims worldwide—through the daily invasions of Western news, film, television, and public discourse—that they can commit honor killings with impunity. Of course, insisting on conflating Islam and honor killings sends the same disinformation to non-Muslims, too, bolstering anti-Muslim prejudice.

FEMALE GENITAL CUTTING

Female genital cutting (FGC) describes a variety of practices that involve cutting the female genitalia. It's a cultural and social practice that predates Islam by a thousand years. FGC is neither unique to Muslims, nor is it practiced by the majority of Muslims.

Globally, FGC is practiced by Christians, Muslims, and Jews, as well as by members of non-Abrahamic religions.[83] In Egypt, where it is practiced by Christians as well as Muslims, it dates back to the times of the

Pharaohs.[84] Historically, it has been virtually unknown in most Muslim societies, including Saudi Arabia. In societies where it *is* practiced, it almost always predates Islamization of those areas.[85]

FGC does not come from Islam. It is completely absent from the Qur'an. The few statements of the Prophet on FGC are considered weak and historically unreliable; even then, they don't advocate the practice but curb it and warn against harming women.[86] Though evidence indicates that the Prophet's grandsons were circumcised, no evidence indicates that any woman in the Prophet's family underwent FGC.[87]

Neither is FGC mandated by shariah. The majority of classical scholars over a thousand years ago tolerated it as an existing practice but did not consider it an obligation. The great majority of Islamic scholars today reject it.

If FGC were Islamic, it could not have remained virtually unknown in most Muslim societies for 1,400 years. Many Muslims in the world even today have never heard of it. Increased immigration in the last fifty years from Africa, where it originated, has spread FGC to wider geographical areas.

FGC violates clear tenets of Islam. First, Muslims must not "change God's creation"—meaning the human body—or damage it. Even tattoos and plucking hairs are considered damaging to the human body; how, then, can cutting into organs be acceptable?

Second, Islam approves of sexual enjoyment for its own sake, not just for procreation. (This is why contraception is not problematic in Islam.) Even in very early Islam, a woman could divorce her husband on grounds of impotence or sexual abandonment.[88] Women have the right to sexual fulfillment, and at least certain types of FGC prevent sexual fulfillment.

Third, the overriding purpose of shariah is to prevent harm, not cause it. Practices that cause harm must be restricted or abolished.

Why, then, did the majority of early Islamic scholars tolerate and even recommend FGC? I can only assume they didn't understand the harm that it caused. At the time, FGC had been a socially acceptable practice in Africa for centuries. They would have taken it for granted, as they did male circumcision.

Many modern Islamic scholars have been forceful in repudiating the practice of FGC. In 2005, Al-Azhar's Dean of the Faculty of Sharia, Ahmed Talib, said that FGC was a "crime that had no relationship to Islam."[89] In 2006, a conference of high-level Islamic religious scholars agreed that FGC was "irreconcilable with Islam."[90] The late Grand Mufti Tantawi of Al-Azhar said that since the Qur'an made no mention of this practice and because the hadiths were weak, the issue should be left to the medical profession to decide.[91]

How can modern scholars repudiate FGC when most late-antiquity Islamic scholars tolerated it? Because fiqh is not static! It was meant to evolve! Just because Islamic scholars from over a millennium ago didn't realize a practice was harmful and were medically misinformed does *not* mean that centuries of Muslims ever after must be bound by their opinions. Fiqh *changes*. Muslims are not bound by their religion to behave exactly the way seventh-century Arabs behaved.

Most people who perform FGC do so because they think it is religiously mandated, so it's important that many Muslim organizations have condemned FGC from both Islamic and secular perspectives. Britain's largest Muslim organization, the Muslim Council of Britain, has explicitly condemned FGC as un-Islamic and against the teachings of religion.[92] The Islamic Circle of North America, joining the International Day of Zero Tolerance for Female Genital Mutilation, condemned FGC as abusing human rights and Islamic tenets.[93]

The Global Muslim Women's Shura Council published a position paper on FGC, absolutely and unconditionally condemning FGC as a harmful practice that violates the spirit and letter of Islam, violates international laws on children's rights and women's rights, and endangers populations. (Full disclosure: I'm a member of this group.) Translations of this paper have been disseminated to villages in Africa, where they practice FGC; as a result, multiple villages have pledged to eradicate this practice.

Linking Muslims and FGC is a common tool for Islam haters, but it's hypocritical. Not only is FGC practiced by people of all religions—in Kenya and Ethiopia by more Christians than Muslims[94]—it's been practiced in the West until relatively recently. In the nineteenth century, while Western colonial officials condemned FGC in Africa, it was practiced in England and America as a way of reducing "female masturbation, hysteria, and mental illness."[95] This practice continued well into the early twentieth century in Britain and America, as evidenced by a 1937 respected medical treatise that mentioned FGC as an acceptable practice; known cases occurred as late as the 1940s.[96]

As in the case of honor killings, both non-Muslims and Muslims who insist on erroneously portraying FGC as Islamic help perpetuate it. Such a stance spreads the erroneous belief amongst Muslims—some who may never have heard of it before—that they must accept FGC as a religious requirement. So the next time you hear someone say that FGC is Islamic, tell them it isn't.

INHERITANCE

I'm periodically assaulted by the assumption that a Muslim woman is worth only half a Muslim man, because Qur'anic rules of inheritance gave a daughter only half the inheritance of a son. By this logic, however, a European woman would have been worth a much smaller fraction of a man. Perhaps even nothing at all. Elizabeth Bennett and her sisters in Jane Austen's *Pride and Prejudice* inherited nothing from her deceased father's estate because the entire estate was entailed to the nearest male relative.

In seventh-century Arabia, the eldest son usually inherited everything. This is because he provided for and defended his tribe. He waged war on other tribes. He needed resources.

This system hardly differed from the European system of primogeniture, which ensured that the oldest son would inherit the entire estate, or at least most of it. Primogeniture operated for centuries, well into the modern era. *Downton Abbey* fans will remember that the earl's estate could not be bequeathed (in the twentieth century!) to his three daughters, because it was entailed to the nearest male heir, their cousin Matthew.

The Qur'an shifted inheritance from the males of the tribe to the nuclear family. It introduced nine new heirs, mostly women and maternal relatives, to the scheme of intestate succession. Before the Qur'an, the wife, daughter, mother, sister, and half-sister—all new Qur'anic heirs—had received nothing.

Fourteen centuries ago, the Qur'an decreed that a daughter, when there was no son to inherit, would receive half the estate. If the deceased left two or more daughters and no son, the daughters shared in two-thirds of the estate. Even in the presence of a son, who received two-thirds of the estate, the daughter would *still* receive one-third. Not just a competence, which the nineteenth-century Bennett sisters would have been happy to receive, but one-third of everything.

This shocked Muhammad's seventh-century followers. How could a male protect the tribe when he could not inherit the entire estate? Women didn't go to war or provide for the tribe; the men did. Imagine the difficulties of conducting any sort of proper tribal raiding when your wealth was reduced by a third!

In the ensuing decades, Islamic religious scholars attempted to interpret inheritance laws in such a way as to limit women's portions whenever possible. Men were in charge, and no one ever wants to relinquish privileges. Therefore, rather than using the rules of inheritance delineated in the Qur'an as a *starting point* to eventually grant equal inheritance rights, they treated the inheritance rules in the Qur'an as the maximum that could ever be allowed. And really, given that they were seventh-century men, it's hard to imagine them doing otherwise.

The inheritance rules in the Qur'an elevated the status of women at that time. Today, though, these same rules seem unfair, because circumstances have changed. But Qur'anic rules need not be read literally, especially when they addressed a specific historical situation.

When I intend to leave half my wealth to my son and half to my daughter, I am not ignoring the Qur'anic verses on inheritance. I am evaluating these verses against historical context—examining their reason for revelation, which was that the son needed more resources because he had to provide for the whole tribe and go to war. Today, the reason for revelation no longer applies, because the historical context has changed. Finally, I am consulting the spirit of the Qur'anic inheritance verses; to take verses that dramatically increased women's rights and use them now to *decrease* them would run counter to the spirit of the verses.

Some Muslims would disagree and insist on the literal reading of the verse. That's okay. All texts, including our Constitution and the Bible, are read literally by some and not by others.

LGBTQI ISSUES

Movies and television overwhelmingly portray Muslims as terrorists or connected to terrorism. Where are the ordinary Muslim characters—the Muslim neighbors, teachers, and families? Only in the last year or two have a few isolated Muslim good guys appeared on television.

When I first saw a Muslim lesbian character on Freeform's *The Bold Type*, my first thoughts unfurled thusly: "Oh no, here we go. Still no mainstream Muslims. . . . But now they've created a lesbian Muslim because so many people assume Muslims are homophobic that they've decided to juxtapose two aspects they assume will result in an edgy, possibly oxymoronic character." My second thoughts crept in soon afterward, though: "Well, at least they have a non-terrorist, somewhat practicing, mostly positive, average, human, even nuanced Muslim character on primetime television—I guess that's progress."

But why do so many assume that Muslims are especially homophobic? Islam seems to be, as Noah Feldman writes, "a canvas on which to project our ideas of the horrible, and as a foil to make us look good." Muslims are bad; therefore, they must be homophobic. Our media perpetuates this perception: hostility toward LGBTQI issues in Muslim-majority countries is emblazoned in *New York Times* headlines,[97] whereas reporting of equivalent hostility in Christian-majority countries requires hours of digging on the internet.

The fact is that some Muslims worldwide are homophobic, and some aren't, just as in other religious communities. In large part, it depends on where they live.

In the US, according to the latest polls, Muslims who favor same-sex marriage far outnumber those not in favor: 52 percent versus 33 percent.[98] That's a majority of Muslim Americans who favor same-sex marriage and a lower level of opposition than in the white evangelical Protestant, black Protestant, Jehovah's Witness, and Mormon communities.[99] What makes this 52 percent additionally significant is that most Muslim Americans are immigrants or the children of immigrants, emigrating mostly from traditional cultures, developing countries, or both, where LGBTQI issues are more taboo than in affluent countries.[100]

Muslim officials have supported LGBTQI rights too. In the US, as of this writing, all past and present Muslim members of Congress have been members of the LGBT Equality Caucus, and mainstream Muslim organizations supported the 2009 hate crimes bill that increased federal legal protections against crimes based on sexual orientation and gender identity.[101] In 2017, in Germany, all six Muslim members of the German parliament voted to approve gay marriage and adoption.[102] The anti-Muslim far-right party, Alternative for Germany, opposed the vote. Angela Merkel also opposed the vote, announcing that "marriage is between a man and a woman."[103]

Of course, acceptance of LGBTQI issues varies across countries. Majorities in many Muslim countries do not accept same-sex marriage, believing religion forbids it—but the same can be said about *non*-Muslims overseas. As of 2017, majorities in Armenia (97 percent), Russia (86 percent), Serbia (75 percent), and Uganda (96 percent) responded that homosexuality should not be accepted by society.[104] Christian-majority Kenya recently affirmed criminalization of same-sex relations.[105] India recriminalized homosexuality (with a jail sentence of ten years) in 2014[106] and only decriminalized it in 2018.[107]

The concept of "LGBTQI rights" is a fairly recent one. Britain did not decriminalize homosexuality until 1967. The United States decriminalized homosexuality on a state-by-state basis from 1962 through 1980. The US Supreme Court did not formally decriminalize sodomy until 2003. Even as of just a few decades ago, not only was homosexuality unacceptable in the United States, but some American laws considerably restricted gay rights; the last state ban on same-sex couples adopting children was not struck down until 2016.[108]

Oh, and when did the Ottoman Empire decriminalize homosexuality? 1858.

Other polls have shown that acceptance of homosexuality worldwide tends to be associated with secular and affluent countries,[109] which is unsurprising as, traditionally, religious interpretations have not sanctioned same-sex relationships, whether Hindu, Buddhist, Christian, Jewish, or Muslim. Religionists have had to actively search for ways to reconcile religious views with acceptance of the LGBTQI community; some have not yet reconciled them. Muslims at this time are wrestling with the same tensions and issues of reconciliation as other religionists. Some Muslims are adamant that homosexuality should be accepted, some are adamant that it should never be accepted, and some are in the middle.

This picture is not always black and white. Iran imposes the death penalty for homosexual acts (which I personally find reprehensible—even under medieval fiqh, the punishment was not necessarily death). However, the Iranian government also provides sex-change operations nearly free of cost, more than any other government in the world.

In Pakistan, which also claims to apply shariah, transgender people (*hijras*) are a legal third gender, with the right to define themselves as they wish; the law says, "'Gender identity' means a person's innermost and individual sense of self as male, female or a blend of both or neither; that can correspond or not to the sex assigned at birth."[110] The law also prohibits discrimination against them.[111] Despite the law, hijras do suffer from discrimination, but they have also been venerated as having special powers and the ability to bestow blessings and cast curses. It's still considered good luck in Pakistan for hijras to come to weddings, because of these powers.

During the rule of the Muslim Mughal emperors in India-Pakistan, some hijras held high positions in court. However, when the British arrived, they were repulsed by the hijra and classified them as a "criminal tribe" in 1871.[112] Today, discrimination notwithstanding, not many modern societies can claim that for centuries they've provided an accepted social position for people of variant gender.

A few years ago, an American general remarked on the radio that, regarding gay issues, lines were much blurrier in Muslim cultures. If you forced Muslims, he said, to directly answer the question of whether homosexuality was permitted in Islam, they would say no. On the other hand, he said, it was much more acceptable in Muslim countries than in Western countries for people of the same sex to hold hands or kiss or show affection, and these actions were not necessarily assumed to be "sinful." Life is not always categorized into binaries.

In sum, Muslims today have varying opinions on LGBTQI issues, still changing, infused with gray areas, their views significantly influenced by their environments and countries of residence. This is no different from other religious groups.

Note again that shariah requires Muslims to live by the law of their country. If same-sex marriage is legal in their country, then that must be accepted, whatever their religious views.

But what does shariah itself "say" about LGBTQI issues? As usual, it doesn't say just one thing.

The Qur'an refers to the Biblical story of Lot and forbids the actions of the men in that story. Traditional fiqh interpreted this to prohibit anal intercourse, which came under the umbrella of illicit sexual intercourse—zina, as discussed in the last chapter. Sexual intercourse between two women lacked penetration and therefore was not considered zina.

Fiqh is more concerned with specific sexual acts than the gender of the participants. Any extramarital phallic penetration of the vagina or anus is illicit sexual intercourse and therefore a hadd offense. But acts of physical love that don't involve such penetration have not been considered major sins, whatever the gender of the participants. Minor sins, yes, perhaps reprehensible, but not major sins and certainly not hudud.[113]

Although Islam, like other religions, forbids same-sex sexual intercourse, homosexuality was historically not as shameful and stigmatized in Islamic civilization as in Europe. Indeed, one of the polemical accusations that medieval Christian Europeans hurled at Muslims was that they were "sodomitical"—too tolerant of homosexuals and openly engaging in same-sex practices.[114]

Muslims of a thousand and more years ago, like everyone else, did not conceive of a homosexual *identity*, which is a fairly recent concept. They simply considered love to be love and desire to be desire, wherever it was directed. That's why male-male love in Islamic history was fairly common and tolerated. Even conservative Islamic religious scholars wrote "folios of poems expounding their love, sometimes their obsession, for male friends and companions."[115]

This wasn't a schizophrenic attitude. Early Muslims accepted that love could flower between opposite sexes and between same sexes, but they also accepted that extramarital sexual intercourse with penetration was prohibited. (European men had similar attitudes about love and sex: writing odes to virtuous women was acceptable, but not fornicating with them.)[116] According to shariah, then, it was not a crime to feel love and attraction, but acting on that attraction and engaging in extramarital sexual acts, whatever your gender, was forbidden.

Because traditional fiqh rules do not allow same-sex couples to marry—the idea would have been inconceivable to medieval people—this leaves no alternative but a life of celibacy. To early Muslim jurists, who assumed that men who desired men could simply redirect that desire at wives, the prohibition on same-sex sexual acts, without recourse to marriage, might not have seemed as unjust as it might seem today. Forced celibacy seems particularly inequitable from an Islamic point of view, because in Islam sexual satisfaction is considered a gift from God (one of the reasons medieval Christian Europeans thought Muslims appallingly licentious), and lifelong celibacy is not valued.

The legal requirements for proving a case of sodomy are the same as for other types of zina, or illicit sexual intercourse. Like other types of zina, sodomy is nearly impossible to prove under shariah. You need four eyewitnesses to the act of intercourse itself, and all the other nearly unattainable requirements, defenses, and ambiguities discussed in the last chapter apply, as well. So do those same principles of avoiding tajassus and providing satr, which prevent catching anyone in the act:

> Wine drinking, fornication, prostitution and homosexuality became widespread in medieval Islamic civilization. Yet Muslim scholars could do little more than complain about this.[117]

In millions of square miles of Islamic lands and in over a thousand years of Islamic history, there were only a few cases of anyone being punished for sodomy.[118]

This general attitude of relative tolerance toward LGBTQI issues in Muslim lands continued until the eighteenth and nineteenth centuries, when British colonialist views influenced it. For example, Malaysia's and Nepal's modern sodomy laws were modeled on India's, which the British had introduced.[119] Political scientists Enze Han and Joseph O'Mahoney have shown that

> the idea that the so-called tolerance towards homosexuality somehow sprang from a western source doesn't hold. As our research shows, this narrative is not only wrong-headed but the opposite of the historical facts. . . . We found that former British colonies are much more likely to have laws that criminalize homosexual conduct than former colonies of other European powers, or other states in general.[120]

In their investigation of 185 countries, Han and O'Mahoney stress, "Furthermore, in our research we show that this finding still holds when we control for other factors like religion, religiosity, democracy, modernity, or wealth."[121]

Today, the great majority of Muslim religious scholars adhere to traditional interpretations of the Qur'an and fiqh and consider same-sex sexual relationships to be unlawful in Islam. The majority would also say that the Qur'an clearly forbids sodomy. A small minority of religious scholars say the Qur'an does not clearly outlaw homosexuality and can be reevaluated in light of modern knowledge and circumstances.

Quite a few Muslim scholars, while agreeing with the traditional fiqh view, believe that in a pluralistic society, Muslims should not be involved in judging others' private sexual practices and rights to same-sex marriage. It's up to God to judge actions between consenting adults that do not injure anyone. Besides, these scholars remind us, shariah does not apply to non-Muslims. In lands under Muslim rule, Muslims allowed Zoroastrians to conduct marriage according to their religion and culture, even though this included incestuous marriage, something prohibited and abhorred in Islam.[122] (I'm *not* saying same-sex marriage is the same as incestuous marriage—I'm simply emphasizing that, historically, Muslims were tolerant of models of behavior other than their own.) Muslim judges historically allowed non-Muslims to charge interest, cultivate wine, and raise pigs,[123] though these were prohibited in Islam.

A minority of scholars do reinterpret the Qur'an and fiqh to allow for same-sex marriage. They assert that the Qur'an is not absolutely clear on same-sex issues.[124] These scholars argue that although the Qur'an refers to the Biblical story of Lot, it does not forbid homosexuality the way we understand it now but rather forbids the *particular acts* in that *particular story*, acts that include all sorts of other reprehensible behavior condemned by the Qur'an, such as violence, rape, spiritual corruption, and disrespect.[125] These scholars would say that early attitudes and misunderstandings about what we now call homosexuality led early Muslims to read the Qur'an in a certain way, but that doesn't mean we must still read the text that way. The legal rules regarding same-sex sexual acts do not come from the Qur'an, after all, but from hadith and fiqh.

There's always been relative de facto tolerance of same-sex relationships in Islam. But Muslims who engaged in these were considered sinners. In contrast, current attempts to categorize same-sex sexual relationships as lawful under shariah is a new thing in Islam, just as it's a new thing for other religious communities vis-à-vis their religious laws.

A complicating factor in discussing LGBTQI issues is that this is one of those areas, like women's rights, that some Muslims, particularly those overseas, perceive as being forced upon them by Western imperialism. Nobody likes being condescended to, but Muslims must remember that tolerance of LGBTQI issues has long been a part of Islamic culture.

Surely we can reclaim that tolerance as their own, without attributing it to imperialism.

WHAT MUSLIMS EAT

Sometimes, I ruminate ruefully on how Muslims cannot even eat without outraged Islam haters branding us as evil and alien. The word *halal* means "allowed," and yet one could reasonably assume it meant "poisoned" from the way some non-Muslims have been carrying on, filing lawsuits and hysterically asserting that the availability of halal meat amounts to "Islamizing" Europe. Apparently, the argument goes, consuming halal meat can make you Muslim. Beware.

In France, in 2017, a court ordered a halal supermarket to close because it did not sell pork or alcohol.[126] The French fast-food chain, Quick, has been sued for offering halal hamburgers. And crowds of Europeans and Americans online have raged against the idea of possibly unknowingly eating halal meat in restaurants.

The halal haters don't make the same allegations about kosher food and, indeed, they avoid acknowledging the similarities between kosher and halal butchering processes. I grew up eating kosher hot dogs at Dodger Stadium, and I never heard of any protests against them. Ironically, most Muslims believe that kosher meat satisfies halal requirements; before my mother found a halal butcher, she bought kosher meat.

Islam haters have resorted to dishonorable tactics, circulating discredited internet calumnies about unsanitary practices in halal butchering. Whether a butcher's practices are unsanitary has nothing to do with whether the meat was butchered according to halal rules. *Every* butcher should be sanitary, halal or not.

The motivation behind the halal rules of butchering was twofold: health and the humane treatment of animals. Scientific evidence confirms that religious slaughter in Jewish and Muslim traditions, carried out properly, is at least as humane as conventional mechanical slaughter.[127]

For meat to be halal (or "allowed"):

- The animal cannot be tortured or mistreated while alive.
- The animal must be killed for food and may not be killed only for sport.

- The animal must be killed outside the presence of other animals.
- Before the animal is killed, a prayer must be said over it, to thank God.
- The animal's throat must be cut swiftly and with a sharp knife, to ensure the most painless death possible.
- The blood must drain from the meat before it is cooked.

That's it. No religious official need be present. Note the lack of requirement that the meat be unsanitary.

Most halal-butchered animals these days are stunned before slaughter, in compliance with the laws of many countries. Some debate percolates about whether stunning increases the animal's suffering: if it does, it would violate halal rules. The Jewish *shechita* method of slaughter cannot involve stunning at all,[128] but the vitriol around this issue revolves almost entirely around halal meat.

Many of today's factory-farm practices invalidate an animal as halal, for several reasons. First, they frequently amount to torture and mistreatment, both of which are prohibited in Islam. For example, often the animals are conscious while their body parts are amputated,[129] while they are skinned, or when they are plunged into the scalding water of defeathering tanks.[130] Second, many modern factory farms *are* unsanitary, because the animals are so packed together that they eat, drink, breathe, and are coated in each other's waste products.[131]

This raises the question of which practice is "barbaric," as France's National Front has accused halal butchering of being.[132] Obviously, for the halal haters, their outrage is not really about the treatment of animals. It's just another way to exteriorize hatred of Islam and Muslims.

Muslims interpret "halal" in a few different ways, in an illustrative example of how shariah operates in daily Muslim life. The halal rules are based on the Qur'an and developed through fiqh. Some Muslims adhere quite strictly to the halal butchering requirements outlined above, never eating meat if it's not specifically certified as halal. Some Muslims rely on a Qur'anic verse that states that the food of Jews and Christians is lawful for Muslims[133]—because the US is a majority Jewish-and-Christian country, they reason, anything sold here (except pork and alcohol) is lawful for Muslims. Still other Muslims simply do not observe the rules regarding halal meat, deeming it a minor regulation too troublesome or too religiously insignificant to matter.

One solution for observant Muslims is to eat fish, which is not subject to halal butchering requirements. This is based on a hadith. These days, I myself prefer vegetarian options—they are environmentally beneficial and render moot the issues of halal slaughter and humane treatment.

Shariah defines some foods as never halal, including carrion (road-kill), animals that eat carrion (like vultures), animals with fangs (no rattlesnake for me), blood (no black pudding, either), or pork. Muslims may not drink alcohol or consume any other intoxicants. A minority opinion decrees that Muslims shouldn't eat shellfish, but the majority opinion allows it.

Unexpected gray areas are subject to interpretation. We cannot consume intoxicants, such as alcohol, but what about the alcohol in vanilla extract? Some would say it's absolutely forbidden. Some would say it's fine if it evaporates during cooking, so the vanilla in cooked items is allowed. Some would say that the amount of vanilla in a dessert is such a small amount that it couldn't possibly make you drunk (which is what the Qur'an clearly prohibits), and therefore it's allowed.

I grew up believing that cooked alcohol was permissible, though I avoided it anyway, except for vanilla extract. Imagine my dismay when I read that alcohol never completely evaporates because it binds with water and forms an azeotrope! Food that contains alcohol retains it even when cooked, as long as water remains in it.

In 2008, Shaykh Yusuf al-Qaradawi gave his opinion that a small amount of alcohol, 0.5 percent, resulting from natural fermentation, is permitted; he based his reasoning on the Prophet's statement, "If drinking a lot of alcohol would make you intoxicated, then you shouldn't drink even a little." Al-Qaradawi argued, then, that if drinking a lot of a drink with some alcohol in it *wouldn't* make one intoxicated, then it was permissible to drink a tiny amount.[134]

Qaradawi's fatwa responded to a specific question about fermentation in energy drinks. I personally do apply Qaradawi's opinion to vanilla extract in baked goods, because even if I ate a whole batch of cookies, I couldn't get drunk on the vanilla extract in them. But other Muslims might follow a different interpretation.

Marshmallows, too, present a potential problem, because they contain gelatin, which often comes from pigs or non-halal animals. If the marshmallows contain gelatin derived from pigs, then Muslims cannot eat them. But usually marshmallows don't specify the origin of the gelatin. What then? Some Muslims would say that, lacking such information, we can assume the gelatin is not porcine; other Muslims would disagree because of the possibility that the gelatin is porcine. Some Muslims would say that such a small amount of gelatin doesn't matter. I say: thank goodness for vegan marshmallows.

All these food rules are subject to an exception—saving a life. Life is sacrosanct in Islam, and a Muslim may eat anything if it is a matter of life or death. If I need a medicine that contains alcohol to save my life, then I am allowed to take that medicine, notwithstanding the age-old excuse of drinking alcohol for medicinal purposes (*Star Trek*'s Dr. McCoy comes to mind). Similarly, if I am literally starving to death and the only comestible available is pork, then I can eat pork.

As a Muslim, if I believe something will harm me, then I shouldn't offer it to someone else. If I believe cocaine will harm me, then I shouldn't offer it to my friend, right? If I believe alcohol will harm me, then I shouldn't offer that to anyone else, either. This rule sometimes presents a problem when we host parties or fundraisers in the US. Is it better to violate the rule of not offering harm to someone else or the rule of hospitality, a near-sacred rule in Islam?[135]

My father, as a young professor, quite often hosted departmental parties. He had a friend who, were there no scotch whiskey available, would excuse himself from the party to locate the nearest liquor store so he could bring back a bottle. After this transpired several times, my father snapped.

"I can't let him do this anymore!" he said. "I feel too ashamed that a guest of mine must go buy his own food! He'll drink it whether I give it to him or not." And that's why grocery shopping for math department parties at our house always included a small bottle of Johnnie Walker.

FINANCE

Fiqh rules of Islamic finance aimed to uplift the downtrodden and eliminate injustice in transactions. Islamic finance emphasizes risk sharing and investment rather than the time value of money. The most significant differences between Islamic finance and Western finance concern the concepts of *riba* (usury) and *gharar* (risk or speculation). Shariah prohibits these.

Islamic scholars have never been unanimous in their definition of riba, usually translated as usury. The Qur'an forbids usury, addressing a common pre-Islamic practice called "doubling." When a loan became due, the lender asked the borrower, "Do you pay or do you double?" If the borrower could not pay back the full amount, he henceforth owed double. This is clearly riba.

Are all types of interest considered riba? Compound interest has generally, though not unanimously, been held to be riba, because it looks a lot like "doubling." Simple interest up to a certain point (say, 7 percent) has generally been tolerated.

But there's a range of opinions. Some scholars would disallow any kind of interest. Others have said that it's not about interest, per se, but about injustice and unlawful gain; exploitation and economic enslavement of the borrower is really what constitutes usury, so we should distinguish between economic loans and loans that help poor people meet basic needs.[136] Quite a few scholars, even a hundred years ago, have allowed Muslims living in non-Muslim countries to engage in transactions involving compound interest, such as the purchase of a house with an interest-bearing loan, because—although traditional fiqh would have disallowed this—practices may be adjusted when Muslims must follow the laws of the country in which they reside.[137]

Gharar, or "risk," means that none of the terms in a contract may be speculative or solely dependent upon chance rather than skill. For example, a contract for the sale of an animal still in the womb contains a speculative term and is disallowed, because you cannot know the animal's precise condition or whether it will be born alive. An insurance contract contains gharar, as well, because it is impossible to know when or if the insured will fall ill or be victimized by theft. Gambling is a type of gharar and is prohibited.

Islamic banks finance transactions in accordance with shariah. Islamic banking usually works to the advantage of the less affluent, emphasizing widely accessible profit-sharing schemes. (Remember, Islamic scholars traditionally came from the middle to lower classes.) According to the International Monetary Fund, during the global financial crisis of

2008, Islamic banks fared better and showed more resilience than conventional banks.[138]

In sum, Muslims interpret shariah in myriad ways in their daily lives. Shariah, as a wide variety of practices around a core set of beliefs, can accommodate this diversity. Muslim Americans, members of one of the most culturally and ethnically diverse American faith groups, are exposed to more varieties of interpretation than many Muslims overseas. We're free to explore and choose our religious practices without government interference. We reconcile our religious practices with American law. You might even say that shariah makes us better Americans.

CHAPTER TWELVE

THE DISINFORMATION CAMPAIGN AND SHARIAH IN AMERICA

*A lie can run round the world before
the truth has got its boots on.*
—from *The Truth* by Sir Terry Pratchett

I HAVE MAINTAINED IN the preceding chapters that shariah is not the law of the land anywhere in the world and that, in America and Europe, shariah resides in the private sphere, in the religious lives of Muslims, in the same way that religious rules are relevant to any faith group: prayer, worship, celebrating holidays, observing dietary restrictions, and living life as a spiritual person. Moreover, shariah itself mandates that Muslims follow the law of the land in which they live, whether the land is "Islamic" or not.

Why, then, have the last several years seen the rise of ominous new concepts like "creeping shariah" and "shariah takeover"? Amazingly enough, the current shariah scare, groundless and vituperative, is due largely to one man. This is his story.

THE DISINFORMATION CAMPAIGN

Between 9/11 and 2010, hate crimes against Muslims had actually declined in the United States. But in 2010, they spiked, for no easily discernible reason—no terrorist attacks by Muslims, no ISIS horror stories.[1] Mark Potok of the Southern Poverty Law Center identifies two causes for the increase in hate crimes: (a) the deliberately engineered controversy about an Islamic cultural center, modeled on Jewish Community Centers, in New York, and (b) a report by lawyer and anti-Muslim propagandist David Yerushalmi and others asserting that Muslims were trying to impose shariah in American criminal courts.[2]

The construction of an Islamic cultural center in a New York neighborhood where multiple mosques had resided for years, where all sorts of other more controversial businesses (like strip clubs) operated, where the center would have improved the neighborhood by replacing an abandoned building, and where city officials had previously approved the project should not even have been newsworthy. It had received widespread support. Even *Fox News*'s Laura Ingraham had commented that the proposed center sounded like a good idea.[3]

But then members of the "Islamophobia industry," a well-documented, loose network of individuals and organizations who disseminate anti-Muslim propaganda into the public discourse, started reframing the project. (The Islamophobia industry is discussed further in the next chapter.) The campaign to oppose the mosque, particularly Pamela Geller, of "Obama is the illegitimate son of Malcolm X" fame,[4] and Robert Spencer, who both earn their livings as vicious anti-Muslim propagandists, dubbed the Islamic cultural center project a "ground zero mosque," a "9/11 monster mosque," and a 9/11 "victory mosque."[5] The *New York Post* published Geller's diatribes, which led to a national, deliberately contrived controversy, causing a remarkable 70 percent of Americans to oppose construction of the mosque. This in turn led to countrywide opposition to mosque construction.[6]

For the Geller/Spencer argument to make any sense, one must believe in one or more of these factually incorrect premises: the developers of the center and al-Qaeda terrorists were one and the same; all Muslims and al-Qaeda terrorists are one and the same; or Islam permits terrorism. Without at least one such premise, preventing Muslims from building a cultural center (or even a mosque) several blocks away from where a group of terrorists committed a heinous crime is nonsensical. One has nothing to do with the other.

The second factor in the 2010 increase in anti-Muslim hate crimes was David Yerushalmi's "anti-shariah law" campaign. Yerushalmi wanted to introduce the idea of a horrific Islamic law ("shariah law," as he framed it), poised to infiltrate the United States and impose Islam on hapless Americans, into the public discourse. He accomplished this goal by drafting model "anti–shariah law" legislation, called "American Laws for American Courts" (ALAC). He then approached state legislatures, warning them of the threat of shariah and urging them to pass anti-shariah legislation modeled (sometimes verbatim) on his own.

Yerushalmi used an approach commonly used by the Islamophobia industry—namely, fixing upon Islamic, Arabic-language *terms of art* (that is, academic terms with specialized meanings) and assigning to them new, sinister definitions. Yerushalmi appropriated the word "shariah," an Islamic academic term, and assigned to it all manner of nightmarish attributes. He is the main reason why, in the last eight years, "shariah" (or "sharia") has transformed from an unknown word to a "scare" word.[7]

Yerushalmi has been criticized by numerous groups, including the Anti-Defamation League, for his "anti-Muslim, anti-immigrant and anti-black bigotry."[8] He has stated, "There is a reason the founding fathers did not give women or black slaves the right to vote."[9] Yerushalmi has advocated criminalizing Islam.[10] A "veteran of the most extreme religious right-wing elements of the Israeli settlers movement,"[11] he has pontificated, completely in opposition to the facts, "The mythical 'moderate' Muslim . . . the Muslim who embraces traditional Islam but wants a peaceful coexistence with the West, is effectively non-existent."[12]

Well, *I'm* a moderate Muslim who embraces traditional Islam! As are the vast majority of Muslims in the world. This is so self-evident I shouldn't even have to say it. Besides, I'm *in* the West, so of course I want a peaceful coexistence with it.

Yerushalmi himself admits deliberately fomenting the shariah scare. He states, "If this thing [his anti-shariah legislation] passed in every state without any friction, it would have not served its purpose. The purpose was heuristic—to get people asking this question, 'What is shariah?'"[13]

Yerushalmi, a lawyer, must know that no religious law can ever take over the United States. His intention was therefore not to prevent such a takeover but rather to introduce a terrifying idea of shariah (stoning! face veils! Arab clothing!) into the public discourse, thus otherizing and discriminating against Muslims. His anti-shariah campaign has heightened shariah hysteria, demonized Muslims by portraying them as outside the American legal system, and denied Muslims the same access to the judicial system as granted to non-Muslims.[14] It's caused pundits and politicians (not to mention laypeople) to wildly hurl around groundless and terrorizing descriptions of shariah.

According to a 2017 report called *Legalizing Othering* by the Haas Institute for a Fair and Inclusive Society, at the University of California at Berkeley,

> The anti-sharia movement has been established, and continues to expand, by an unfounded fear of "creeping sharia," proliferated by fabrications, lies, and intentionally misconstrued information surrounding Muslims in the United States.[15]

Unfortunately, state and federal lawmakers and politicians have heeded Yerushalmi and others in the Islamophobia industry, with little or no fact-checking. Over two hundred anti-shariah bills have been introduced in forty-three states.[16] A proposed Tennessee law would have made adherence to shariah a felony—which means I would have become a criminal for saying my prayers![17]

To date, at least twenty anti-shariah laws have passed in fourteen states,[18] though no Muslim American organization has *ever* sought to establish shariah as the law of the United States.[19]

SHARIAH AND THE US CONSTITUTION

In the United States, our well-established legal doctrines, based on our Constitution, already prohibit any foreign law—including any religious law—from taking over our country. The First Amendment to the Constitution contains two clauses: the Free Exercise Clause and the Establishment Clause. Here they both are: "Congress shall make no law respecting an establishment of religion, or prohibiting the free exercise thereof."[20]

The Free Exercise Clause allows Americans to practice whichever religion they want, or no religion at all, as long as such practice doesn't violate American laws or public policy. The government cannot prevent religious behavior simply because it's religious, and the government cannot prevent the belief in or advocacy of a religion. The Free Exercise

Clause is why we allow people to take days off work for their religious holidays and wear yarmulkes or headscarves.

The Establishment Clause prevents the government from *establishing* any religion. That means the government (including public schools and other government-funded institutions) cannot promote or proselytize any religion or apply any religious law. In other words, no religious law can ever take over—be established as—the law of the United States.

The Establishment Clause also means that our government cannot discriminate against any particular religion. Additionally, it's been interpreted to mean that our government cannot discriminate against non-religion over religion, or religion over nonreligion.[21] As Justice Sonia Sotomayor points out in her dissent to the Supreme Court's ruling on the Trump administration's "Muslim ban," the government cannot favor or disfavor one religion over another, nor can it adopt programs or practices that aid or oppose any religion.[22]

I encounter quite a bit of confusion regarding the Establishment Clause and the Free Exercise Clause, as well as the general constitutional concept of freedom of religion. At a recent authors' dinner, a man asked me why I wrote my second (teen) book. I answered, "Mostly because several middle school and high school teachers asked me to write something age-appropriate for their students."

The man responded, "Oh, we're not supposed to teach religion in public schools, so they can't use your book."

Actually, they can! Public schools cannot teach *faith*—that is, they cannot teach students to believe in a religion or otherwise proselytize a religion, because that would be violating the Establishment Clause. But public schools in virtually every American state have been required to teach *about* world religions. Learning what people believe is just part of learning about history and humanity.

The American Academy of Religion has published guidelines for teaching religion in public schools in constitutionally sound and intellectually responsible ways, noting that "illiteracy regarding religion 1) is widespread, 2) fuels prejudice and antagonism, and 3) can be diminished by teaching about religion in public schools using a non-devotional, academic perspective, called religious studies."[23] Indeed, though some parents always fear world-religions courses will convert their children to other religions, research shows that such courses help reduce intolerance among students without undermining their own personal religious beliefs.[24] Teaching about religion is not only constitutional but also necessary in today's world.

ANTI-SHARIAH LAWS

Because no religious law can ever take over the United States, anti-shariah laws are pointless. As so many have remarked, anti-shariah laws are a solution in search of a problem.[25]

The first anti-shariah law, passed by the Oklahoma state legislature, was defeated as unconstitutional, because, among other things, it specifically identified shariah as the object of the ban. The law clearly discriminated among religions.[26] Since then, in an attempt to appear constitutional, explicit references to "shariah" have been removed in many anti-shariah laws. Instead, lawmakers have enacted laws that ban "any foreign law, legal code, or system."[27]

Most such laws are based on David Yerushalmi's ALAC model legislation,[28] which does not specifically mention the word "shariah." However, Yerushalmi and other legislators have never hidden their goals of specifically targeting shariah with ALAC and its copycat laws.[29] These laws have not yet been litigated.

Anti-shariah laws harbor serious constitutional issues. Amazingly, they potentially violate the Supremacy Clause, the Establishment Clause, the Free Exercise Clause, and the Contracts Clause of our Constitution. Quite an accomplishment.

The Supremacy Clause states that all treaties are "the supreme law of the land." Treaties are a source of international law that are applicable to cases in state courts. But anti-shariah laws bar the courts from considering international law,[30] thus running afoul of the Supremacy Clause.

Anti-shariah laws also potentially violate the Establishment Clause, because they explicitly or in application prefer one religion over another. For a law to be unconstitutional under the Establishment Clause, its language need not specifically discriminate against a particular religion, if the practical effect is discriminatory. Courts apply the following test to see if the law is unconstitutional: (a) the law must have a secular legislative purpose, (b) the law's primary effect must be one that neither advances nor inhibits religion, and (c) the law must not result in an excessive government entanglement with religion.[31]

Anti-shariah laws violate the Free Exercise Clause because they impinge on the right of Muslims to freely practice their religion. For example, a Muslim might be disallowed, under such laws, from making an enforceable shariah-compliant will, even if that will is otherwise perfectly valid under American law.[32] In the lawsuit challenging the Oklahoma anti-shariah law (*Awad v. Ziriax*), Mr. Awad argued that the law prevented him from specifying in his will that he wanted to be interred with his head pointed toward Mecca.[33]

The free exercise of religion is circumscribed by the government's interest in protecting its citizens. If a particular religious practice is against American law or policy, then the government may indeed have a compelling interest that supersedes the free exercise of religion in that case. That's why we don't allow people to perform human sacrifices, even if their religion requires it.

However, even if the government has a compelling interest and wishes to restrict a religious practice because of it, the restriction must be *narrowly tailored* to that particular practice. The government cannot simply bar the whole religion. For example, if the government believes polygamy is socially harmful, then the government may ban polygamy. But the government may not ban an entire religion that allows it. Judaism, Islam, and Mormonism, for example, have all at least at some point allowed polygamy.[34]

Anti-shariah laws are likely unconstitutional under the Contracts Clause, as well, which gives us our constitutional right to enter into contracts. We all should be able to choose which law will govern our contracts. Muslims should be able to enter into contracts that comply with shariah principles. Anti-shariah laws would restrict these rights of contract.

Suppose I want to lend money to someone, but I don't want to charge them interest, because I feel that would be un-Islamic. I draw up a contract loaning the money and specifying conditions for the repayment of the loan, but only for the original amount of the loan—I don't include any additional fees or interest. If the borrower refuses to pay me back, I might go to court to have my contract enforced and retrieve my money.

But if I live in a state that's passed an anti-shariah law, my contract may very well be thrown out and invalidated because it complies with shariah. I wouldn't get my money back, even though there's nothing in the contract that would violate any state or federal law or public policy!

And that's a violation of my constitutional rights. I should be able to enter into any contract I want to, just as non-Muslims can, as long as my contract doesn't violate American law or policy. If I don't have the same rights as non-Muslims simply because I'm Muslim, then that's a violation of our Constitution. And if I can't enter into contracts that comply with shariah, even if they are otherwise valid under American law, that's also a violation of my constitutional rights.

Look at it this way: any contract should be valid in the United States if it satisfies American legal requirements for a contract and if it does not violate any law or public policy. If such a contract *also* satisfies Islamic law or Jewish law or Biblical law or Hindu law, so what? The only question is whether it is valid under American law.

Professors, attorneys, judges, and legislators have denounced the anti-shariah movement for multiple reasons. They know it's a gargantuan waste of time that depicts Muslims as unable to follow any law but shariah and impinges on Muslims' legal rights. And they know anti-shariah laws, whether or not they identify shariah by name, are harmful to the American judicial system, both generally and specifically.

Anti-shariah laws harm our judicial system in specific ways by preventing judges from doing their jobs and even forcing them into inequitable legal decisions. They prevent American courts from freely evaluating any foreign law that applies to a dispute, which they must be able to do if, for example, they're going to recognize overseas marriages (my American college roommate got married in Jamaica!) or international adoptions.[35] Anti-shariah laws hinder American companies from doing business overseas, since such transactions often require any disputes to be governed by the laws of a foreign country. Such laws may even undo anti-kidnapping (child abduction) statutes, because such statutes depend on reciprocity: if we don't recognize foreign law, foreign jurisdictions won't enforce our custody decrees, making it harder to recover abducted children.[36]

Anti-shariah laws harm our country in general ways, as well. They promote the demonization of Muslim Americans. They bolster the erroneous characterization of Muslims as un-American and our beliefs as incompatible with the Constitution. Anti-shariah laws and the campaigns to pass them cause Muslims to be treated as enemies seeking to impose our own laws on Americans instead of complying with American law. These laws legalize discrimination against Muslims and escalate Islamophobia. Once Muslims are branded as enemies, violence against us becomes much easier, as evidenced by the sharp rise in hate crimes against Muslims since the start of the anti-shariah campaign.

More than that, though, these laws and their appended campaigns harm all Americans. They undermine our Constitution, which guarantees freedom from religious discrimination. They damage our democracy by targeting some citizens over others. They stoke fear and hysteria, which increases the likelihood of policy choices based on fear rather than facts. And, of course, they promote warfare, because if Muslim *Americans* are worthy of discrimination and fear, how much more evil must Muslims *overseas* be?

As journalist Tim Murphy writes, "The sharia ban would replace a non-existent problem . . . with a bunch of very real ones."[37]

The American Bar Association has announced its opposition to any blanket prohibitions on consideration or use of foreign law, international law, or "the entire body of law or doctrine of a particular religion."[38] The ABA gives these reasons: anti-shariah laws have enormous constitutional concerns, and the US Constitution already protects the individual rights and freedoms such laws purport to protect.[39]

Lawyers Christine Albano and Laura W. Morgan comment:

> That the American Bar Association would have to come out with such a resolution is a sad commentary on our times, for it betrays not only a current anti-Muslim sentiment, it reveals some of the public's misunderstanding of how the courts apply the law, whether statutory or case law, to the facts of a given case and always within a constitutional framework.[40]

That's the key: the courts can only apply law within a constitutional framework. That means that, however shariah arises before US courts, whether and to what extent it applies is *always* subject to American law.

SHARIAH IN AMERICAN COURTS

Shariah appears in our justice system only insofar as any religious or foreign law would appear. It arises primarily when relevant to a dispute: either in the way that any foreign law does, or as a source of information necessary to understanding the facts of a case.

As a source of information, an American court might consult shariah to find evidence of the intention or expectation of the parties.[41] Or understanding a point of shariah might be essential to clarifying an ambiguous term in an agreement or determining customary practices.[42]

Like any other foreign law, shariah might arise as relevant to a private contract dispute between parties. In one case, a contract between Exxon Mobil and a Saudi oil company was governed by Saudi law, which incorporates elements of shariah (the Saudis would likely say their law is *all* shariah). When a dispute arose, the American court had to hear testimony on Saudi law.[43] The court returned a $400 million verdict in favor of Exxon Mobil and against the Saudi company.[44] If an anti-shariah law had been in place, the jury would not have been able to return a $400 million verdict in favor of Exxon Mobil.[45]

Another common context in which shariah arises is the enforcement of a marriage contract between two Muslims. Under shariah, when two people marry, they sign a marriage contract in which they can agree to any number of provisions.

One of the standard provisions of an Islamic marriage contract is the *mahr* provision. This directs the husband, upon marriage, to give the wife an agreed-upon sum of money or property, called a mahr. This is her separate property and remains hers, so that she has a financial cushion in case her husband divorces her or dies. The mahr provision is a necessary part of the Islamic marriage contract, though the amount itself can be waived. If the contract lacks a mahr provision, the judge must assume it's *implied*—that is, the judge must assume it was intended to be in the contract and proceed as if it were.

The mahr was a radical idea in the seventh century because, before Islam and even much later all over the world, money was paid not to the bride but to the *groom* by the bride or her family. This sum was called a dowry, and it was commonplace everywhere until recently, including in America and Europe.

The mahr is the opposite of the dowry; instead of a bride paying the groom, the groom pays the bride. The mahr is also not necessarily the *only* piece of property a wife gets under shariah upon divorce or death of the husband. It's a supplement to, not a substitution for, any other property she might inherit or receive upon divorce.[46]

What happens if two Muslims enter into a marriage with a contract that specifies a mahr, then get divorced, and then the husband refuses to pay the mahr? If she takes him to court, the judge must review the terms of the contract. In such a case, the judge would need to consult shariah to determine what the mahr is and how it works.

Courts have upheld Islamic marriage contracts when they don't violate American law or public policy. When a court has found such a contract invalid, it's because the contract doesn't conform to American law or policy. For example, it might be too vague, or perhaps one party signed it under duress, or maybe (as in one case) it was sprung on the husband fifteen minutes before the wedding, when all the guests were already present.[47]

If a court enforces a mahr provision in a contract, this does not mean that the court is violating the Establishment Clause of the First Amendment. This does not mean that shariah is taking over our court system. It means that the court is accommodating religious practice under the Free Exercise Clause.

But in states that have enacted anti-shariah laws, the court would be barred from evaluating shariah or perhaps any foreign law. That means that a court would be allowed—perhaps even be required—to invalidate a contract simply because it's based on shariah. Of the 194 anti-shariah bills considered by the *Legalizing Othering* report, 191 bar courts from enforcing contracts and agreements between individuals.[48] This has real-world, often unjust consequences.

One such unjust result occurred in Kansas, in a case directly affected by the state's anti-shariah law, which was disguised as an anti-foreign-law ban. In *Soleimani v. Soleimani*, after her divorce, a wife sought enforcement of the mahr provision in her marriage contract, which required her husband (whose assets had amounted to $7 million before his marriage) to pay her a mahr of $677,000.[49] At the time of the court case, she had recently immigrated to the US, spoke little English, and lived in a shelter.[48] Because of the Kansas anti-shariah law, the trial court could neither interpret the contract by applying Islamic law nor honor the mahr provision; the trial court judge said he was precluded from considering shariah because of the anti-shariah legislation adopted in Kansas.[51]

The result? Instead of receiving her $677,000, the wife received $692 per month for two years.[52]

Ironically, the state senator who had introduced and pushed for the anti-shariah law in Kansas, Susan Wagle, had corralled votes for it by censuring any votes against it as "votes against women."[53]

SHARIAH AND ARBITRATION

Arbitration and mediation can also be affected by anti-shariah laws. Any party to a contract can always agree to submit contract disputes to arbitration, rather than sue in court. Arbitration is usually faster and cheaper. Additionally, arbitrators can be chosen for their expertise; if you're in a particular industry, like making widgets, you might prefer that your dispute be arbitrated by a widget expert, rather than adjudicated by a judge who may not know widgets from gizmos.

Arbitrators and mediators may be religious officials. Like the widget experts, they may be chosen for their expertise in the subject matter of the contract. Religious arbitration has long been an established part of our legal system. Some Jews use arbitration to resolve their disputes under Jewish rabbinical law; Beth Din of America is a rabbinic tribunal that arbitrates disputes according to halakha (Jewish law).[54] Similarly, some organizations in the US require contract disputes to be resolved by "Biblically based mediation."[55] Muslim Americans can also agree to dispute resolution by Islamic religious scholars.

Why choose religious officials to arbitrate? It's often a matter of conscience—I might want to know that I'm following my religious law *as well as* the civil law of my country. Or the state law system may not be relevant to the particular issue in dispute. Or perhaps the state law system is insufficient for my issue.

In Britain, for example, Muslim women whose marriages had not been registered by the state were unable to get divorced—in the view of the state, if there's no marriage, there can be no dissolution of marriage. For such cases and for cases in which their husbands refused to cooperate, shariah councils were set up to help Muslim women obtain religious divorces. This allowed them to remarry with clear consciences.[56]

If two parties obtain an arbitrator's (or mediator's) decision, but then one party refuses to comply with the decision, then the other party can ask a court to enforce it. The court would determine if the arbitrator's decision was valid. If the arbitration concerned Muslim parties, the judge might need to evaluate shariah. This doesn't mean the civil court judge would be imposing shariah! Rather, the judge would be determining whether the arbitration should be enforceable by applying the law agreed upon by the parties themselves.

In 2011, a mosque and its trustees agreed to have their disputes resolved by an Islamic scholar. When a dispute arose, the Islamic scholar decided in favor of the trustees. The mosque, not liking this result, then took the case to Florida state court.[57] Because the parties had agreed that Islamic law would govern the dispute, the judge said he would use it to decide whether to enforce the arbitration agreement.[58]

This caused great furor in anti-shariah groups, which accused the judge of allowing "creeping shariah" and "forcing shariah law onto the parties against their will."[59] But the judge wasn't seeking to impose Islamic law on anyone. The court was simply ensuring that the arbitration proceedings conformed to the rules *already agreed upon by the parties*; that they happened to be Islamic rules made no difference.[60]

This is a key point. The law that governs an arbitration or a contract is the law to which *all parties agree*, whether it's shariah or French law or something else. Nobody can force anyone to follow a foreign or religious law.

American courts routinely interpret foreign law. Markus Wagner, professor of international law, explains:

> If we both sign a contract agreeing to be governed by German law, then Florida courts will interpret German law. . . . It happens all the time, it's just that no one writes about it. We could use Jewish law, Canaanite law, so long as it doesn't contravene public policy.[61]

The bottom line is, if Jewish arbitration and Christian arbitration are permitted, but Muslim arbitration is not permitted, then this difference is not about law—it's about prejudice. And in case you're thinking, "But shariah allows for stoning," well, so do the Ten Commandments and the Old Testament, and the stoning in these religious laws would never be allowed in the United States because *every case* concerning the application of religious law is always subject to American law and public policy. Anti-shariah laws that ban all religious law would affect not only Muslims who seek decisions from religious tribunals but also Jews, Christians, and other religious groups who desire religious arbitration.

American courts already possess safeguards to protect our legal system from infiltration. Anti-shariah bans are unnecessary and cause harm not only to Muslims but to other religious minorities and our entire legal system. Anti-shariah legislation should be exposed for what it is: an intentional, unconstitutional attempt to discriminate against Muslims and manipulate the public into erroneously believing that Muslims cannot abide by American law or be loyal Americans.

PART III

RECOGNIZING THE PROBLEM

CHAPTER THIRTEEN

ISLAMOPHOBIA AND WHY WE HAVE THE STEREOTYPES

Prejudice is a great time saver.
You can form opinions
without having to get the facts.
—E. B. White

WHENEVER I EMBARK on an explanation of shariah, I'm dogged by the slightly desperate feeling that my words will be disbelieved, because the real shariah so little resembles the villainous law described by David Yerushalmi, Frank Gaffney, other Islamophobes, and far-right politicians. How can I explain what's true when what's normalized is baseless fiction or, at best, an unrecognizable caricature?

This chapter explains why such an enormous difference between reality and perception has appeared in our discourse and why the shadowy evil caricature of shariah—and of Islam generally—is so easily accepted. Specifically, it answers a baffling question: why is it that so many politicians and others swallowed David Yerushalmi's lies about shariah, rather than engaging in some simple fact-checking? A brief consultation with an Islamic studies professor would have sufficed.

The answer to this question is multifaceted but can be distilled into two broad categories. First, Yerushalmi is part of the "Islamophobia industry," so his disinformation campaign was organized and connected to media and policymakers. Second, we all tend to believe stories that confirm our fears, and the West has had a long historical tradition, similar to anti-Semitism, of fearing and loathing Islam and Muslims. In other words, Yerushalmi's disinformation was easy to believe, because we in the West were already culturally primed to believe it.

But before discussing these two categories, a brief definition is in order.

ISLAMOPHOBIA DEFINED

"Islamophobia" refers neither to an individual problem nor a mental illness but to anti-Muslim prejudice. Some people prefer "anti-Muslim bigotry" to "Islamophobia." At a recent conference, a high school teacher (white, male, Christian) scoffed at the term "Islamophobia" and said to me, "It's anti-Muslim hatred! Why don't we call it what it is?"

Islamophobia is also sometimes called "anti-Muslim racism." Racisms are not biological classifications but sociopolitical constructs. In nineteenth-century America, Christian Syrians were legally classified as white, but Muslim Syrians as nonwhite.[1] This mattered, because whiteness included more legal privileges. Non-Muslims today have been attacked because they "look" Muslim, though being Muslim is a state of belief, not appearance. If you believe Muslims are despicable or fanatical or violent *because they're Muslim*, then that's racism.[2]

It's important to understand that Islamophobia need not arise from intentional hatred or malicious intentions. Islamophobic tropes are normalized in our Western culture; they bombard us from all directions—textbooks, internet, film and television, news media, and books. We're all conditioned to think a certain way about Islam and Muslims, to the point where we don't even really question our assumptions.

Islamophobia can refer not only to individual prejudice but also to structural prejudice, which means discrimination embedded into our institutions, government, policies, and media. The two dimensions of Islamophobia—individual and structural—feed on each other. For example, governmental policies (like war-on-terror and surveillance policies) endorse anti-Muslim stereotypes and validate individual Islamophobia. In return, individuals with Islamophobic views spur those in government to enact more policies targeting Muslims.[3]

Quite frequently, people defend Islamophobia by protesting that they have a "rational fear" of Islam or that they are simply "criticizing" Islam. However, what's being feared or criticized is not Islam but the tall-tale, bogeyman version of Islam—which is produced by Islamophobia in the first place. Similarly, those who claim a "rational fear" of Muslims and therefore believe them to be innately villainous—which is Islamophobia—defend their views by pointing to real threats from Muslims but ignoring real threats from other groups (like white men). I've never heard anyone claim to have a rational fear of Buddhism because of the brutal violence in Myanmar.

Some people attempt to disguise their bigotry by insisting that they don't hate Muslims; they just hate *Islam*. This is a spurious, oxymoronic argument. Muslims are defined as those who follow Islam.

THE ISLAMOPHOBIA INDUSTRY

Yerushalmi's anti-shariah disinformation campaign is one segment of a larger "Islamophobia industry," introduced in the previous chapter, which aims to incite fear of Islam and Muslims by disseminating disinformation into the public discourse through media and politicians. A well-funded, profitable, loose network of individuals and organizations, the Islamophobia industry has been extensively documented.[4] This network's fabrications and disinformation have been used by politicians, public figures, and media personalities to foment fear and garner power.

Here's how it works. Individuals and organizations fund Islamophobic groups, many of which are classified as hate groups. These groups use anti-Muslim propagandists (virtually none of whom have any credentials in Islam, Islamic studies, or Islamic law) to feed false information (through lectures, books, "policy reports," and consultations) to the media, politicians, and the religious right—who, in turn, use public platforms to disseminate the disinformation to the public. The disinformation is a jumble of fabrications, distortions, accusations, and co-options of Islamic terms. These anti-Muslim propagandists intend to scare the public into taking action against Muslims here and abroad.

Why would people devote their lives to demonizing Muslims? For some, perhaps the tragedy of 9/11 ignited fear and hatred of all Muslims—though only nineteen men perpetrated that crime, hardly representative of almost a quarter of the world's population. Perhaps some need a scapegoat: scapegoating and derision of those perceived as different is nothing new, and Muslims are perceived as outwardly different—often brown or black, sometimes differently dressed. Some anti-Muslim propagandists probably believe their own disinformation, just as some Nazis believed that Jews were subhuman. Some probably do believe in a worldwide mass "Islamic threat," just as some Americans in the McCarthy era believed that fighting soulless, godless Communists was their raison d'être. And some clearly strive to influence US foreign policy in the Middle East, specifically Israel-Palestine.

But an additional, enormous reason for the Islamophobia industry is profit. Islam bashing is profitable. Hundreds of millions of dollars—at the very least—have been funneled to Islamophobic groups and individuals. The industry generates personal wealth and fame. In just five years (2008–13), thirty-three Islamophobic groups had access to at least $205 million in revenue.[5]

Because blaming all American and European national problems on Islam, or "Islamization," is quite far-fetched, anti-Muslim propagandists resort to warnings of "secret" shariah. They accuse Muslims of "secretly" taking over government positions. Indeed, Islamophobia parallels the anti-Semitism of the early twentieth century in the way it foments fear of an alien minority secretly taking over the country.

The nonpartisan organization People for the American Way notes that Islamophobes use the following strategies "to cast doubt on the validity of Islam as a religion and the integrity of Muslim Americans in order to justify prejudice and illegal discrimination:

- Framing Muslim Americans as dangerous to America
- Twisting statistics and using fake research to 'prove' the Muslim threat
- Inventing the danger of "creeping sharia"
- Justifying taking away freedoms and liberties from Muslims in order to "defend liberty"
- Denying the validity of Islam as a religion[6]

The common tactic of asserting that Islam is not a religion but an "ideology" or a "cult" is designed to ensure that Muslims are not protected under our Constitution. For example, the Center for American Progress notes:

In a 2007 interview with Reason magazine, Hirsi Ali [author and anti-Muslim activist] said "we are at war with Islam," called Islam "a violent ideology," claimed "there is no moderate Islam," and advocated for closing all Islamic schools. During the interview, she also called for amending the U.S. Constitution in order to discriminate against Muslim Americans and criticized President George W. Bush for saying that the United States is not at war with Islam.[7]

Hirsi Ali's statements have been widely discredited, but she continues to be beloved by the media, educators, and the general public.

Another, related, Islamophobia-industry strategy accuses all Muslims and Islam itself of incompatibility with our Constitution. Constitutional law professor Jared Goldstein maintains that nativists who believe "being American means being white and Christian" are often not recognized as nativists, because they couch their views in the language of "constitutional nationalism."[8] As Goldstein explains:

In recent years, those on the far-right have frequently justified anti-Muslim bigotry with the claim that Islam is incompatible with the Constitution.[9]

Historically, Congress used this tactic to exclude various immigrant groups, such as Jews, Italians, Chinese, and Catholics.[10] After federal legislation terminated this tactic—not until 1965!—white nationalists continued to promote it.

David Yerushalmi, Frank Gaffney, and others within the Islamophobia industry have championed this view to incite prejudice and shariah hysteria. Consequently, research in 2018 found that two in five Americans believe that Islam "is incompatible with US values."[11] And although larger percentages of Republicans and far-right political groups harbor negative views of Muslims, fully 32 percent of Democrats favor targeting Muslims at airports and 12 percent of Democrats would deny Muslim citizens the right to vote.[12]

The ultimate effect of the Islamophobia industry (in common with propagandistic attacks on other minority groups) is violence. Anders Breivik, the Norwegian terrorist who killed 77 people and injured 240 in

2011, left a manifesto in which he himself attributed his deadly inspiration—to combat the "Islamization of Europe"—to several anti-Muslim propagandists of the American and European Islamophobia networks, including Robert Spencer, Pamela Geller, Geert Wilders, and Bat Ye'or. In 2019, the Australian-born suspected killer of over fifty worshippers at two New Zealand mosques left a manifesto praising Donald Trump and Anders Breivik.[13] Thousands of Muslim individuals, organizations, and mosques have been the object of hate incidents since 2001, including arson, assault, and murder. Terrorism expert Marc Sageman remarks that the Islamophobes "and their writings are the infrastructure from which Breivik emerged. . . . This rhetoric is not cost-free."[14]

THE HISTORICAL FRAMEWORK

Instead of marginalizing the Islamophobia industry and fact-checking its propaganda, we in the West have offered platforms to its members, allowed them to profit from demonizing Muslims, and hired them to consult for the government. Why are we so eager to believe the worst of Muslims that we enthusiastically pay unqualified, uncredentialed fearmongers to vilify almost a quarter of the world's population?

It's not because of the oft-repeated canard that "Muslims are more violent than others." Political scientist Steven Fish uses empirical statistical data to examine some of the tropes that our public discourse repeatedly recycles. He reasons that if Muslims were more prone to violence than others, then homicide rates in Muslim populations would be higher. Right? He finds, instead, that homicide rates in Muslim populations are *lower*:

> Homicide is markedly rarer in Muslim societies than non-Muslim societies. The proportion of the country that is made up of Muslims is a good predictor of the murder rate, with a larger Muslim population associated with less homicide.[15]

Furthermore, between 1970 and 2012, only 2.5 percent of terrorist attacks on US soil were perpetrated by Muslims.[16] Historian Juan Cole, examining twentieth-century deaths from war and political violence, estimates that Christians of European heritage killed over fifty times as many people as Muslims killed (102 million to 2 million).[17]

Al-Qaeda and ISIS didn't create the negative stereotypes of Islam. Although they and groups like them validate Islamophobic narratives, all major religions include groups that commit violence without being stereotyped the way Muslims are stereotyped. For example, Latin America has been plagued with decades of violence—gang and drug warfare,[18] terrorists,[19] women sold into sex slavery,[20] violence against women and severe gender inequality[21]—and yet none of that is characterized as "Christian violence" (nor should it be) the way violence in the Middle East is characterized as "Muslim"—or worse, "Islamic"—violence.

If anti-Muslim stereotypes predate 9/11 and Muslims are not more violent than others, then where do these stereotypes come from? In large part, they come from 1,400 years of the West viewing Islam as the enemy. The Islamophobia industry is simply the newest vehicle in a Western Christian historical tradition that has perceived Muslims through the lens of fear and hostility.

This tradition comes from Christian European texts over the centuries. But, according to historian Michael Penn, in the first several centuries of Islam, up to *half* the Christians in the world lived in Muslim-ruled lands, not Europe. Their everyday interactions with Muslims (which belie the "clash of civilizations" trope) were recorded in Syriac, which few Western scholars understood. Therefore, our modern Western views of Islam and Muslims come from European texts, not Syriac texts—that is, from people who didn't interact with Muslims and met them primarily on battlefields.[22]

For over a millennium, apocryphal tales of Islam and Muslims have infused Western art, culture, literature, and historical narratives. Christian Europeans from the seventh century onward knew little of what Muslims believed, but they understandably viewed Islam as a false religion (how could they not, as Christians?) and Muhammad as Satan, the anti-Christ, a false prophet, a lecher, an epileptic, and all manner of other monsters.

Muslims may have disagreed and clashed militarily with Jews and Christians, but they didn't harbor the same sorts of tall tales about them, because they knew Jews and Christians personally. And they regarded the Judeo-Christian tradition as part of Islam. Muhammad had Christian relatives. There's evidence that Muhammad considered himself allied with Christian Byzantine Rome.[23] The Qur'an considers Jews, Christians, and other monotheists to be believers, not "infidels."

By the year 1100, an entire body of continually expanding mythology about Islam and Muhammad had developed in Europe, to which successive generations added new tall tales to the old tall tales. It was a closed system of European myths unaffected by facts; even eyewitness accounts from visitors to Muslim lands failed to penetrate it. Norman Daniel writes:

> It was with very great reluctance that what Muslims said Muslims believed was accepted as what they did believe. There was a Christian picture in which the details (even under the pressure of facts) were abandoned as little as possible, and in which the general outline was never abandoned.[24]

The image of the feared and loathsome Muslim mutated over the centuries, from "Saracens" in the earlier centuries to monsters of the Middle Ages (often depicted with blue, black, or purple skin![25]) to mainly Ottomans or Turks in the Renaissance, to the Victorian savages of Orientalism and colonialism, fanatics and barbarians whom the white man had an obligation to colonize and civilize. Some Europeans treated Muhammad and his teachings fairly, even admired them, but these were comparatively few. As political power shifted from the Ottomans to the Europeans, fear decreased and contempt replaced it, but the negative stereotypes never abated.

These tropes survive largely intact, sometimes verbatim, into the present day. Modern stereotypes of Muslims, as religion professor Sophia Rose Arjana writes, are simply

> old anxieties that lie within a multiplicity of times and spaces on the pages of manuscripts and canvases of paintings, in works of great drama, poetry, and fiction, within travel diaries and government documents, and on the screens of movie theaters.[26]

In other words, these "old anxieties" still infuse all aspects of our culture, including the secondary-school textbooks that educate us, the literature we still read, the narratives from which we learn world history, the artwork we study, the internet we find indispensable, the news media that conditions us and has been conditioned itself by our cultural biases, and the television and movies that overwhelmingly portray the only good Muslims as dead Muslims. Or, at best, "secular" Muslims.

In America, we inherited this historical and cultural tradition—this *framework*—from the British, though it was mostly dormant until the Iranian Revolution of 1979. Then, almost overnight, it resurged, and negative current events began to be fitted into that same historical tradition, framed as confirmation that Muslims were to be feared and loathed and not like us. Around the same time, the Soviet Union and Communism as enemies had declined as threats. This left an opening for a new villain. Or rather, a resuscitated villain, the Islamic one.

WHY YOU SHOULD CARE

Islamophobia and its subtopics have each had entire books written about them and cannot all be discussed here. But I do urge you to read further on these topics, because we all need to care about them, whether we're Muslim or not.

Islamophobia lacerates the social fabric of our country, and that damages us all. It corrodes the wisdom of our domestic policy, premising it on fear rather than facts and influencing the treatment of those living within US borders. Islamophobia divides Americans. It hampers our ability to intelligently evaluate the rhetoric of politicians.

Islamophobia undermines the wisdom of our foreign policy, as well, increasing the appeal and likelihood of warfare. After all, if Islam is evil and Muslims are innately violent, then why address their grievances or attempt diplomatic solutions? Just bomb their countries.

This violence in turn leads to increasing anger and resentment on the part of Muslims, the dismissal of their legitimate grievances, and the creation of more terrorists. Islamophobic rhetoric—such as the shariah hysteria—distracts and blinds us to the actual reasons why and venues where extremism might burgeon next.[27] Not least, Islamophobia incessantly broadcast, through news media and film, to 1.7 billion or so Muslims worldwide provides the fuel that extremists burn to recruit potential terrorists.

Thus, Islamophobia endangers us all, and we all have a responsibility to combat it. Individually, or via groups that fight Islamophobia, we must all hold accountable those who peddle it. We must stop electing politicians who hawk it. We must refuse to provide platforms to the Islamophobes who seek to spread it: if paying Nazis to "educate" people about Jews would be (quite rightly) unthinkable, then paying anti-Muslim propagandists to "educate" people about Muslims should be unthinkable too.

In sum, we can move from an "us vs. them" framework to an "all-of-us" framework. What's best for *all* of us?

The world is too small for any other alternative.

CONCLUSION

THE SHARIAH-BASED SYSTEM OF LAW AND ETHICS would never have survived for over a millennium had it not been equitable. Despite its disruption and dismantling, new generations of scholars, men and women, are engaging in the study of the Islamic legal tradition, modernizing, arguing, disputing, and creating new solutions to religious issues—just as Islamic scholars have done for centuries. Modernization cannot transpire overnight, though; nor can it proceed easily without education or in repressive societies.

I perceive cause for optimism. Since the early 1990s, at least twenty-three Muslim-majority countries have become more democratic.[1] This number was published before the Arab uprisings of 2010, which saw democracy established in Tunisia and briefly in Egypt. Had the US supported the newly birthed democratic government in Egypt, rather than the Egyptian military, the uprisings may well have resulted in a lasting democratic government there too. In April 2019, after weeks of peaceful protests, Algerians ousted their dictator of twenty years. Senegal is 95 percent Muslim and has been a beacon of democracy since independence. And Indonesia, with the largest Muslim population on earth, transitioned to democracy relatively peacefully.

As discussed, studies indicate that Muslims show no greater propensity toward a mixture of government and religion than other religious groups. Nevertheless, Islamists succeed because they typically present the most viable alternatives to dictatorship. As Noah Feldman writes:

> For many Muslims today, living in corrupt autocracies, the call for shariah is not a call for sexism, obscurantism, or savage punishment but for an Islamic version of what the West considers its most prized principle of political justice: the rule of law.[2]

How grateful I am that my parents emigrated from India to the US, a country with a strong rule of law! Those Muslims overseas fighting for freedom and the rule of law deserve the chance to figure it all out for themselves, just as our Founders did. Whether the rule of law is based on shariah or something else should be their decision.

Fiqh tells us that every rule in Islam must further the protection of life, family, intellect, religion, human dignity, and resources. The Prophet Muhammad said, "None of you has faith until he loves for his brother or neighbor what he loves for himself." The Qur'an authorizes Muslims to defend churches and synagogues, states clearly that Muslims should not be even discourteous to people of other faiths, forbids forced conversion, and tells us that God made us into different races and tribes so that we can learn from one another. This is shariah, in all these words. Now, more than ever, in our world of internet-magnified hatred and tribalism and racism, these words are still well worth following.

I grew up in Southern California, watching *Star Trek* reruns, crushing on Captain Kirk, learning about aliens. Lacking Muslim friends in my daily life, I myself often felt like the alien species with whom the crew warily made "first contact." When I write, I periodically detect *Star Trek* lessons sidling into my consciousness, perhaps because the overarching message of that iconic show was that aliens were worthy of communication, compassion, and friendship—and the unknown was to be embraced and accepted, not feared and evaded. Naïve though it may sound, I believe that's a lesson that still commands great power. Muslims may seem like aliens, and shariah may seem like a language impossible to understand, but we can be embraced and accepted. We are American, after all. And French and German and Canadian and everything else.

Mr. Spock once remarked, "One man cannot summon the future."

"But," replied Captain Kirk, my hero, "one man can change the present!"

Thank you for helping to change the present.

ACKNOWLEDGMENTS

IN THE INTEREST of keeping transliteration accurate but simple, I've dispensed with some of the markings on Arabic words. I've also opted for English over Arabic whenever possible. *Shariah* would more accurately be transliterated as *shari'ah* or *sharī'a*, but we left out the apostrophe (which represents the Arabic letter, *'ayn*) to make the book more reader-friendly.

I offer my heartfelt thanks to the following people who helped me realize this book project: my wonderful team at Beacon and especially my editor, Amy Caldwell, for her vision and compassion; Sally Falkenhagen for closely reading the entire manuscript (more than once!) and sending me her excellent, thoughtful, and practical suggestions; Eve La Puma and Lina Karamali, for their enthusiastic research assistance; Asifa Quraishi-Landes, Greg Surman, and Irwin Keller for generously reading sections and offering valuable comments; Karen Connolly and Shehnaz Khan for talking over legal issues; Munir Jiwa, friend, mentor, and unfailing source of support; and the many Islamic scholars who have helped and supported me in my work.

Above all, the love and boundless support of my husband empowers the work I do. This book is for him, as are they all.

NOTES

3. In this book, I have consulted several works for translations (called "interpretations") of Qur'anic verses: Asma Afsaruddin, *The First Muslims: History and Memory* (Oxford, UK: Oneworld, 2008); Ahmed Ali, *Al-Qur'an: A Contemporary Translation* (Princeton, NJ: Princeton University Press, 1993); A. J. Arberry, *The Koran Interpreted* (New York: Touchstone, 1996); and Muhammad Asad, *The Message of the Qur'an* (Gibraltar: Dar al-Andalus, 1980).

CHAPTER ONE: SHARIAH IN A NUTSHELL

1. Noah Feldman, "Why Shariah?," *New York Times Magazine*, Mar. 16, 2008.

2. Khaled Abou El Fadl, *Reasoning with God: Reclaiming Shari'ah in the Modern Age* (Lanham, MD: Rowman & Littlefield, 2014), xxxii.

3. Jonathan A. C. Brown, *Misquoting Muhammad: The Challenge and Choices of Interpreting the Prophet's Legacy* (London: Oneworld, 2014), 32.

4. Jonathan A. C. Brown, "The Issue of Apostasy in Islam," Yaqeen Institute for Islamic Research, July 5, 2017, yaqeeninstitute.org.

CHAPTER TWO: MUHAMMAD AND THE BIRTH OF ISLAM

1. Daryl Johnson, "Hate in God's Name," Southern Poverty Law Center, Sept. 25, 2017, splcenter.org.

2. It's hard to estimate exactly how many Muslims there are in the US. When I wrote my first book, estimates were as high as 3 percent but have since been reduced. Other population estimates are from the CIA World Factbook at https://www.cia.gov/library/publications/the-world-factbook/.

3. Jonathan A. C. Brown, *Muhammad: A Very Short Introduction* (New York: Oxford University Press, 2011), 96. Aside from Brown's *Muhammad* as a source for the life of Muhammad as set forth herein, additional sources include Asma Afsaruddin, *The First Muslims: History and Memory* (Oxford, UK: Oneworld, 2008); Juan Cole, *Muhammad: Prophet of Peace Amid the Clash of Empires* (New York: Nation Books, 2018); Hugh Kennedy, *The Prophet and the Age of the Caliphates: The Islamic Near East From the Sixth to the Eleventh Century* (New York: Longman, 1991); and Omid Safi, *Memories of Muhammad: Why the Prophet Matters* (New York: HarperOne, 2010).

4. Instead of *Anno Domini*, or "the Year of the Lord," I'm using the more neutral *Common Era* (CE).

5. For a survey of this notion of woman as evil, see Alvin J. Schmidt, *Veiled and Silenced: How Culture Shaped Sexist Theology* (Macon, GA: Mercer University Press, 1989), ch. 3.

6. For a full, readable text of the sermon, see, e.g., Imam Abdullah Antepli, "The Last Sermon of the Prophet Muhammad," *Huffington Post*, Feb. 3, 2012.

7. Norman Daniel, *Islam and the West: The Making of an Image* (1960; Oxford, UK: Oneworld, 2009), 314.

8. Cole, *Muhammad*, 2–3, 97.

9. See, generally, Cole, *Muhammad*.

10. See, e.g., John L. Esposito and Natana J. DeLong-Bas, *Shariah: What Everyone Needs to Know* (New York: Oxford University Press, 2018), 133.

11. Esposito and DeLong-Bas, *Shariah*, 133.

12. See Cole, *Muhammad*, 137–43.

13. See Cole, *Muhammad*, 145.

14. F. E. Peters, *A Reader on Classical Islam* (Princeton, NJ: Princeton University Press, 1994), 261.

CHAPTER THREE: THE QUR'AN

1. Akbar S. Ahmed, *Islam Today: A Short Introduction to the Muslim World* (London: I.B. Tauris, 2001), 28-29.

2. A.J. Arberry, *The Koran Interpreted* (New York: Touchstone, 1996), 12-16.

3. Occasionally, we amend the Constitution, too, but we can't amend the Qur'an.

4. Fazlur Rahman, *Major Themes of the Qur'an* (1980; Minneapolis: Bibliotheca Islamica, 1989), 48, discussing Surah 24, verse 33, and noting that some Muslim scholars interpreted this as a "recommendation" and not a "command."

5. Arun Kundnani's keynote lecture on Islamophobia at Rutgers Law School, Sept. 10, 2018, https://youtube.com/watch?v=eDnyyng_H14.

6. See, generally, Rahman, *Major Themes of the Qur'an*.

7. See, e.g., Madani Azzeddine, Ertan Düzgüneş, Valentina-Mariana Manoiu, "Environmental Education in the Holy Quran," conference paper, Oct. 2016, ResearchGate, https://researchgate.net/publication/309428496_ENVIRONMENTAL_EDUCATION_IN_THE_HOLY_QURAN.

8. See Basil H. Aboul-Enein, "'The Earth Is Your Mosque': Narrative Perspectives of Environmental Health and Education in the Holy Quran," *Journal of Environmental Studies and Sciences* 8 (2018): 22–31.

CHAPTER FOUR: THE SUNNA

1. Jonathan A. C. Brown, *Hadith: Muhammad's Legacy in the Medieval and Modern World* (Oxford, UK: Oneworld, 2009), 15–24.

2. Stuart A. P. Murray, *The Library: An Illustrated History* (New York: Skyhorse Publishing, 2009), 50–51, 56. See, also, Anver M. Emon and Rumee Ahmed, eds., *The Oxford Handbook of Islamic Law* (Oxford, UK: Oxford University Press, 2018), 415.

3. Brown, *Hadith*, 23.

4. See, e.g., Brown, *Hadith*, 69–75.

5. Wael B. Hallaq, *Shari'a: Theory, Practice, Transformations* (Cambridge, UK: Cambridge University Press, 2009), 39–40.

6. Rik Smits, "Lefties Aren't Special After All," *New York Times*, Apr. 13, 2012.

7. Sebastian Murdock, "Teacher Allegedly Suggests Kid Is 'Evil, Sinister' for Being Left-Handed," *Huffington Post*, Sept. 22, 2015.

8. See, e.g., website of the Landover Baptist Church, http://landoverbaptist.net.

9. Simon Singh, *The Code Book: The Science of Secrecy from Ancient Egypt to Quantum Cryptography* (New York: Anchor, 2000), 14–19.

10. Singh, *The Code Book*, 14–19.

11. Ibrahim al-Kadi, "Origins of Cryptology: The Arab Contributions," in *Selections from Cryptologia*, ed. C.A. Deavours (London: Artech House, 1998), 94.

12. See, generally, Brown, *Hadith*, also 77–95.

13. Brown, *Hadith*, 78–79.

14. Brown, *Hadith*, 79–92.

15. Brown, *Hadith*, 92–96.

16. Brown, *Misquoting Muhammad*, 225.

17. Brown, *Hadith*, 219, 235.

18. Abou El Fadl, *Reasoning with God*, xxxv.

19. Amina Wadud, *Qur'an and Woman: Rereading the Sacred Text from a Woman's Perspective* (New York: Oxford University Press, 1999), 39–40.

20. Brown, *Misquoting Muhammad*, 138.

21. Brown, *Misquoting Muhammad*, 138.

22. Asghar Ali Engineer, *The Rights of Women in Islam*, 3rd. ed. (1992; New Delhi: Sterling Publishers, 2008), 91–92.

23. Engineer, *The Rights of Women in Islam*, 91–92.

24. Fatima Mernissi, *The Forgotten Queens of Islam*, trans. Mary Jo Lakeland (France: Polity Press, 1993), 89–90, 115–16.

CHAPTER FIVE: SUNNI, SHI'A, AND OTHERS

1. I'm talking about extremists such as the Salafis and criminal extremists such as ISIS. See Mustafa Akyol, "We Need More Sushi Muslims," *Hurriyet Daily News*, Jan. 9, 2016, http://hurriyetdailynews.com/opinion/mustafa-akyol/we-need-more-sushi-muslims-93619.

2. See, e.g., Esposito and DeLong-Bas, *Shariah*, 71.

3. John L. Esposito, *Islam: The Straight Path* (New York: Oxford University Press, 1988), 47.

4. Khaled Abou El Fadl, *The Great Theft: Wrestling Islam from the Extremists* (New York: HarperCollins, 2005), 53.

5. Abou El Fadl, *The Great Theft*, 47, 74.

6. Abou El Fadl, *The Great Theft*, 48.

7. Abou El Fadl, *The Great Theft*, 52.

8. Abou El Fadl, *The Great Theft*, 60–61.

9. In the 1950s the Eisenhower administration sought to fight communism by bolstering King Saud into a globally recognized Islamic leader, though most Muslims thought the Saudis to be bafflingly extremist. See, e.g., Zack Beauchamp, "Beyond Oil: The US-Saudi Alliance, Explained," *Vox*, Jan. 6, 2016, www.vox.com/2016/1/6/10719728/us-saudi-arabia-allies.

10. Abou El Fadl, *The Great Theft*, 75.

11. Carl W. Ernst, *Following Muhammad: Rethinking Islam in the Contemporary World* (Chapel Hill: University of North Carolina Press, 2003), 166.

12. Carl W. Ernst, *Sufism: An Introduction to the Mystical Tradition of Islam* (1997; Boston: Shambhala, 2011), 5–16.

13. Khaled Beydoun, "Antebellum Islam," *Howard Law Journal* 58 (2014): 141. See, also, Sylviane A. Diouf, *Servants of Allah: African Muslims Enslaved in the Americas* (1998; New York: New York University Press, 2013); and Jonathan Curiel, "Muslim Roots of the Blues: The Music of Famous American Blues Singers Reaches Back through the South to the Culture of West Africa," *San Francisco Chronicle*, Aug. 15, 2004.

14. Kambiz GhaneaBassiri, *A History of Islam in America: From the New World to the New World Order* (New York: Cambridge University Press, 2010), 223–27.

15. Clifton E. Marsh, *The Lost-Found Nation of Islam in America* (Lanham, MD: Scarecrow Press, 2000), 61.

16. GhaneaBassiri, *A History of Islam in America*, 284–89.

CHAPTER SIX: WHAT SHARIAH IS AND HOW IT WORKS

1. Abdullahi An-Na'im, *Toward an Islamic Reformation: Civil Liberties, Human Rights, and International Law* (Syracuse, NY: Syracuse University Press, 1990), 20.

2. Wael B. Hallaq, *An Introduction to Islamic Law* (New York: Cambridge University Press, 2009), 9.

3. Hallaq, *Shari'a*, 104.

4. Hallaq, *Shari'a*, 104. See, also, Abou El Fadl, *Reasoning with God*, xlii.

5. See, generally, Mohammad Akram Nadwi, *Al-Muḥddithāt: The Women Scholars in Islam* (Oxford, UK: Interface Publications, 2009).

6. Hallaq, *An Introduction to Islamic Law*, 22.

7. Brown, *Misquoting Muhammad*, 35.

8. Hallaq, *An Introduction to Islamic Law*, 23.

9. Hallaq, *An Introduction to Islamic Law*, 23; Hallaq, *Shari'a*, 101.

10. Brown, *Misquoting Muhammad*, 41.

11. Abou El Fadl, *Reasoning with God*, xxxvii.

12. Abou El Fadl, *Reasoning with God*, xxxiv.

13. Brown, *Misquoting Muhammad*, 27.

14. Hallaq, *An Introduction to Islamic Law*, 26; Hallaq, *Shari'a*, 104.

15. Chibli Mallat, *Introduction to Middle Eastern Law* (New York: Oxford University Press, 2007), 104–5.

16. Mallat, *Introduction to Middle Eastern Law*, 104–5.

17. Sachiko Murata and William C. Chittick, *The Vision of Islam* (St. Paul, MN: Paragon House, 1994), 23–25.

18. Hallaq, *An Introduction to Islamic Law*, 23; Hallaq, *Shari'a*, 162.

19. Hallaq, *An Introduction to Islamic Law*, 23; Hallaq, *Shari'a*, 162.

20. Abou El Fadl, *Reasoning with God*, 196.

21. Anver M. Emon, "Conceiving Islamic Law in a Pluralistic Society," *Singapore Journal of Legal Studies* (2006): 335.

22. Hallaq, *An Introduction to Islamic Law*, 27.

23. Abou El Fadl, *Reasoning with God*, xxxix.

24. Mallat, *Introduction to Middle Eastern Law*, 41.

25. Hallaq, *An Introduction to Islamic Law*, 27.

26. Brown, *Misquoting Muhammad*, 50.

27. Nadwi, *Al-Muḥddithāt*, 8.

28. Nadwi, *Al-Muḥddithāt*, 9.

29. Nadwi, *Al-Muḥddithāt*, 43; Carla Powers, "A Secret History," *New York Times Magazine*, Feb. 25, 2007.

30. Nadwi, *Al-Muḥddithāt*, 81, 150, 179.

31. Powers, "A Secret History."

32. "Amrah bint Abd Al-Rahman," Women's Islamic Initiative in Spirituality & Equality, http://wisemuslimwomen.org/muslim-woman/umrah-bint-abdur-rahman-7, accessed Aug. 23, 2019. See, also, Nadwi, *Al-Muḥddithāt*, 7.

33. Khaled Abou El Fadl, *And God Knows the Soldiers: The Authoritative and Authoritarian in Islamic Discourses* (Lanham, MD: University Press of America, 2001), 137.

34. For example, implicit bias tests show that 80 percent of women "display the automatic gender stereotype of *male = work* and *female = family*." This includes women who have never been without careers in their adult lives! See Mahzarin R. Banaji and Anthony G. Greenwald, *Blindspot: Hidden Biases of Good People* (New York: Delacorte, 2013), 115.

35. Abou El Fadl, *Reasoning with God*, xxxiii.

36. Hallaq, *An Introduction to Islamic Law*, 10.

37. Hallaq, *An Introduction to Islamic Law*, 12.

38. Hallaq, *An Introduction to Islamic Law*, 12.

39. Brown, *Misquoting Muhammad*, 24.

40. Hallaq, *An Introduction to Islamic Law*, 73.

41. Hallaq, *Shari'a*, 51.

42. Hallaq, *Shari'a*, 130.

43. Joseph Schacht, *An Introduction to Islamic Law* (1964; Oxford, UK: Clarendon Press, 1991), 188.

44. Nadia Sonneveld and Monika Lindbekk, eds., *Women Judges in the Muslim World: A Comparative Study of Discourse and Practice* (Leiden: Brill, 2017), 155.

45. Mernissi, *The Forgotten Queens of Islam*, 42–43; Wiebke Walther, *Women in Islam: From Medieval to Modern Times* (1981; Princeton, NJ: Markus Wiener, 2006), 123.

46. Engineer, *The Rights of Women in Islam*, 96.

47. Hallaq, *Shari'a*, 162–66.

48. Hallaq, *Shari'a*, 178.

49. Hallaq, *Shari'a*, 162–64.

50. John A. Makdisi, "The Islamic Origins of the Common Law," *North Carolina Law Review* 77 (1999): 1718–27.

51. Makdisi, "The Islamic Origins of the Common Law," 1726.

52. Makdisi, "The Islamic Origins of the Common Law," 1727.

53. Makdisi, "The Islamic Origins of the Common Law," 1729.

54. See, generally, Makdisi, "The Islamic Origins of the Common Law."

55. Makdisi, "The Islamic Origins of the Common Law," 1731.

56. Manlio Lima, "English Common Law and Islam: A Sicilian Connection," *Best of Sicily Magazine*, 2008, http://bestofsicily.com/mag/art283.htm.

57. Lima, "English Common Law and Islam."

58. Emon, "Conceiving Islamic Law in a Pluralistic Society."

59. Over two hundred scholars met in Jordan and reaffirmed the legitimacy of these schools and their followers in the Amman Message (see ammanmessage.com). See, also, Esposito and DeLong-Bas, *Shariah*, 50, and Abou El Fadl, *Reasoning with God*, xliii.

60. Hallaq, *An Introduction to Islamic Law*, 47.

61. Hallaq, *An Introduction to Islamic Law*, 48–49.

62. Hallaq, *An Introduction to Islamic Law*, 48–49.

63. Hallaq, *An Introduction to Islamic Law*, 50–54.

64. Hallaq, *An Introduction to Islamic Law*, 68.

65. Hallaq, *An Introduction to Islamic Law*, 69.

66. Reza Aslan, *No god but God: The Origins, Evolution, and Future of Islam* (New York: Random House, 2005), 143.

67. Hallaq, *Shari'a*, 70.

68. Hallaq, *Shari'a*, 70.
69. Noah Feldman, *The Fall and Rise of the Islamic State* (Princeton, NJ: Princeton University Press, 2008), 29.
70. Abou El Fadl, *Reasoning with God*, xlii-xliii.
71. Feldman, *The Fall and Rise of the Islamic State*, 31.
72. Feldman, *The Fall and Rise of the Islamic State*, 32.
73. Feldman, *The Fall and Rise of the Islamic State*, 35.
74. Feldman, *The Fall and Rise of the Islamic State*, 40.
75. Linda T. Darling, *A History of Social Justice and Political Power in the Middle East: The Circle of Justice from Mesopotamia to Globalization* (New York: Routledge, 2013), 2.
76. Hallaq, *Shari'a*, 199–200.
77. Darling, *A History of Social Justice and Political Power in the Middle East*, 211–12.

CHAPTER SEVEN: RELIGIOUS MINORITIES WITHIN THE SHARIAH SYSTEM

1. Anver M. Emon, *Religious Pluralism and Islamic Law: Dhimmis and Others in the Empire of Law* (Oxford, UK: Oxford University Press, 2012), 223.
2. Michael Bonner, *Jihad in Islamic History: Doctrines and Practice* (Princeton, NJ: Princeton University Press, 2008), 89–90.
3. Cole, *Muhammad*, 206.
4. Gerald Hawting, *The First Dynasty of Islam: The Umayyad Caliphate AD 661–750* (1986; London: Routledge, 2000), 4.
5. Ernst, *Following Muhammad*, 119–20.
6. Ernst, *Following Muhammad*, 120.
7. Arthur Goldschmidt Jr., *A Concise History of the Middle East*, 7th ed. (1979; Boulder, CO: Westview Press, 2002), 54.
8. Al-Kadi, "Origins of Cryptology," 95.
9. Jane I. Smith, "Islam and Christendom," in *The Oxford History of Islam*, ed. John Esposito (Oxford, UK: Oxford University Press, 1999), 312–13.
10. Smith, "Islam and Christendom," 313.
11. John L. Esposito, *The Islamic Threat: Myth or Reality?* (New York: Oxford University Press, 1992), 40–41.
12. Smith, "Islam and Christendom," 312.
13. See Khaled Abou El Fadl, "Terrorism Is at Odds with Islamic Tradition," *Los Angeles Times*, Oct. 11, 2001; An-Na'im, *Toward an Islamic Reformation*, 149–50, 156; and Surah 59, verses 7–9.
14. 'Abd Allah bin al-Sheikh Mahfuz bin Bayyah, *The Culture of Terrorism: Tenets and Treatments*, trans. Hamza Yusuf (Berkeley, CA: Sandala, 2014), 16.
15. Khaled Abou El Fadl, "The Place of Tolerance in Islam," *Boston Review*, Dec. 1, 2001.
16. See Afsaruddin, *The First Muslims*, 110–15; see, also, Asma Afsaruddin, *Striving in the Path of God: Jihad and Martyrdom in Islamic Thought* (New York: Oxford University Press, 2013).
17. Afsaruddin, *The First Muslims*, 110–15.
18. Afsaruddin, *The First Muslims*, 110–15.
19. Ernst, *Following Muhammad*, 119–120.
20. Khaled A. Beydoun, "Convert or Die: Ethnic Cleansing in CAR," *Al Jazeera*, Aug. 18, 2015, https://aljazeera.com/indepth/opinion/2015/08/convert-die-ethnic-cleansing-car-150811113005080.html.
21. "'No Other Conclusion,' Ethnic Cleansing of Rohingyas in Myanmar Continues—Senior UN Rights Official," *UN News*, Mar. 6, 2018, https://news.un.org/en/story/2018/03/1004232.
22. Emran Qureshi and Michael A. Sells, eds., *The New Crusades: Constructing the Muslim Enemy* (New York: Columbia University Press, 2003), 9.
23. Qureshi and Sells, *The New Crusades*, 9.
24. Keith Doubt, "Scapegoating and the Simulation of Mechanical Solidarity in Former Yugoslavia: 'Ethnic Cleansing' and the Serbian Orthodox Church," *Humanity & Society* 31, no. 1 (2007): 65–82.
25. Campana Aurélie, "The Massive Deportation of the Chechen People: How and Why Chechens Were Deported," *Online Encyclopedia of Mass Violence* (Sciences Po Paris, Nov. 5,

2007), https://sciencespo.fr/mass-violence-war-massacre-resistance/en/document/massive
-deportation-chechen-people-how-and-why-chechens-were-deported, accessed Apr. 23, 2018.

26. Kamal Mitra Chenoy, Vishnu Nagar, Prasenjit Bose, and Vijoo Krishnan, *Ethnic Cleansing in Ahmedabad: A Preliminary Report* (South Asia Citizens Web, 2002), http://sacw
.net/Gujarat2002/sahmatreport032002.html. See, also, Victor Mallet, "Hindus Convicted over 2002 Muslim Massacre," *Financial Times*, June 2, 2016.

27. "China's Re-Education Camps: An Affront to Religious Freedom," Muslim Public Affairs Council, Aug. 16, 2018, mpac.org. As of Sept. 2018, over a million Muslims have been forced into "reeducation camps," where they are "retrained," forced to drink alcohol and eat pork, and even tortured. See, also, Chris Buckley, "China Is Detaining Muslims in Vast Numbers. The Goal: Transformation," *New York Times*, Sept. 8, 2018.

28. Emon, *Religious Pluralism and Islamic Law*, 59–62.

29. Emon, *Religious Pluralism and Islamic Law*, 78.

30. Emon, *Religious Pluralism and Islamic Law*, 89–90.

31. Cole, *Muhammad*, 303–4.

32. Cole, *Muhammad*, 208.

33. Emon, *Religious Pluralism and Islamic Law*, 67–68; Afsaruddin, *The First Muslims*, 181.

34. Afsaruddin, *The First Muslims*, 181.

35. Afsaruddin, *The First Muslims*, 181.

36. Emon, *Religious Pluralism and Islamic Law*, 71, n. 105.

37. Cole, *Muhammad*, 208.

38. Afsaruddin, *The First Muslims*, 181.

39. Afsaruddin, *The First Muslims*, 43.

40. Afsaruddin, *The First Muslims*, 43.

41. Bonner, *Jihad in Islamic History*, 90.

42. Bonner, *Jihad in Islamic History*, 91.

43. Bonner, *Jihad in Islamic History*, 91.

44. Emon, *Religious Pluralism and Islamic Law*, 223.

45. Michael Goodich, ed., *Other Middle Ages: Witnesses at the Margins of Medieval Society* (Philadelphia: University of Pennsylvania Press, 1998), 8.

46. Maria Rosa Menocal, *Ornament of the World: How Muslims, Jews, and Christians Created a Culture of Tolerance in Medieval Spain* (New York: Little, Brown, 2002), 244–52.

47. Huston Smith, *The World's Religions* (New York: HarperSanFrancisco, 1991), 256.

48. Lauren Benton, *Law and Colonial Cultures: Legal Regimes in World History, 1400–1900* (New York: Cambridge University Press, 2002), 117.

49. Stephanie Nicole Hassell, "Slavery, Conversion, and Religious Geography in Portuguese India in the Sixteenth and Seventeenth Centuries," PhD diss., Stanford University, 2014, 69, 134.

50. Maria Jesús Rubiera Mata and Mikel de Epalza, "Al-Andalus: Between Myth and History," *History and Anthropology* 18, no. 3 (Sept. 2007): 269–73.

51. Emon, *Religious Pluralism and Islamic Law*, 73n113, citing Michael G. Morony, *Iraq after the Muslim Conquest* (Princeton, NJ: Princeton University Press, 1984), 306, 317–20.

52. K. Theodore Hoppen, *The Mid-Victorian Generation: 1846–1886* (Oxford: Clarendon Press, 1998), 442–47. See, also, Patrick Allitt, *Victorian Britain, Part I*, course guidebook and lecture recording (Teaching Company, 2002), 34.

53. See "The 24th Amendment," history.house.gov.

54. See, generally, Emon, *Religious Pluralism and Islamic Law*.

55. Emon, *Religious Pluralism and Islamic Law*, 3.

56. C. J. Werleman, "Slovakia's Deplorable Move to Criminalise Islam," *New Arab*, Sept. 18, 2018, alaraby.co.uk. Slovakia has passed a law decreeing that a religion must have fifty thousand followers to be deemed a state religion; as only about five thousand Muslims live in Slovakia, this bill prevents them from building a single mosque, restricts basic rights of freedom of expression, and prevents them from engaging religious leaders or holding religious ceremonies (such as marriages). The bill also prevents schools from teaching students about Islam, which means Slovakian students will grow up ignorant of Slovakia's Muslim history. The proponents of the bill have "publicly stated it's intended to outlaw all aspects of Muslim life in the country forever."

57. "Muslims in U.S. Face Challenges Erecting Mosques," *All Things Considered*, NPR, July 15, 2010, https://npr.org/templates/story/story.php?storyId=128545975.

58. "Austria Proposes Headscarf Ban for Girls Under 10," *BBC News*, Apr. 4, 2018 (ban proposed as a "child protection law"), and "The Islamic Veil Across Europe," *BBC News*, Jan. 31, 2017 (noting that debates on this piece of scarf that women wear is associated with "religious freedom, female equality, secular traditions and even fears of terrorism").

59. Martha Nussbaum, *The New Religious Intolerance: Overcoming the Politics of Fear in an Anxious Age* (Cambridge, MA: Harvard University Press, 2012), 134.

60. Nick Cumming-Bruce and Steven Erlanger, "Swiss Ban Building of Minarets on Mosques," *New York Times*, Nov. 29, 2009.

61. Robert Barnes, "Supreme Court Stops Execution Because of Religious Concerns, a Contrast to Last Month," *Washington Post*, Mar. 28, 2019.

62. Maryam Saleh, "US Courts Have Been Treating Muslims Differently for a Very Long Time," *Intercept*, Dec. 7, 2017.

63. Glenn Greenwald, "The FBI's Anticipatory Prosecution of Muslims to Criminalize Speech," *Guardian*, Mar. 19, 2013.

64. Shirin Sinnar and Robert Weisberg, "A 'Terrorist' Reconsidered: Lodi Man's 2006 Conviction Was Injustice," *Mercury News*, July 17, 2014.

65. Carrie Johnson and Margo Williams, "'Guantanamo North': Inside Secretive US Prisons," *All Things Considered*, NPR, Mar. 3, 2011.

66. Rylee Sommers-Flanagan, "The Legal Story of Guantanamo North," *University of Pennsylvania Journal of Constitutional Law* 19 (2017): 1171.

67. Elsadig Elsheikh, Basima Sisemore, and Natalia Ramirez Lee, *Legalizing Othering: The United States of Islamophobia* (Berkeley, CA: Haas Institute for a Fair and Inclusive Society, 2017), 24.

68. See Institute for Social Policy and Understanding, *Equal Treatment? Measuring the Legal and Media Responses to Ideologically Motivated Violence in the United States* (Dearborn, MI: Institute for Social Policy and Understanding, Apr. 2018), https://www.ispu.org/public-policy/equal-treatment.

69. *Trump v. Hawaii*, No. 17–965, Decided June 26, 2018, Sotomayor, J., dissenting, p.2.

70. Dalia Mogahed and Youssef Chouhoud, *American Muslim Poll 2017: Muslims at the Crossroads* (Dearborn, MI: Institute for Social Policy and Understanding, 2017).

71. "The Marrakesh Declaration," January 25–27, 2016, marrakeshdeclaration.org.

CHAPTER EIGHT: SHATTERING A MILLENNIUM AND DISRUPTING A CIVILIZATION

1. See, e.g., Tamim Ansary, *Destiny Disrupted: A History of the World through Islamic Eyes* (New York: Public Affairs, 2009), 217–46.

2. Ansary, *Destiny Disrupted*, 217–46.

3. Ernst, *Following Muhammad*, 18.

4. Hallaq, *An Introduction to Islamic Law*, 103.

5. S.V. R. Nasr, "European Colonialism and the Emergence of Modern Muslim States," in Esposito, *The Oxford History of Islam*, 572.

6. Nasr, "European Colonialism and the Emergence of Modern Muslim States," 575.

7. Nasr, "European Colonialism and the Emergence of Modern Muslim States," 553.

8. Reinhardt Schulze, *A Modern History of the Islamic World* (London: I. B. Tauris, 2000), 85–86.

9. Albert Hourani, *A History of the Arab Peoples* (Cambridge, MA: Belknap Press of Harvard University Press, 1991), 270.

10. See Hallaq, *An Introduction to Islamic Law*, 85–114.

11. Leila Ahmed, *A Quiet Revolution: The Veil's Resurgence, from the Middle East to America* (New Haven, CT: Yale University Press, 2011), 29.

12. Cynthia Talbot, "Inscribing the Other, Inscribing the Self: Hindu-Muslim Identities in Pre-Colonial India," *Comparative Studies in Society and History* 37, no. 4 (1995): 693.

13. Shalom Goldman, "Evangelical Islamophobia as American as Apple Pie," *Religion Dispatches*, Dec. 1, 2010.

14. Esposito, *The Islamic Threat*, 49, quoting Maxime Rodinson, *Europe and the Mystique of Islam* (Seattle: University of Washington Press, 1987), 66.

15. Esposito, *The Islamic Threat*, 52.

16. Esposito, *The Islamic Threat*, 52.

17. Ernst, *Following Muhammad*, 20.

18. Edward Said, *Orientalism* (1978; New York: Penguin, 1991), 38.

19. Said, *Orientalism*, 38–39.

20. Ernst, *Following Muhammad*, 24.

21. Aslan, *No god But God*, 73

22. Nour Kteily and Emile Bruneau, "Backlash: the Politics and Real-World Consequences of Minority Group Dehumanization," *Personality and Social Psychology Bulletin* 43, no. 1 (2016).

23. Singh, *The Code Book*, 16.

24. Akbar S. Ahmad, *Islam Today* (London: I. B. Tauris, 1999), 62.

25. Jonathan Bloom and Sheila Blair, *Islam: A Thousand Years of Faith and Power* (New Haven, CT: Yale University Press, 2002), 127–28.

26. Al-Kadi, "Origins of Cryptology," 116.

27. Salim T. S. Al-Hassani, Elizabeth Woodcock, and Rabah Saoud, eds., *1001 Inventions: Muslim Heritage in Our World* (Manchester, UK: Foundation for Science, Technology, and Civilisation, 2007), 12.

28. Rebecca Mileham, ed., *1001 Inventions and Awesome Facts from Muslim Civilization* (Washington DC: National Geographic, 2012), 44.

29. Mileham, *1001 Inventions and Awesome Facts from Muslim Civilization*, 34.

30. George Beshore, *Science in Early Islamic Cultures* (New York: Franklin Watts, 1998), 35.

31. Beshore, *Science in Early Islamic Cultures*, 35.

32. Michael Hamilton Morgan, *Lost History: The Enduring Legacy of Muslim Scientists, Thinkers, and Artists* (Washington, DC: National Geographic, 2008), 158.

33. Bloom and Blair, *Islam*, 111.

34. Brown, *Misquoting Muhammad*, 11; Ernst, *Following Muhammad*, 27.

35. Morgan, *Lost History*, 186.

36. Brown, *Misquoting Muhammad*, 229; Salah Zaimeche, Salim Al-Hassani, and Ahmed Salem, "Lady Montagu and the Introduction of the Smallpox Inoculation to England," *Muslim Heritage*, http://muslimheritage.com/article/lady-montagu-and-introduction-smallpox-inoculation-england#ftn118, accessed Aug. 23, 2019; and Al-Hassani, Woodcock, and Saoud, *1001 Inventions*, 178–79.

37. Ernst, *Following Muhammad*, 30.

38. John L. Esposito and Dalia Mogahed, *Who Speaks for Islam? What a Billion Muslims Really Think* (New York: Gallup Press, 2007), 40.

39. Hallaq, *Introduction to Islamic Law*, 96.

40. Hallaq, *Introduction to Islamic Law*, 95–96.

41. Hallaq, *Introduction to Islamic Law*, 112.

42. Emon, "Conceiving Islamic Law in a Pluralistic Society," 347.

43. Ernst, *Following Muhammad*, 128–29.

44. Emon, "Conceiving Islamic Law in a Pluralistic Society," 339.

45. Emon, "Conceiving Islamic Law in a Pluralistic Society," 339.

46. Emon, "Conceiving Islamic Law in a Pluralistic Society," 347.

47. Emon, "Conceiving Islamic Law in a Pluralistic Society," 346.

48. Hallaq, *An Introduction to Islamic Law*, 87, quoting Nicholas Dirks, *The Scandal of Empire: India and the Creation of Imperial Britain* (Cambridge, MA: Belknap Press, 2006), 221.

49. G. M. Trevelyan, *English Social History: A Survey of Six Centuries, Chaucer to Queen Victoria* (1942; Middlesex, UK: Pelican Books, 1974), 363.

50. Emon, "Conceiving Islamic Law in a Pluralistic Society," 342–46.

51. Emon, "Conceiving Islamic Law in a Pluralistic Society," 340.

52. Emon, "Conceiving Islamic Law in a Pluralistic Society," 342–46.

53. Abou El Fadl, *Reasoning with God*, 49.

54. Emon, "Conceiving Islamic Law in a Pluralistic Society," 348.

55. Emon, "Conceiving Islamic Law in a Pluralistic Society," 346.

56. Emon, "Conceiving Islamic Law in a Pluralistic Society," 340.

57. Hallaq, *Shari'a*, 458.

58. Frantz Fanon is generally credited with this concept.

59. Emon, "Conceiving Islamic Law in a Pluralistic Society," 346.

60. Emon, "Conceiving Islamic Law in a Pluralistic Society," 334.

61. Wael Hallaq, "On the Origins of the Controversy about the Existence of Mujtahids and the Gate of Ijtihad," *Studia Islamica* 63 (1986): 129–41.

62. Hallaq, "On the Origins of the Controversy about the Existence of Mujtahids and the Gate of Ijtihad," 129–41.

63. See, e.g., Wael Hallaq, "Was the Gate of Ijtihad Closed?," *International Journal of Middle East Studies* 16 (1984); Ali-Karamali and Dunne, "The Ijtihad Controversy," *Arab Law Quarterly* 9, pt. 3 (1994); Hallaq, *Shari'a*, 445; and Abou El Fadl, *Reasoning with God*, liii.

64. Abou El Fadl, *Reasoning with God*, liii.

65. Ahmed, *A Quiet Revolution*, 23.

66. Feldman, "Why Shariah?"

67. Feldman, "Why Shariah?"

68. Eugene Hecker, *A Short History of Women's Rights* (1914; Westport, CT: Greenwood Press, 1971), 137.

69. Amira El Azhary Sonbol, ed., *Women, the Family, and Divorce Laws in Islamic History* (Syracuse, NY: Syracuse University Press, 1996), 279.

70. Sonbol, *Women, the Family, and Divorce Laws in Islamic History*, 281.

71. John L. Esposito with Natana J. DeLong-Bas, *Women in Muslim Family Law* (Syracuse, NY: Syracuse University Press, 2001), 29.

72. Sonbol, *Women, the Family, and Divorce Laws in Islamic History*, 285.

73. Ernst, *Following Muhammad*, 128.

74. Hecker, *A Short History of Women's Rights*, 124–27. English women didn't receive even minimal legal protections against domestic violence until the Matrimonial Causes Act of 1878. See "Custody Rights and Domestic Violence," https://parliament.uk/about/living-heritage/transformingsociety/private-lives/relationships/overview/custodyrights.

75. Ernst, *Following Muhammad*, 146.

76. Ahmed, *A Quiet Revolution*, 36–37.

77. Miriam Cooke, "Islamic Feminism before and after September 11," *Duke Journal of Gender Law & Policy* 9 (2002): 227.

78. Leila Ahmed, *Women and Gender in Islam: Historical Roots to a Modern Debate* (New Haven, CT: Yale University Press, 1992), 128.

79. World Bank, "Proportion of Seats Held by Women in National Parliaments (%)," https://data.worldbank.org/indicator/SG.GEN.PARL.ZS, accessed Aug. 23, 2019; see also "Women in National Parliaments," data from the Inter-Parliamentary Union, Apr. 1, 2018, http://archive.ipu.org/wmn-e/classif.htm.

80. Hecker, *A Short History of Women's Rights*, 155–56, 168.

81. Cynthia Sewell, "This Bill Would Have Ended Child Marriage for Those Under Age in Idaho. The House Voted It Down," *Idaho Statesman*, Feb. 28, 2019.

82. Ziba Mir-Hosseini, "Muslim Women's Quest for Equality: Between Islamic Law and Feminism," *Critical Inquiry* 32 (2006): 638–39.

83. Brown, *Misquoting Muhammad*, 110.

84. See, generally, Mir-Hosseini, "Muslim Women's Quest for Equality."

85. Mir-Hosseini, "Muslim Women's Quest for Equality," 635–36.

86. Nasr, "European Colonialism and the Emergence of Modern Muslim States," 565.

87. Nasr, "European Colonialism and the Emergence of Modern Muslim States," 566.

88. Nasr, "European Colonialism and the Emergence of Modern Muslim States," 566.

89. Nasr, "European Colonialism and the Emergence of Modern Muslim States," 566.

90. Mark Fathi Massoud, "Don't Blame Sharia for Islamic Extremism—Blame Colonialism," *Conversation*, Apr. 8, 2019, https://theconversation.com.

91. Feroz Ahmad, "Turkey," in *The Oxford Encyclopedia of the Modern Islamic World*, ed. John Esposito (New York: Oxford University Press, 1995), 242.

92. Nasr, "European Colonialism and the Emergence of Modern Muslim States," 590–91.

93. Nasr, "European Colonialism and the Emergence of Modern Muslim States," 596.

94. Nasr, "European Colonialism and the Emergence of Modern Muslim States," 557, 598.

95. Nasr, "European Colonialism and the Emergence of Modern Muslim States," 587.

96. Nasr, "European Colonialism and the Emergence of Modern Muslim States," 587.

CHAPTER NINE: SHARIAH IN POSTCOLONIAL MUSLIM-MAJORITY COUNTRIES

1. Samer Ghamroun, "Lebanese Sharia Courts: When Women Litigants Turn into Reformers," *Legal Agenda*, Dec. 1, 2013, legal-agenda.com.

2. Sharough Akhavi, "Iran," in Esposito, *Oxford Encyclopedia of the Modern Islamic World,* 229.

3. Esther van Eijk, "Sharia and National Law in Saudi Arabia," in *Sharia Incorporated: A Comparative Overview of the Legal Systems of Twelve Muslim Countries to Past and Present,* ed. Jan Michiel Otto (Leiden: Leiden University Press, 2010), 158.

4. Rudolph Peters, *Crime and Punishment in Islamic Law* (Cambridge, UK: Cambridge University Press, 2005), 153.

5. James M. Dorsey, "Crown Prince Mohammad's Vow to Moderate Saudi Islam: Easier Said Than Done," *Huffington Post,* Oct. 28, 2017.

6. See, e.g., "Saudi Arabia: Religion Textbooks Promote Intolerance," Human Rights Watch, Sept. 13, 2107, hrw.org.

7. Abou El Fadl, *The Great Theft,* 23.

8. Abou El Fadl, *The Great Theft,* 23.

9. Abou El Fadl, *The Great Theft,* 23.

10. Feldman, *The Fall and Rise of the Islamic State,* 100.

11. Feldman, *The Fall and Rise of the Islamic State,* 98.

12. Abou El Fadl, *The Great Theft,* 23.

13. Charles Kurzman, "Introduction: Liberal Islam and Its Islamic Context," in *Liberal Islam: A Sourcebook,* ed. Kurzman (New York: Oxford University Press, 1998), 20.

14. Abdulaziz Sachedina, *The Islamic Roots of Democratic Pluralism* (Oxford, UK: Oxford University Press, 2001), 5. This refers to obsolete concepts such as how the world is divided into "the abode of war" versus the "abode of Islam." This does not come from Qur'an or Sunna, and it was defunct by the twelfth century. Even before that, this concept wasn't universally accepted or used. The rules of war in Islam were basically the same as the rules of war in Christianity; scapegoating Islam as any more political than Christianity is just applying a double standard.

15. M. Steven Fish, *Are Muslims Distinctive? A Look at the Evidence* (New York: Oxford University Press, 2011), 63.

16. Fish, *Are Muslims Distinctive?,* 63.

17. Fish, *Are Muslims Distinctive?,* 63.

18. Esposito and Mogahed, *Who Speaks for Islam?,* 56.

19. Frederick Clarkson, "'Project Blitz' Seeks to Do for Christian Nationalism What ALEC Does for Big Business," *Religion Dispatches,* Apr. 27, 2018. See, also, Katherine Stewart, "A Christian Nationalist Blitz," *New York Times,* May 26, 2018.

20. Clarkson, "'Project Blitz' Seeks to Do for Christian Nationalism What ALEC Does for Big Business." See, also, Stewart, "A Christian Nationalist Blitz."

21. Esposito and Mogahed, *Who Speaks for Islam?,* 49.

22. Esposito and Mogahed, *Who Speaks for Islam?,* 48.

23. Esposito and Mogahed, *Who Speaks for Islam?,* 50.

24. Esposito and Mogahed, *Who Speaks for Islam?* 63.

25. Esposito and Mogahed, *Who Speaks for Islam?,* 55–57.

26. Esposito and Mogahed, *Who Speaks for Islam?,* 47, 51, 58.

27. Magali Rheault and Dalia Mogahed, "Majorities See Religion and Democracy as Compatible," Gallup News Service, Oct. 3, 2007.

28. Mohamad Abdalla, "Islamic Australia? What Place Is There for Sacred Law in a Secular Land?" *ABC Religion and Ethics,* May 10, 2013; an expanded version of the article appears in Mohamad Abdalla, "Sacred Law in a Secular Land" in *Griffith Law Review* 21, no. 3 (2012).

29. Abdalla, "Islamic Australia? What Place Is There for Sacred Law in a Secular Land?"

30. Khaled A. El Fadl, "Muslim Minorities and Self-Restraint in Liberal Democracies," *Loyola of Los Angeles Law Review* 29 (1996): 1535.

31. Asifa Quraishi-Landes, "Five Myths About Sharia," *Washington Post,* June 24, 2016.

32. El Fadl, "Muslim Minorities and Self-Restraint in Liberal Democracies," 1534.

33. Esposito and DeLong-Bas, *Shariah,* 133.

34. Sharough Akhavi, "Iran" in Esposito, *Oxford Encyclopedia of the Modern Islamic World,* 229.

35. See Raymond William Baker, *Islam Without Fear: Egypt and the New Islamists* (Cambridge, MA: Harvard University Press, 2003). The countries that deem the Muslim

Brotherhood a terrorist organization are those whose governments are most threatened by social and political participation—monarchies and authoritarian governments like Saudi Arabia and Egypt.

36. John L. Esposito, *The Future of Islam* (New York: Oxford University Press, 2010), 63.

37. Darling, *A History of Social Justice and Political Power in the Middle East*, 212.

38. Darling, *A History of Social Justice and Political Power in the Middle East*, x.

39. Darling, *A History of Social Justice and Political Power in the Middle East*, 212.

40. Wendy Pearlman, "The Syrian Civil War Exiled Millions and Produced ISIL; But How Did It Start?," *Conversation*, Mar. 14, 2019, theconversation.com.

41. Abou El Fadl, *Reasoning with God*, 49.

42. Abbas Amanat and Frank Griffel, eds., *Shari'a: Islamic Law in the Contemporary Context* (Stanford, CA: Stanford University Press, 2007), 12.

43. Amanat and Griffel, *Shari'a*, 12–14.

44. Nicholas Kristof, "Islam, Virgins and Grapes," *New York Times*, Apr. 22, 2009.

45. Amanat and Griffel, *Shari'a*, 12–14.

46. Feldman, *The Fall and Rise of the Islamic State*, 118.

47. Meriem El Haitami, "Islamist Feminism in Morocco: (Re)defining the Political Sphere," *Frontiers: A Journal of Women Studies* 7, no. 3 (2016): 74–91.

48. Noah Feldman, *After Jihad: America and the Struggle for Islamic Democracy* (New York: Farrar, Straus and Giroux, 2003), 228.

49. Nathan J. Brown, Amr Hamzawy, and Marina Ottaway, "Islamist Movements and the Democratic Process in the Arab World: Exploring the Gray Zones," Carnegie Papers Middle East Series, no. 67 (2006): 9.

50. See, e.g., Sherman Jackson, "Shari'ah, Democracy, and the Modern Nation-State: Some Reflections on Islam, Popular Rule, and Pluralism," *Fordham International Law Journal* 27 (2003): 105–7; and Jonathan Brown, "The Sharia, Homosexuality & Safeguarding Each Other's Rights in a Pluralist Society," *Iman Wire*, Al-Madina Institute, June 18, 2016.

51. Brown, Hamzawy, and Ottaway, "Islamist Movements and the Democratic Process in the Arab World," 8–10.

52. Brown, Hamzawy, and Ottaway, "Islamist Movements and the Democratic Process in the Arab World," 17; William L. Cleveland and Martin Bunton, *A History of the Modern Middle East*, 6th ed. (1994; Boulder, CO: Westview Press, 2016), 544–45.

53. See, generally, Brown, Hamzawy, and Ottaway, "Islamist Movements and the Democratic Process in the Arab World: Exploring the Gray Zones."

54. Zvi Bar'el, "Islamic Party's Secret Weapon in Tunisia Local Elections: A Jewish Candidate," *Haaretz*, Feb. 26, 2018, haaretz.com.

55. Francesca Mannocchi, "The First Female Mayor of Tunis on Her Chequered Battle to Empower Women," *National*, 25 Oct. 2018, thenational.ae.

56. Monica L. Marks, "Convince, Coerce, or Compromise? Ennahda's Approach to Tunisia's Constitution," Analysis Paper No. 10, Brookings Doha Center, Feb. 2014, brookings.edu.

57. Feldman, *After Jihad*, 5. See also John L. Esposito, *Islam and Politics* (Syracuse, NY: Syracuse University Press, 1998), 302–7.

58. Feldman, *After Jihad*, 5.

59. Cleveland and Bunton, *A History of the Modern Middle East*, 544.

60. Cleveland and Bunton, *A History of the Modern Middle East*, 544.

61. Omayma Abdel Latif and Marina Ottaway, "Women in Islamist Movements: Toward an Islamist Model of Women's Activism," Carnegie Papers, No. 2, Carnegie Endowment for International Peace, June 2007.

62. Ghamroun, "Lebanese Sharia Courts."

63. Nadia Guessous, "Having a Conversation on Other Terms: Gender and the Politics of Representation in the New Moroccan Government," *Jadaliyya*, Jan. 9, 2012, jadaliyya.com.

64. Andrea Khalil, ed., *Gender, Women and the Arab Spring* (New York: Routledge, 2015), 5.

65. See Yesim Arat, "Feminists, Islamists, and Political Change in Turkey," *Political Psychology* 19, no. 1 (1998): 125.

66. Sachedina, *The Islamic Roots of Democratic Pluralism*, 133.

67. Pew Research Center, *Many Countries Favor Specific Religions, Officially or Unofficially* (Washington, DC: Pew Research Center, Oct. 3, 2017. "Christian churches receive

preferential treatment in more countries—28—than any other unofficial but favored faith," and in Apr. 2018, Israel passed the "Nation-State bill," which thirteen top American Jewish organizations opposed on the grounds that it legalized, on a constitutional level, discrimination in Israel against Israeli non-Jews. See "Top American Jewish Organizations in Letter to Herzog: 'Nation-State Bill Would Enshrine Discrimination Into Israel's Basic Laws,'" press release, J Street, July 12, 2018.

68. Esposito and DeLong-Bas, *Shariah*, 139.

69. Associated Press, "The Secret to ISIS's Success: Over 100 Former Saddam Hussein-Era Officers Run Jihadi Group's Military and Intelligence Operations in Iraq and Syria," *Daily Mail*, Aug. 8, 2015.

70. See Southern Poverty Law Center, "Ku Klux Klan," https://www.splcenter.org/fighting-hate/extremist-files/ideology/ku-klux-klan, accessed September 29, 2019.

71. Charles Kurzman, "Chasing the Ghosts of Violent Extremism in the Middle East," briefing for Samuel Brownback, US ambassador at large for international religious freedom, May 1, 2018, https://kurzman.unc.edu/islamic-terrorism/chasing-ghosts.

72. Charles Kurzman, *The Missing Martyrs: Why There Are So Few Muslim Terrorists* (New York: Oxford University Press, 2011), 27.

73. Kurzman, *The Missing Martyrs*, 7.

74. Ruth Alexander and Hannah Moore, "Are Most Victims of Terrorism Muslim?," *BBC News*, Jan. 20, 2015, bbcnews.com.

75. James Rush, "Isis Captors 'Didn't Even Have the Koran,' Says French Journalist Held Prisoner by Group for More Than 10 Months," *Independent*, Feb. 4, 2015.

76. Aya Batrawy, Paisley Dodds, and Lori Hinnant, "Leaked ISIS Documents Reveal Recruits Have Poor Grasp of Islamic Faith," *Independent*, Aug. 16, 2016.

77. Batrawy, Dodds, and Hinnant, "Leaked ISIS Documents Reveal Recruits Have Poor Grasp of Islamic Faith."

78. Lydia Wilson, "What I Discovered from Interviewing Imprisoned ISIS Fighters: They're Drawn to the Movement for Reasons That Have Little to Do with Belief in Extremist Islam," *Nation*, Oct. 21, 2015.

79. Lydia Wilson, "What I Discovered from Interviewing Imprisoned ISIS Fighters."

80. Mick Krever, "ISIS Captors Cared Little About Religion, Says Former Hostage," CNN.com, Feb. 4, 2015, in which released ISIS prisoner Didier Francois remarked, "There was never really discussion about texts or—it was not a religious discussion. It was a political discussion."

81. Peter Byrne, "Anatomy of Terror: What Makes Normal People Become Extremists?" *New Scientist*, Aug. 16, 2017.

82. Byrne, "Anatomy of Terror."

83. Marc Sageman, *Misunderstanding Terrorism* (Philadelphia: University of Pennsylvania Press, 2017), 10.

84. Nafeez Ahmed, "Food Scarcity Is Fanning Flames of 'War on Terror,'" *Middle East Eye*, May 1, 2015, middleeasteye.net.

85. Robert Pape, *Dying to Win: The Strategic Logic of Suicide Terrorism* (New York: Random House, 2005), 13.

86. Pape, *Dying to Win*, 4.

87. Pape, *Dying to Win*, 245.

88. Pape, *Dying to Win*, 245.

89. Pape, *Dying to Win*, 260.

90. Pape, *Dying to Win*, 256, 260–61.

91. Jared A. Goldstein, "A Good American: How Trump's Immigration Ban Explicitly Smears Muslims as Being Potentially Hostile to the Constitution," *Slate*, Feb. 14, 2017.

92. Ernst, *Following Muhammad*, 140.

93. Charles Kurzman, "Introduction: Liberal Islam and Its Islamic Context," in *Liberal Islam: A Sourcebook*, ed. Kurzman (New York: Oxford University Press, 1998), 20.

94. Feldman, *After Jihad*, 206.

95. Esposito and De Long-Bas, *Shariah*, 144.

96. See, generally, Wael B. Hallaq, *The Impossible State: Islam, Politics, and Modernity's Moral Predicament* (New York: Columbia University Press, 2013).

97. See, generally, Hallaq, *The Impossible State*.

98. Hallaq, *The Impossible State*, 13.

99. Abdullahi An-Na'im, *Islam and the Secular State: Negotiating the Future of Shari'a* (Cambridge, MA: Harvard University Press, 2008), 7.

100. An-Na'im, *Islam and the Secular State*, 30.

101. An-Na'im, *Islam and the Secular State*, 29.

102. Emon, "Conceiving Islamic Law in a Pluralistic Society," 352.

103. Emon, "Conceiving Islamic Law in a Pluralistic Society," 354.

104. Emon, "Conceiving Islamic Law in a Pluralistic Society," 354.

105. Emon, "Conceiving Islamic Law in a Pluralistic Society," 354.

106. See, generally, Asifa Quraishi-Landes, "Islamic Constitutionalism: Not Secular. Not Theocratic. Not Impossible," *Rutgers Journal of Law and Religion* 16 (2015): 553.

107. Quraishi-Landes, "Islamic Constitutionalism," 568–70.

108. Quraishi-Landes, "Islamic Constitutionalism," 564.

109. Quraishi-Landes, "Islamic Constitutionalism," 568–70.

110. William Dalrymple, "Scribes of the New Racism," *Independent*, Sept. 25, 2001.

111. Cole, *Muhammad*, 78.

112. Cole, *Muhammad*, 62–63.

113. Karen Armstrong, *Islam: A Short History* (New York: Modern Library/Random House, 2000), 10.

114. Cole, *Muhammad*, 78.

115. Surah 16, verse 36.

116. Craig Considine, "What Studying Muhammad Taught Me about Islam," *Huffington Post*, Mar. 23, 2014. See, also, John Andrew Morrow, *The Covenants of the Prophet Muhammad with the Christians of the World* (Brooklyn, NY: Angelico/Sophia Perennis, 2013).

117. Peters, *Crime and Punishment in Islamic Law*, 65.

118. Cole, *Muhammad*, 156.

119. Brown, "The Issue of Apostasy in Islam."

120. Taha Jabir Alalwani, *Apostasy in Islam: A Historical & Scriptural Analysis* (London: International Institute of Islamic Thought, 2011), 99.

121. Nazir Khan, "Forever on Trial: Islam and the Charge of Violence," Yaqeen Institute for Islamic Research, Nov. 16, 2016.

122. Brown, "The Issue of Apostasy in Islam."

123. Brown, "The Issue of Apostasy in Islam."

124. Brown, "The Issue of Apostasy in Islam."

125. Brown, "The Issue of Apostasy in Islam."

126. Amanat and Griffel, *Shari'a*, 13.

127. Sophie Gorman, "Blasphemy Is a Crime Not Only in Pakistan, but Europe Too," *France24*, Oct. 31, 2018, https://france24.com.

128. Louise Nyholm Kallestrup and Raisa Maria Toivo, eds., *Contesting Orthodoxy in Medieval and Early Modern Europe: Heresy, Magic, and Witchcraft* (Cham, Switzerland: Palgrave Macmillan, 2017), 2.

129. Abdullahi Ahmed An-Na'im, "Apostasy, Heresy, and Freedom of Belief in Islam," ABC Religion & Ethics, Mar. 15, 2017, https://www.abc.net.au.

130. Deuteronomy, 13:6–12

131. Kallestrup and Toivo, *Contesting Orthodoxy in Medieval and Early Modern Europe*, 9, 46.

132. El Fadl, *The Great Theft*, 159.

133. Esposito and DeLong-Bas, *Shariah*, 227.

134. Esposito and DeLong-Bas, *Shariah*, 225.

CHAPTER TEN: THE SCARY STUFF

1. Jonathan Brown, "Stoning and Hand Cutting—Understanding the Hudud and Shariah in Islam," Yaqeen Institute for Islamic Research, Jan. 12, 2017, yaqeeninstitute.org.

2. "Sarah Palin Supports Stoning and Slavery?," Loonwatch, May 14, 2010, loonwatch .com.

3. Trevelyan, *English Social History*, 363.

4. Jonathan Brown, "Stoning and Hand Cutting—Understanding the Hudud and Shariah in Islam," Yaqeen Institute for Islamic Research, Jan. 12, 2017, yaqeeninstitute.org.

5. Brown, "Stoning and Hand Cutting."

6. Hisham M. Ramadan, "On Islamic Punishment," in *Understanding Islamic Law: From Classical to Contemporary*, ed. Hisham M. Ramadan (Oxford, UK: AltaMira Press, 2006), 45.

7. Kecia Ali, *Sexual Ethics and Islam: Feminist Reflections on Qur'an, Hadith, and Jurisprudence* (Oxford, UK: Oneworld, 2006), 75.

8. Esposito and DeLong-Bas, *Shariah*, 192.

9. Brown, "Stoning and Hand Cutting."

10. Abou El Fadl, *Reasoning with God*, li; Peters, *Crime and Punishment in Islamic Law*, 27.

11. Luqman Zakariyah, "Confession and Retraction: The Application of Islamic Legal Maxims in Safiyyatu and Amina's Cases in Northern Nigeria," *Journal of Muslim Minority Affairs* 30, no. 2 (2010).

12. Abou El Fadl, *Reasoning with God*, l–li.

13. Peters, *Crime and Punishment in Islamic Law*, 13.

14. Peters, *Crime and Punishment in Islamic Law*, 15.

15. Abu Amina Elias, "Application of Hudud Punishments in Sharia Law," December 17, 2015, abuaminaelias.com.

16. Peters, *Crime and Punishment in Islamic Law*, 14.

17. See, e.g., Peters, *Crime and Punishment in Islamic Law*, 55.

18. Peters, *Crime and Punishment in Islamic Law*, 13–14.

19. Feldman, "Why Shariah?"

20. Classical fiqh scholars (like other ancient peoples) allowed a man to also have lawful sexual intercourse with his slaves, with their consent and in a legal relationship similar to marriage, but that was in ancient times. The vast majority of Islamic scholars would agree that slavery is no longer allowed in Islam anymore.

21. Cole, *Muhammad*, 205, 308.

22. Brown, "Stoning and Hand Cutting."

23. Peters, *Crime and Punishment in Islamic Law*, 12–16; Schacht, *An Introduction to Islamic Law*, 177.

24. Peters, *Crime and Punishment in Islamic Law*, 15.

25. Peters, *Crime and Punishment in Islamic Law*, 55.

26. Ahmed Ali, *Al-Qur'an: A Contemporary Translation* (Princeton, NJ: Princeton University Press, 1993), 113.

27. Ahmed Ali, *Al-Qur'an*, 113.

28. Sources for this entire list: Hallaq, *Shari'a*, 317; Peters, *Crime and Punishment in Islamic Law*, 56–57; Brown, "Stoning and Hand Cutting."

29. Schacht, *An Introduction to Islamic Law*, 176.

30. Peters, *Crime and Punishment in Islamic Law*, 27.

31. Esposito and DeLong-Bas, *Shariah*, 216–17.

32. Peters, *Crime and Punishment in Islamic Law*, 20–28.

33. Brown, "Stoning and Hand Cutting."

34. Hallaq, *Shari'a*, 317.

35. Brown, "Stoning and Hand Cutting."

36. Hallaq, *Shari'a*, 312

37. Hallaq, *Shari'a*, 312

38. Esposito and DeLong-Bas, *Shariah*, 197.

39. Esposito and DeLong-Bas, *Shariah*, 197.

40. Brown, "Stoning and Hand Cutting."

41. Brown, "Stoning and Hand Cutting."

42. Brown, "Stoning and Hand Cutting."

43. Brown, "Stoning and Hand Cutting."

44. Peters, *Crime and Punishment in Islamic Law*, 55.

45. Brown, "Stoning and Hand Cutting."

46. Peters, *Crime and Punishment in Islamic Law*, 66.

47. Peters, *Crime and Punishment in Islamic Law*, 66.

48. Ahmad Abd al-Aziz al-Alfi, "Punishment in Islamic Criminal Law," in *Islamic Criminal Justice System*, ed. Cherif M. Bassiouni (London: Oceana Publications, 1982), 236.

49. Hallaq, *Shari'a*, 312.

50. Peters, *Crime and Punishment in Islamic Law*, 35.

51. ACLU Foundation, *A Living Death: Life without Parole for Nonviolent Offenses* (New York: American Civil Liberties Union, 2013).

52. Peters, *Crime and Punishment in Islamic Law*, 106.

53. Brown, *Hadith*, 288; "By the Book: Why Harsh Punishments Are More Prevalent in the Muslim World," *Economist*, July 2, 2015; Niki Gamm, "Adultery in Islam and among Ottomans," *Hurriyet Daily News*, Feb. 21, 2015.

54. Sadakat Kadri, *Heaven on Earth: A Journey through Shari'a Law from the Deserts of Ancient Arabia to the Streets of the Modern Muslim World* (New York: Farrar, Straus and Giroux, 2012), 217–18.

55. Abou El Fadl, *Reasoning with God*, 292.

56. Abou El Fadl, *Reasoning with God*, 292.

57. Esposito and DeLong-Bas, *Shariah*, 198–99.

58. Esposito and DeLong-Bas, *Shariah*, 186.

59. Abou El Fadl, *Reasoning with God*, 292.

60. Peters, *Crime and Punishment in Islamic Law*, 145.

61. Peters, *Crime and Punishment in Islamic Law*, 145.

62. Peters, *Crime and Punishment in Islamic Law*, 145.

63. Peters, *Crime and Punishment in Islamic Law*, 145.

64. Esposito and DeLong-Bas, *Shariah*, 194.

65. Abou El Fadl, *Reasoning With God*, 292–93.

66. Mohammad S. El-Awa, *Punishment in Islamic Law: A Comparative Study* (Indianapolis: American Trust Publications, 1982), 136, 137.

67. Peters, *Crime and Punishment in Islamic Law*, 184.

CHAPTER ELEVEN: SHARIAH IN EVERYDAY LIFE

1. See, e.g., Pew Research Center, "Beliefs About Sharia," survey findings, Apr. 30, 2013, http://pewforum.org/2013/04/30/the-worlds-muslims-religion-politic s-society-beliefs-about-sharia.

2. Since 1962, Israeli pork production has been banned in areas not mostly populated by Christians. See "Israel's Pork Problem: What a Change to One of the Most Controversial Laws in Israeli History Could Mean for the Country's Christian Arabs," *Slate*, Aug. 8, 2012.

3. Deuteronomy 21:18–21.

4. Titus 2:9–10.

5. See, e.g., "Bomb Plot Charge Only Latest JDL Controversy," ABC News, Mar. 19, 2002.

6. Brown, "The Issue of Apostasy in Islam."

7. Brown, "The Issue of Apostasy in Islam."

8. Brown, "The Issue of Apostasy in Islam."

9. Kalpana Jain, "Why Muslim Women Wear a Hijab: 3 Essential Reads," *Conversation*, Feb. 1, 2019, theconversation.com.

10. Khaled M. Abou El Fadl, *Conference of the Books: The Search for Beauty in Islam* (Lanham, MD: University Press of America, 2001), 295.

11. Esposito and DeLong-Bas, *Women in Muslim Family Law*, 11.

12. Abou El Fadl, *And God Knows the Soldiers*, 135.

13. Abou El Fadl, *Conference of the Books*, 297.

14. Abou El Fadl, *Conference of the Books*, 291–96.

15. Abou El Fadl, *Conference of the Books*, 291–96.

16. Abou El Fadl, *And God Knows the Soldiers*, 131.

17. Asma Barlas, *"Believing Women" in Islam: Unreading Patriarchal Interpretations of the Qur'an* (Austin: University of Texas Press, 2002), 55.

18. Abou El Fadl, *Conference of the Books*, 295.

19. Abou El Fadl, *Conference of the Books*, 294.

20. Mohammad Asad, *The Message of the Qur'an* (Gibraltar: Dar al-Andalus, 1980), 538n37.

21. Saba Mahmood, *Politics of Piety: The Islamic Revival and the Feminist Subject* (Princeton, NJ: Princeton University Press, 2005), 160.

22. Abou El Fadl, *And God Knows the Soldiers*, 125.

23. Alessandra Stanley, "Ruling on Tight Jeans and Rape Sets Off Anger in Italy," *New York Times*, Feb. 16, 1999.

24. See Siobhan Hegarty, "Islamophobia: Women Wearing Head Coverings Most at Risk of Attacks, Study Finds," Australian Broadcasting Commission News, Oct. 23, 2017, abc.net.au; Harriet Agerholm, "Women 'Bearing Brunt' of Rising Islamophobic Attacks in

the UK: Street-Level Anti-Muslim Acts Jump Almost a Half in One Year, Says Hate-Monitoring Group," *Independent*, Nov. 3, 2017.

25. See Bridge Initiative at https://bridge.georgetown.edu.

26. See, e.g., Khaled Abou El Fadl's fatwa on hijab, which states, in part, "In my view, it is an error for a Muslim woman to continue wearing the headscarf, or the hijab if doing so brings such a person undue attention, or puts her at risk of harm of any sort." Jan. 2, 2016, https://www.searchforbeauty.org/2016/01/02/fatwa-on-hijab-the-hair-covering-of-women.

27. Jain, "Why Muslim Women Wear a Hijab."

28. Nabila Ramdani, "Laïcite and the French Veil Debate," *Guardian*, May 23, 2010.

29. Sahar Amer, *What Is Veiling?* (Chapel Hill: University of North Carolina Press, 2014), 145–47.

30. See 1 Corinthians 11:6. Valerie Vande Panne, "Don't Make Any Assumptions about the Next Headscarf You See," *Mashable*, May 29, 2015, https://mashable.com/2015/05/29/headscarf-diversity/#eoFRbrOO4ZqX.

31. "A Jewish Movement to Shroud the Female Form," NPR, Mar. 17, 2008.

32. Panne, "Don't Make Any Assumptions about the Next Headscarf You See."

33. Mehdi Mozaffari, "The Rushdie Affair," in Esposito, *Oxford Encyclopedia of the Modern Islamic World*, 445.

34. Esposito, *The Islamic Threat*, 191.

35. An-Na'im, *Toward an Islamic Reformation*, 183.

36. Mozaffari, "The Rushdie Affair," 444.

37. Faisal Kutty, "Blasphemy and Islam: A Colonial Legacy," *Counterpunch*, Apr. 17, 2014.

38. Harriet Sherwood, "Rights Groups Push for Yes Vote in Irish Blasphemy Referendum," *Guardian*, Oct. 25, 2018.

39. Brown, "The Issue of Apostasy in Islam."

40. Ed Pilkington, "Children's Writer Philip Pullman Ranked Second on US Banned Books List," *Guardian*, Sept. 30, 2009.

41. "Students' Reading of Koran Text Is Upheld," *Los Angeles Times*, Aug. 20, 2002.

42. Nancy Kranich, "What's Daddy's Roommate Doing in Wasilla?," *Nation*, Sept. 29, 2008.

43. Carol Kuruvilla, "DC Relinquishes Rights to Comic Book Series about Jesus after Conservative Backlash," *Huffington Post*, Feb. 18, 2019.

44. Sharon Waxman, "Gibson to Delete a Scene in Passion," *New York Times*, Feb. 4, 2004.

45. See Brian Hauss, "The New Israel Anti-Boycott Act Is Still Unconstitutional," blog post, ACLU, Mar. 7, 2018, https://aclu.org/blog/free-speech/rights-protesters/new-israel-anti-boycott-act-still-unconstitutional; "Cardin Unveils Amended, But Still Unconstitutional, Israel Anti-Boycott Act," Palestine Legal, Mar. 8, 2018, https://palestinelegal.org.

46. See NAACP v. Claiborne Hardware Co., No. 81–202 (1982), in which the US Supreme Court held that boycotts were protected under the First Amendment.

47. Gillian Brockell, "'Jesus Christ Superstar': Why Jews, Christians and Even Its Composer Hated It at First," *Washington Post*, April 2, 2018.

48. Brockell, "'Jesus Christ Superstar.'" See, also, Talia Ralph, "'Jesus Christ Superstar Banned in Russia," *PRI*, September 29, 2012.

49. Peter Gottschalk and Gabriel Greenberg, *Islamophobia: Making Muslims the Enemy* (Lanham, MD: Rowman & Littlefield, 2008), 145.

50. Gottschalk and Greenberg, *Islamophobia*, 145.

51. Peter Gottschalk and Gabriel Greenberg, "From Muhammad to Obama: Caricatures, Cartoons, and Stereotypes of Muslims," in *Islamophobia: The Challenge of Pluralism in the 21st Century*, ed. John L. Esposito and Ibrahim Kalin (New York: Oxford University Press, 2011), 194.

52. Gwladys Fouché, "Danish Paper Rejected Jesus Cartoons," *Guardian*, Feb. 6, 2006.

53. Gottschalk and Greenberg, *Islamophobia*, 145.

54. Esposito and Mogahed, *Who Speaks for Islam?*, 144.

55. Esposito and Mogahed, *Who Speaks for Islam?*, 143.

56. Gottschalk and Greenberg, "From Muhammad to Obama," 192.

57. Gottschalk and Greenberg, "From Muhammad to Obama," 192.

58. John L. Esposito, *What Everyone Needs to Know about Islam: Answers to Frequently Asked Questions from One of America's Leading Experts* (New York: Oxford University Press, 2002), 138.

59. Charles Kurzman, "America Is Holding Itself Hostage to Terrorism," *Huffington Post*, Dec. 17, 2015.

60. Esposito and Mogahed, *Who Speaks for Islam?*, 73.

61. Tom Verde, "Malika I: Khayzuran & Zubayda," *Aramco World Magazine*, Jan./Feb. 2016, aramcoworld.com.

62. Rashid Ergener, *About Turkey: Geography, Economy, Politics, Religion, and Culture* (Santa Fe, NM: Pilgrims Process, 2002), 19.

63. Max Fisher, "It's Not Just Fox News: Islamophobia on Cable News Is Out of Control," *Vox*, Jan. 13, 2015.

64. Conrad Hackett and Dalia Fahmy, "Education of Muslim Women Is Limited by Economic Conditions, Not Religion," *Fact Tank: News in the Numbers*, Pew Research Center, June 12, 2018.

65. Hackett and Fahmy, "Education of Muslim Women Is Limited by Economic Conditions, Not Religion."

66. Mohammad Younis, "Muslim Americans Exemplify Diversity, Potential," *Gallup News*, Mar. 2, 2009.

67. Younis, "Muslim Americans Exemplify Diversity, Potential."

68. Esposito and Mogahed, *Who Speaks for Islam?*, 121.

69. Esposito and Mogahed, *Who Speaks for Islam?*, 123.

70. Ole Danbol Mjøs, chairman of the Norwegian Nobel Committee, presentation speech, Dec. 10, 2003, https://nobelprize.org/prizes/peace/2003/ceremony-speech/; Reza Aslan, *No god But God*, 74.

71. Ali, *Sexual Ethics and Islam*, 64.

72. Hallaq, *Shari'a*, 314.

73. Brown, "Islam Is Not the Cause of Honor Killings. It's Part of the Solution," Yaqeen Institute for Islamic Research, Oct. 25, 2016, yaqeeninstitute.org.

74. Brown, *Misquoting Muhammad*, 180.

75. Peters, *Crime and Punishment in Islamic Law*, 124.

76. Peters, *Crime and Punishment in Islamic Law*, 124.

77. Brown, "Islam Is Not the Cause of Honor Killings. It's Part of the Solution."

78. "Honour Killings by Region," Honour Based Violence Awareness Network, hbv-awareness.com, accessed Aug. 26, 2019.

79. Anna Momigliano, "Italy's Views on Violence against Women Are Finally Changing," *Washington Post*, Nov. 3, 2016.

80. James Brooke, "'Honor' Killing of Wives Is Outlawed in Brazil," *New York Times*, Mar. 29, 1991.

81. An executive decree was issued in July 2005 to repeal Article 269 of the Haiti Criminal Code. "The Right of Women in Haiti to Be Free from Violence and Discrimination," Inter-American Commission on Human Rights, Organization of American States, III.A.136, Mar. 10, 2009, https://cidh.oas.org/countryrep/Haitimujer2009eng/HaitiWomen09.toc.htm.

82. Magali Rheault and Dalia Mogahed, "Common Ground for Europeans and Muslims among Them," *Gallup News*, May 28, 2008.

83. Global Muslim Women's Shura Council, "Female Genital Cutting: Harmful and Un-Islamic," Women in Islamic Spirituality and Equality, wisemuslimwomen.org, 5, citing Carla Makhlouf Obermeyer, "Female Genital Surgeries: The Known, the Unknown, and the Unknowable," *Medical Anthropology Quarterly* 13, no. 1 (1999): 79–106.

84. Ahmed, *Women and Gender in Islam*, 175–76.

85. Ali, *Sexual Ethics and Islam*, 100.

86. Esposito and DeLong-Bas, *Shariah*, 214.

87. Global Muslim Women's Shura Council, "Female Genital Cutting," 6.

88. Esposito and DeLong-Bas, *Shariah*, 119.

89. Esposito and DeLong-Bas, *Shariah*, 215.

90. Esposito and Mogahed, *Who Speaks for Islam?*, 117.

91. Ali, *Sexual Ethics and Islam*, 110.

92. Renee Lewis, "Largest UK Muslim Organization Declares Female Circumcision Un-Islamic," *Al Jazeera*, June 23, 2014.

93. "ICNA Joins International Day of Zero Tolerance for FGM," Feb. 6, 2016, https://www.icna.org/icna-joins-international-day-of-zero-tolerance-for-fgm.

94. Esposito and DeLong-Bas, *Shariah*, 213.

95. Pat Caplan, "Campaign against FGM Exposes How Differently We View Our Own Obsessions," *Conversation*, Aug. 19, 2014; Ali, *Sexual Ethics and Islam*, 99.

96. Martha Coventry, "Making the Cut," *Ms.*, Oct./Nov. 2000.

97. See, e.g., Mike Ives and Muktita Suhartono, "'Gay Muslim' Comic Strip Vanishes after Indonesia Calls It Pornographic," *New York Times*, Feb. 13, 2019.

98. "Like Americans Overall, Muslims Now More Accepting of Homosexuality," survey, Pew Research Center, July 25, 2017, https://www.pewforum.org/2017/07/26/political-and -social-views/pf_2017-06-26_muslimamericans-04new-06; "Most US Christian Groups Grow More Accepting of Homosexuality," Fact Tank, Pew Research Center, Dec. 18, 2015.

99. See the following studies by Pew Research Center, Religion & Public Life, pewforum.org: "Attitudes on Same-Sex Marriage," May 14, 2019; "Views about Same-Sex Marriage among Mormons," 2014; and "Views about Same-Sex Marriage among Jehovah's Witnesses," March 1, 2019. See, also, Alex Vandermaas-Peeler, Daniel Cox, Molly Fisch-Friedman, Rob Griffin, and Robert P. Jones, "Emerging Consensus on LGBT Issues: Findings from the 2017 American Values Atlas," *PRRI*, May 1, 2018.

100. Pew Research Center, *The Global Divide on Homosexuality: Greater Acceptance in More Secular and Affluent Countries* (Washington, DC: Pew Research Center, June 4, 2013).

101. Peter Montgomery, "LGBT and Muslim? A New Report Busts Stereotypes," *Religion Dispatches*, Nov. 3, 2011.

102. Moustafa Bayoumi, "How the 'Homophobic Muslim' Became a Populist Bogey-man," *Guardian*, Aug. 7, 2017.

103. Greg Wilford, "All of Germany's Muslim MPs Voted in Favour of Same-Sex Mar-riage," *Independent*, July 2, 2017.

104. Pew Research Center, *Religious Belief and National Belonging in Central and Eastern Europe* (Washington, DC: Pew Research Center, May 10, 2017); Pew Research Center, *The Global Divide on Homosexuality*.

105. Pauline Mpungu, "Kenya's High Court Upholds Ban on Same-Sex Relations," *Al Jazeera*, May 24, 2019.

106. Andrew Buncombe, "India's Gay Community Scrambling after Court Decision Recriminalises Homosexuality," *Independent*, Feb. 23, 2014.

107. Adam Withnall, "India's Supreme Court Rules Gay Sex Is No Longer a Crime in Historical Section 377 Judgment," *Independent*, Sept. 6, 2018.

108. See "Adoption and Same-Sex Couples: Overview," FindLaw, https://family.findlaw .com/adoption/adoption-and-same-sex-couples-basics.html, accessed Aug. 26, 2019.

109. Pew Research Center, *The Global Divide on Homosexuality*.

110. "A Bill to provide for the protection, relief and rehabilitation of rights of the transgender persons and their welfare and for matters connected therewith and incidental thereto," passed on Mar. 7, 2018, www.senate.gov.pk/uploads/documents/1521612511_419. pdf, accessed Oct. 14, 2019. See, also, Asad Hashim, "Pakistan Passes Landmark Transgen-der Rights Law," *Al Jazeera*, May 9, 2018.

111. Hashim, "Pakistan Passes Landmark Transgender Rights Law."

112. Sabrina Toppa, "Pakistan's Transgender Community Takes Another Step Forward," *Al Jazeera*, Mar. 5, 2018.

113. Khaled El-Rouayheb, *Before Homosexuality in the Arab-Islamic World, 1500–1800* (Chicago: University of Chicago Press), 138.

114. See Scott Siraj Al-Haqq Kugle, "Sexuality, Diversity, and Ethics," in *Progressive Muslims: On Justice, Gender, and Pluralism*, ed. Omid Safi (Oxford, UK: Oneworld, 2003).

115. Jonathan Brown, "LGBTQ and Islam Revisited: The Days of the Donald," Yaqeen Institute for Islamic Research, Dec. 14, 2017.

116. El-Rouayheb, *Before Homosexuality in the Arab-Islamic World, 1500-1800*, 5.

117. Brown, "Stoning and Hand Cutting."

118. Jonathan Brown, "The Sharia, Homosexuality & Safeguarding Each Other's Rights in a Pluralist Society," *Iman Wire*, Al-Madina Institute, June 18, 2016.

119. Amy Bhatt, "India's Sodomy Ban, Now Ruled Illegal, Was a British Colonial Leg-acy," *Conversation*, Sept. 12, 2018, https://theconversation.com/indias-sodomy-ban-now -ruled-illegal-was-a-british-colonial-legacy-103052.

120. Enze Han and Joseph O'Mahoney, "The British Colonial Origins of Anti-Gay Laws," *Washington Post*, Oct. 30, 2014.

121. Enze Han and Joseph O'Mahoney, "The British Colonial Origins of Anti-Gay Laws," *Washington Post*, Oct. 30, 2014.

122. Munir Shaikh, "Contemporary Developments within Muslim Societies and Communities Regarding LGBT Identity and Rights," in *Muslim LGBT Inclusion Project: Final Report* (New York: Intersections International, Nov. 4, 2011).

123. Brown, "The Sharia, Homosexuality & Safeguarding Each Other's Rights in a Pluralistic Society."

124. See, e.g., Scott Siraj al-Haqq Kugle, *Homosexuality in Islam: Critical Reflections on Gay, Lesbian, and Transgender Muslims* (Oxford, UK: Oneworld, 2010).

125. Ali, *Sexual Ethics and Islam*, 82.

126. Samuel Osborne, "France: Court Orders Halal Supermarket in Paris to Close Because It Does Not Sell Pork or Wine," *Independent*, Dec. 5, 2017.

127. Shuja Shafi and Jonathan Arkush, "Jewish and Muslim Methods of Slaughter Prioritise Animal Welfare," *Guardian*, Mar. 6, 2014.

128. James Meikle, "What Exactly Does the Halal Method of Animal Slaughter Involve?," *Guardian*, May 8, 2014.

129. Jo Warrick, "They Die Piece by Piece," *Washington Post*, Apr. 10, 2001.

130. "Factory Farming: Misery for Animals," People for the Ethical Treatment of Animals, https://www.peta.org/issues/animals-used-for-food/factory-farming, accessed Oct. 7, 2019.

131. The torture, horrifying living conditions, and sadistic abuse of animals destined for slaughter has been widely documented in books (e.g., Ken Midkiff, *The Meat You Eat* [New York: St. Martin's Griffin, 2005]); documentaries (e.g., *Food, Inc.*); and articles (e.g., Paul Solotaroff, "In the Belly of the Beast," *Rolling Stone*, Dec. 10, 2013; and "Exposing Abuse on the Factory Farm," editorial, *New York Times*, Aug. 8, 2015).

132. Jonathan Laurence, "France's Beef with Islam," *Foreign Policy* (Mar. 7, 2012).

133. Surah 5, verse 5.

134. Frances Harrison, "Alcohol Fatwa Sparks Controversy," *BBC News*, Apr. 11, 2008.

135. The Prophet Muhammad is reported to have said, "There is no good in the one who is not hospitable," as well as other statements on hospitality. See, e.g., Mona Siddiqui, *Hospitality and Islam: Welcoming in God's Name* (London: Yale University Press, 2015), 10.

136. Ibrahim Warde, *Islamic Finance in the Global Economy* (Edinburgh: Edinburgh University Press, 2000), 56.

137. Abdalla, "Islamic Australia? What Place Is There for Sacred Law in a Secular Land?"; an expanded version of the article appears in Mohamad Abdalla, "Sacred Law in a Secular Land," *Griffith Law Review* 3 (2012): 21. See, also, Khaled Abou El Fadl, "Islamic Law and Muslim Minorities," *Islamic Law and Society* 1, no. 2 (1994): 185.

138. International Monetary Fund, "IMF Survey: Islamic Banks: More Resilient to Crisis?," Oct. 4, 2010, imf.org.

CHAPTER TWELVE: THE DISINFORMATION CAMPAIGN AND SHARIAH IN AMERICA

1. Elsheikh, Sisemore, and Lee, *Legalizing Othering*, 23.

2. Elsheikh, Sisemore, and Lee, *Legalizing Othering*, 23.

3. See, e.g., Steve Rendall, "The Media's Construction of the 'Ground Zero Mosque': How Islamophobic Blogs Manufactured a Controversy," *Extra!*, Fairness & Accuracy in Reporting, October 1, 2010.

4. Alex Pareene, "Bombshell: Obama Malcolm X Love Child?," *Gawker*, Oct. 30, 2008.

5. Elsheikh, Sisemore, and Lee, *Legalizing Othering*, 19.

6. For a good summary and timeline of these events, see, e.g., Justin Elliott, "How the 'Ground Zero Mosque' Fear Mongering Began," *Salon*, Aug. 16, 2010.

7. See, e.g., Elsheikh, Sisemore, and Lee, *Legalizing Othering*.

8. See Anti-Defamation League, *David Yerushalmi: A Driving Force behind Anti-Sharia Efforts in the U.S.* (New York: ADL, 2013).

9. "On Race: A Tentative Discussion," *The McAdam Report*, May 12, 2006, as quoted in Southern Poverty Law Center, "David Yerushalmi," https://www.splcenter.org/fighting-hate/extremist-files/individual/david-yerushalmi, accessed Oct. 7, 2019.

10. Nathan Lean, *The Islamophobia Industry: How the Right Manufactures Fear of Muslims* (London: Pluto Press, 2012), 123.

11. Southern Poverty Law Center, "David Yerushalmi," https://www.splcenter.org/fighting-hate/extremist-files/individual/david-yerushalmi, accessed Aug. 26, 2019.

12. Swathi Shanmugasundaram, "Anti-Sharia Law Bills in the United States," Feb. 5, 2018, Southern Poverty Law Center; see, also, Robert Steinback, "'Study' of Mosques Reflects Anti-Muslim Bias of Co-Author," Southern Poverty Law Center, June 13, 2011, and the Council on American-Islamic Relations' profile on Yerushalmi at islamophobia.org.

13. Andrea Elliott, "The Man behind the Anti-Shariah Movement," *New York Times*, July 30, 2011.

14. ACLU Program on Freedom of Religion and Belief, *Nothing to Fear: Debunking the Mythical "Sharia Threat" to Our Judicial System* (New York: American Civil Liberties Union, May 2011).

15. Elsheikh, Sisemore, and Lee, *Legalizing Othering.*

16. Shanmugasundaram, "Anti-Sharia Bills in the United States."

17. Tanya Somanader, "Tennessee Bill Dubs Sharia Law 'Treasonous,' Would Punish Muslims with 15 Years in Jail," *ThinkProgress*, Feb. 23, 2011.

18. United States of Islamophobia Database, launched April 25, 2018, https://haasinstitute.berkeley.edu/global-justice/islamophobia#islamophobia-database, accessed Oct. 7, 2019.

19. Esposito and DeLong-Bas, *Shariah*, 10.

20. US Constitution, Amendment I.

21. Nussbaum, *The New Religious Intolerance*, 90–91.

22. Trump v. Hawaii, No. 17–965, Decided June 26, 2018, Sotomayor, J., dissenting, p.2.

23. "Guidelines for Teaching about Religion in K-12 Public Schools in the United States," American Academy of Religion, Apr. 2010, aarweb.org.

24. Carrie Kilman, "One Nation, Many Gods," *Teaching Tolerance* 32 (Fall 2007), tolerance.org.

25. See, e.g., Daniel Mach and Jamil Dakwar, "Anti-Sharia Law: A Solution in Search of a Problem," Religion News Service, May 19, 2011, https://davidgibson.religionnews.com.

26. "The Fight against Anti-Shariah Measures," Council on American Islamic Relations, Oklahoma Chapter, June 2, 2016, https://cairoklahoma.com/initiative.

27. Ryan H. Boyer, "'Unveiling' Kansas's Ban on Application of Foreign Law," *Kansas Law Review* 61 (2013): 1068.

28. Elsheikh, Sisemore, and Lee, *Legalizing Othering*, 38.

29. See, e.g., Boyer, "'Unveiling' Kansas's Ban on Application of Foreign Law," 1069.

30. American Bar Association Resolution 113A, adopted by the House of Delegates, Aug. 8–9, 2011, 6.

31. The *Lemon* Test, from Lemon v. Kurtzman, 403 US 602 (1971); Dave Pantzer and Asma T. Uddin, "A First Amendment Analysis of Anti-Sharia Initiatives," Institute of Social Policy and Understanding, May 2012, 20, ispu.org.

32. American Bar Association Resolution 113A, 7.

33. Pantzer and Uddin, "A First Amendment Analysis of Anti-Sharia Initiatives," 20.

34. Some adherents of these religions still practice it. See, e.g., David Sedley, "In Defiance of Israeli Law, Polygamy Sanctioned by Top Rabbis," *Times of Israel*, Dec. 27, 2016; see, also, Mette Ivie Harrison, "Do Mormons Still Practice Polygamy?," *Huffington Post*, Mar. 23, 2017. Polygamy is still allowed under majority fiqh, though most Muslim-majority countries either prohibit it or restrict its implementation.

35. Mach and Dakwar, "Anti-Sharia Law."

36. Tim Murphy, "SD Rep. Who Authored Abortion Bill Nixes Sharia Ban," *Mother Jones*, Feb. 18, 2011, motherjones.com.

37. Murphy, "SD Rep. Who Authored Abortion Bill Nixes Sharia Ban."

38. See, generally, American Bar Association Resolution 113A, Adopted by the House of Delegates, Aug. 8–9, 2011, americanbar.org.

39. See, generally, American Bar Association Resolution 113A.

40. Christine Albano and Laura W. Morgan, "The Intersection of Sharia and Family Law: A Policy and Case Summary," *Journal of the American Academy of Matrimonial Lawyers* 30, no. 1 (2017): 219–20.

41. Abed Awad, "Islamic Family Law in American Courts: A Rich, Diverse and Evolving Jurisprudence," in *Muslim Family Law in Western Courts*, Durham Modern Middle East and Islamic World Series, ed. Elisa Guinchi (New York: Routledge, 2014), 170.

42. Awad, "Islamic Family Law in American Courts," 170.

43. Abed Awad, "The True Story of Sharia in American Courts," *Nation*, June 14, 2012.

44. Awad, "The True Story of Sharia in American Courts."

45. Awad, "The True Story of Sharia in American Courts."

46. Awad, "Islamic Family Law in American Courts," 174.

47. Awad, "Islamic Family Law in American Courts," 170–75.

48. Elsheikh, Sisemore, and Lee, *Legalizing Othering*, 39.

49. Boyer, "'Unveiling' Kansas's Ban on Application of Foreign Law," 1078.

50. Boyer, "'Unveiling' Kansas's Ban on Application of Foreign Law," 1078.

51. Abed Awad, "Islamic Law in US Courts: Anti-Shari'a Ban in Kansas," *ShariaSource*, Harvard Law School, July 14, 2017, https://shariasource.blog; Boyer, "'Unveiling' Kansas's Ban on Application of Foreign Law," 1078.

52. Boyer, "'Unveiling' Kansas's Ban on Application of Foreign Law," 1078–79.

53. Simon Brown, "Shariah Charade: Kansas Lawmakers Needlessly Ban Islamic Law," Americans United for the Separation of Church and State, May 16, 2012, au.org.

54. See Beth Din of America, https://bethdin.org.

55. Sarah Posner, "Hypocritical Freakout over Shari'ah, but Not Biblical Law," *Religion Dispatches*, Mar. 22, 2011, religiondispatches.org.

56. Homa Khaleeli, "Inside Britain's Sharia Councils: Hardline and Anti-Women—or a Dignified Way to Divorce?," *Guardian*, Mar. 1, 2017.

57. Posner, "Hypocritical Freakout over Shari'ah, but Not Biblical Law."

58. Laura Figueroa, "Adam Hasner Says Florida Judge Using Islamic Law in the Courtroom," *Politifact*, May 4, 2011, politifact.com.

59. Michael A. Helfand, "Between Law and Religion: Procedural Challenges to Religious Arbitration Awards," *Chicago-Kent Law Review* 90, no. 1 (2015): 142.

60. Helfand, "Between Law and Religion," 142.

61. Figueroa, "Adam Hasner Says Florida Judge Using Islamic Law in the Courtroom"; Adam Serwer, "Sharia Panic Hits Florida," *American Prospect*, Mar. 23, 2011.

CHAPTER THIRTEEN: ISLAMOPHOBIA AND WHY WE HAVE THE STEREOTYPES

1. Khaled Beydoun, *American Islamophobia: Understanding the Roots and Rise of Fear* (Oakland: University of California Press, 2018), 68–69.

2. See Craig Considine, "Muslims Aren't A Race, So I Can't Be Racist, Right? Wrong," *Huffington Post*, Nov. 19, 2016.

3. Khaled Beydoun, "Toward a Legal Definition and Framework," *Columbia Law Review Online* 116 (2019), https://columbialawreview.org/content/islamophobia-toward-a-legal-definition-and-framework.

4. Sources on Islamophobia are too numerous to list, but islamophobianetwork.com outlines the network concisely. See, also, Elsheikh, Sisemore, and Lee, *Legalizing Othering*; Nathan Lean, *The Islamophobia Industry: How the Right Manufactures Fear of Muslims* (London: Pluto Press, 2012); the Center for American Progress's report *Fear, Inc.: The Roots of the Islamophobia Network in America* (Wajahat Ali et al. [Washington, DC: CAP, 2011]); and the report *Pedlars of Hate: The Violent Impact of the European Far Right* from the Institute for Race Relations (Liz Fekete [London: 2012]).

5. Joint report from the Council on American-Islamic Relations and the University of California at Berkeley's Center for Race and Gender, *Confronting Fear: Islamophobia and Its Impact in the US 2013–2015* (Washington, DC: CAIR, 2017), islamophobia.org.

6. Right Wing Watch Staff, "The Right Wing Playbook on Anti-Muslim Extremism," July 2011, a project of People for the American Way, rightwingwatch.org.

7. See profile on Ayaan Hirsi Ali in Center for American Progress, *Fear, Inc.*, islamophobianetwork.com.

8. Jared A. Goldstein, "Unfit for the Constitution: Nativism and the Constitution, from the Founding Fathers to Donald Trump," *Journal of Constitutional Law* 20, no. 3 (2018): 557.

9. Jared A. Goldstein, "A Good American: How Trump's Immigration Ban Explicitly Smears Muslims as Being Potentially Hostile to the Constitution," *Slate*, Feb. 14, 2017.

10. Goldstein, "A Good American."

11. Research by the New America Foundation and American Muslim Institution found that nearly half of Americans (42 percent) said Islam was not compatible with American values, with Republicans more likely to hold negative views. Shafik Mandhai, "Two in Five Americans Say Islam 'Is Incompatible with US Values,'" *Al Jazeera*, Nov. 1, 2018.

12. Sophia A. McClennen, "America's Real Muslim Problem Is Islamophobia," *Salon*, July 7, 2018.

13. "New Zealand Mosques' Attack Suspect Praised Trump in Manifesto," *Al Jazeera*, Mar. 15, 2019.

14. Scott Shane, "Killings in Norway Spotlight Anti-Muslim Thought in US," *New York Times*, July 24, 2011.

15. Fish, *Are Muslims Distinctive?*, 130.

16. This is based on FBI data, as well as on data from the National Consortium for the Study of Terrorism and Responses to Terrorism (START): "Non-Muslims Carried Out More Than 90% of All Terrorist Attacks in America," *Global Research* (Centre for Research on Globalization), Jan. 8, 2018 (first published May 1, 2013), globalresearch.ca.

17. Juan Cole, "Terrorism and Other Religions," *Informed Comment*, Apr. 23, 2013, juancole.com.

18. "Shining Light on Latin America's Homicide Epidemic," *Economist*, Apr. 5, 2018.

19. See, e.g., Claire Felter and Danielle Renwick, "Colombia's Civil Conflict," Council on Foreign Relations, Jan. 11, 2017, cfr.org.

20. Timothy Pratt, "Sex Slavery Racket a Growing Concern in Latin America," *Christian Science Monitor*, Jan. 11, 2001 (estimating that 35,000 women are trafficked every year out of Colombia alone).

21. "Latin America, Caribbean Most Violent Region for Women—UN," *Jamaica Observer*, Nov. 24, 2017; Johanna Mendelson Forman, "What Gender Inequality Looks Like in Latin America," *Huffington Post*, Jan. 23, 2014.

22. See, generally, Michael Philip Penn, *Envisioning Islam: Syriac Christians and the Early Muslim World* (Philadelphia: University of Pennsylvania Press, 2015).

23. See, generally, Cole, *Muhammad*.

24. Daniel, *Islam and the West*, 291.

25. Sophia Rose Arjana, *Muslims in the Western Imagination* (New York: Oxford University Press, 2015), 28.

26. Arjana, *Muslims in the Western Imagination*, 1.

27. Jon Queally, "The US-Led Global War on Terrorism Has Succeeded . . . in Creating More Global Terrorism," *Common Dreams*, Sept. 17, 2018, noting, "Since 9/11, the regions where the US military has been most active—countries in Africa, the Middle East, and South Asia—have seen a five-fold increase in violent attacks."

CONCLUSION

1. John Feffer, *Crusade 2.0: The West's Resurgent War on Islam* (San Francisco: City Lights, 2012), 74.

2. Feldman, "Why Shariah?

INDEX